T0298425

Cooperative Security and the Balance of Power in ASEAN and the ARF

The Association of Southeast Asian Nations (ASEAN) and the ASEAN Regional Forum (ARF) – the key multilateral security institutions in Southeast Asia and the Asia-Pacific – are frequently viewed as exemplars of cooperative security rather than operating on a more traditional 'balance of power' basis.

Emmers questions the dichotomy implicit in this interpretation and investigates what role the balance of power really plays in such cooperative security arrangements and in the calculations of their participants. He offers a thorough analysis of the influence the balance of power has had on the formation and evolution of ASEAN and the ARF and reveals the co-existence and interrelationship between both approaches within the two institutions.

The book contains case studies of Brunei's motives in joining ASEAN in 1984, ASEAN's response to the Third Indochina Conflict, the workings of the ARF since 1994 and ASEAN's involvement in the South China Sea dispute. It will interest students and researchers of ASEAN and the ARF, the international politics of the Asia-Pacific, regionalism and the balance of power theory.

Ralf Emmers is a Post-Doctoral Fellow in Asian Security at the Institute of Defence and Strategic Studies, Nanyang Technological University, Singapore.

Politics in Asia series
Formerly edited by Michael Leifer
London School of Economics

Korea versus Korea
A case of contested legitimacy
B.K. Gills

Taiwan and Chinese Nationalism
National identity and status in international society
Christopher Hughes

Managing Political Change in Singapore
The elected presidency
Kevin Y.L. Tan and Lam Peng Er

Islam in Malaysian Foreign Policy
Shanti Nair

Political Change in Thailand
Democracy and participation
Kevin Hewison

The Politics of NGOs in South-East Asia
Participation and protest in the Philippines
Gerard Clarke

Malaysian Politics under Mahathir
R.S. Milne and Diane K. Mauzy

Indonesia and China
The politics of a troubled relationship
Rizal Sukma

Arming the Two Koreas
State, capital and military power
Taik-young Hamm

Engaging China
The management of an emerging power
Edited by Alastair Iain Johnston and Robert S. Ross

Singapore's Foreign Policy
Coping with vulnerability
Michael Leifer

Philippine Politics and Society in the Twentieth Century
Colonial legacies, post-colonial trajectories
Eva-Lotta E. Hedman and John T. Sidel

Constructing a Security Community in Southeast Asia
ASEAN and the problem of regional order
Amitav Acharya

Monarchy in South-East Asia
The faces of tradition in transition
Roger Kershaw

Korea After the Crash
The politics of economic recovery
Brian Bridges

The Future of North Korea
Edited by Tsuneo Akaha

The International Relations of Japan and South East Asia
Forging a new regionalism
Sueo Sudo

Power and Change in Central Asia
Edited by Sally N. Cummings

The Politics of Human Rights in Southeast Asia
Philip Eldridge

Political Business in East Asia
Edited by Edmund Terence Gomez

Singapore Politics under the People's Action Party
Diane K. Mauzy and R.S. Milne

Media and Politics in Pacific Asia
Duncan McCargo

Japanese Governance
Beyond Japan Inc
Edited by Jennifer Amyx and Peter Drysdale

China and the Internet
Politics of the digital leap forward
Edited by Christopher R. Hughes and Gudrun Wacker

Challenging Authoritarianism in Southeast Asia
Comparing Indonesia and Malaysia
Edited by Ariel Heryanto and Sumit K. Mandal

Cooperative Security and the Balance of Power in ASEAN and the ARF
Ralf Emmers

Cooperative Security and the Balance of Power in ASEAN and the ARF

Ralf Emmers

RoutledgeCurzon
Taylor & Francis Group
LONDON AND NEW YORK

First published 2003
by RoutledgeCurzon
2 Park Square, Milton Park, Abingdon, Oxon, OX14 4RN

Simultaneously published in the USA and Canada
by RoutledgeCurzon
270 Madison Ave, New York NY 10016

RoutledgeCurzon is an imprint of the Taylor & Francis Group

Transferred to Digital Printing 2005

© 2003 Ralf Emmers

Typeset in Times by Exe Valley Dataset Ltd, Exeter

British Library Cataloguing in Publication Data
A catalogue record for this book is available from the British Library

Library of Congress Cataloging in Publication Data
Emmers, Ralf, 1974
  Cooperative security and the balance of power in ASEAN and ARF/
    Ralf Emmers.
      p. cm.
  Includes bibliographical references and index.
  1. ASEAN. 2. ASEAN Regional Forum.
  3. Asia, Southeastern – Politics and government – 1945. 4. Pacific Area –
  Politics and government. 5. National security – Asia, Southeastern.
  6. National security – Pacific Area. 7. Security, International.
  8. Asia, Southeastern – Foreign relations – Pacific Area. 9. Pacific Area –
  Foreign relations – Asia, Southeastern. I. Title.

DS520.E46 2003
327.1'7'0959–dc21   2002154337

ISBN 0–415–30992–1

This book is dedicated to the memory of my
PhD supervisor, the late Professor Michael Leifer

Contents

Foreword

The major achievement of this book is the reintroduction of the balance of power as a conceptual category for explaining the evolution of the key security associations in Southeast Asia, namely the long-standing Association of Southeast Asian Nations (ASEAN) that was founded in 1967 and the ASEAN Regional Forum (ARF) that was established in 1994. Ralf Emmers uses the concept of the balance of power in two basic ways. First, he demonstrates the continuing significance of the well-established way of using it to explain how in managing security relations between the great powers so as to prevent the emergence of regional hegemony the balance also contributes to sustaining the independence of other lesser states. With regard to Southeast Asia this refers particularly to relations between the United States and China. Second, and more strikingly, Emmers shows how the balance of power, conceived in political (as opposed to conventional security) terms has been central to the inner development of ASEAN itself.

This approach runs counter to contemporary mainstream explanations that stress constructivism or modes of expressing particular group identities for the development of ASEAN and cooperative security for the development of the ARF. It is one of the strengths of this book that instead of engaging in a polemic against these approaches, Emmers concentrates on demonstrating how his balance of power approach actually helps us to understand the internal dynamics of the evolution of these two key organizations. Indeed the book may be seen as a text for explaining the underlying forces driving security cooperation and what constrains that cooperation in the Southeast Asian region.

Unusually for a book based on a PhD thesis, it is free of much of the scholasticism that is often so tiresome for the interested reader. Instead its arguments and narratives of events are fluently presented without sacrificing the core scholarly strengths that underpin them. This is very much to the credit of Dr Emmers himself, but it also reflects the influence of his supervisor, the great scholar of Southeast Asian politics, the late Professor Michael Leifer, to whose memory the book is dedicated.

MICHAEL YAHUDA

Acknowledgements

Research for this book was conducted while I was a doctoral student at the Department of International Relations at the London School of Economics (LSE). My greatest debt of gratitude is to my supervisor, the late Professor Michael Leifer. He carefully read each chapter more than once before critically appraising the entire manuscript. His guidance and encouragements during a period of more than three years were inestimable. Professor Leifer's academic interest in the concept of the balance of power, as displayed both in his own publications and in his supervision of my PhD dissertation, has had a profound influence on this monograph. I will always remember him as my academic mentor. I am also grateful to Professor Michael Yahuda for guiding me through the last few months of the PhD programme. Moreover, I would like to thank him and Dr Christopher Hughes for twice inviting me to present my work at the Seminar on Asia and the Pacific in International Relations, LSE.

The Institute of Southeast Asian Studies (ISEAS) and the Centre for Strategic and International Studies (CSIS) hosted my field research in Singapore and Jakarta. I wish to thank all the governmental officials, former ambassadors, retired foreign ministers and academics of various universities and research institutes who shared with me their thoughts and experiences of ASEAN, the ARF and the international politics of Southeast Asia. While some of the interviewees demanded not to be named in the text, all answered frankly to my questions. I am grateful to the Central Research Fund, University of London, for sponsoring my field research to Southeast Asia in the spring of 2000.

I would like to express my deepest gratitude to the Institute of Defence and Strategic Studies (IDSS), in particular to Director Barry Desker and Deputy Director Amitav Acharya, for giving me the time and support to transform my PhD dissertation into the present book. I wish also to thank Heidi Bagtazo and Grace McInnes at Routledge as well as the three anonymous reviewers for their valuable comments. 'The Influence of the Balance of Power Factor within the ASEAN Regional Forum', first appeared in *Contemporary Southeast Asia*, vol. 23, no. 2, August 2001, pp. 275–291. It is reproduced as Chapter 5 with the kind permission of the publisher, Institute of Southeast Asian Studies, Singapore.

Finally, I would like to thank my parents for their love and constant support, my brother for introducing me to Southeast Asia and above all my wife for her patience, editorial skills and indispensable insights. I am solely responsible for any factual errors and remaining shortcomings.

RALF EMMERS
Singapore
November 2002

Abbreviations

ABRI	Armed Forces of the Republic of Indonesia
AMM	ASEAN Ministerial Meeting
APEC	Asia-Pacific Economic Cooperation
ARF	ASEAN Regional Forum
ASA	Association of Southeast Asia
ASEAN	Association of Southeast Asian Nations
ASEM	Asia–Europe Meeting
CBM	Confidence-building measure
CGDK	Coalition Government of Democratic Kampuchea
COMECON	Council for Mutual Economic Assistance
CPM	Communist Party of Malaya
CPT	Communist Party of Thailand
CSBM	Confidence- and security-building measure
CSCAP	Council for Security Cooperation in the Asia-Pacific
CSCE	Conference on Security and Cooperation in Europe
CSIS	Centre for Strategic and International Studies
DK	Democratic Kampuchea
DRV	Democratic Republic of Vietnam
EAEC	East Asian Economic Caucus
EAEG	East Asian Economic Group
EEC	European Economic Community
EEZ	Exclusive Economic Zone
EU	European Union
FPDA	Five Power Defence Arrangements
Fretilin	Revolutionary Front for an Independent East Timor
FUNCINPEC	National United Front for an Independent, Neutral, Peaceful and Cooperative Cambodia
G7	Group of Seven
GCC	Gulf Cooperation Council
ICJ	International Court of Justice
ICK	International Conference on Kampuchea
IDSS	Institute of Defence and Strategic Studies
IISS	International Institute for Strategic Studies

IMF	International Monetary Fund
INTERFET	International Force in East Timor
IR	International Relations
ISG	Inter-Sessional Support Group
ISM	Inter-Sessional Meeting
ISIS	Institutes of Strategic and International Studies
JI	*Jemaah Islamiah*
JIM	Jakarta Informal Meeting
KPNLF	Khmer People's National Liberation Front
LSE	London School of Economics
MFA	Ministry of Foreign Affairs (Singapore)
NATO	North Atlantic Treaty Organization
NPT	Nuclear Non-Proliferation Treaty
NUS	National University of Singapore
PD	preventive diplomacy
PKI	Indonesian Communist Party
PLA	People's Liberation Army
PMC	Post-Ministerial Conference
PRC	People's Republic of China
PRK	People's Republic of Kampuchea
SAARC	South Asian Association for Regional Cooperation
SAF	Singapore Armed Forces
SEANWFZ	Southeast Asia Nuclear Weapon-Free Zone
SEATO	South-East Asia Treaty Organization
SOM	Senior Officials Meeting
TAC	Treaty of Amity and Cooperation
TNI	Tentara Nasional Indonesia (Indonesian Armed Forces)
UN	United Nations
UNCLOS III	Third United Nations Convention of the Law of the Sea
UNGA	United Nations General Assembly
UNSC	United Nations Security Council
UNTAET	United Nations Transitional Administration in East Timor
ZOPFAN	Zone of Peace, Freedom and Neutrality

Introduction

The central theme of this monograph is the role and relevance of the balance of power factor within inter-state regimes for regional cooperative security with special reference to the Association of Southeast Asian Nations (ASEAN)[1] and the ASEAN Regional Forum (ARF).[2] ASEAN and the ARF are normally depicted as associative forms of security arrangements that may be defined as alternatives to those characteristic of and employing the traditional concept of the balance of power. This book addresses one core question: to what extent may the balance of power, defined in political terms, play a part in such associative security arrangements and in the calculations of the participants? Hence, it judges to what extent the balance of power may become a factor in cooperative security regimes. To that end, it assesses the role of the balance of power as a disposition to promote countervailing arrangements to deny hegemony within and beyond cooperative security even if devoid of direct military content.

A central question addressed in this book is what impact, if any, may balance of power have on the modalities of regimes for cooperative security. Depending on the answers, it may be possible to argue that balance of power and cooperative security can coexist in a complementary way within the same security arrangement. Yet, care should be taken in employing the term 'complementary'. For example, traditional balance of power and associative dimensions may complement one another through separate structures within the same region. Indeed, military alliances and regional cooperative security regimes can exist independently from and simultaneously in complement to one another. Both may work together in the interest of preserving stable regional security relations. In short, collective defence alignments and co-operative security institutions may operate side by side, but separately. The aim of this project, however, is to study the factor of the balance of power as one consideration within a cooperative security regime and discuss its possible coexistence with an associative dimension part of the cooperative process.

This monograph seeks to contribute to the study of regimes/institutions and should therefore be located in a specific body of the International Relations (IR) literature. It argues that an analysis of the balance of power is required to achieve a good understanding of the history of ASEAN and the

ARF. Consequently, the primary contribution made to the study of both cooperative security arrangements will be the systematic application of the balance of power concept to an examination of their modalities. The book aims to reject the notion that cooperative security regimes should be defined as alternatives to balance of power by arguing that ASEAN and the ARF were informed with some reference to the concept. As a result, it attempts to demonstrate the coexistence of associative and balance of power dimensions within the same arrangement.

In the IR literature, ASEAN and the ARF are discussed in the context of security theory, international cooperation and institution building. In particular, many scholars of Southeast Asian relations have classified ASEAN as a security regime.[3] Regimes are defined as 'sets of implicit or explicit principles, norms, rules, and decision-making procedures around which actors' expectations converge in a given area of international relations'.[4] The existence of a security regime does not make the use of force unthinkable nor does it lead to the existence of converging interests only. Bilateral tensions, territorial disputes and other forms of potential threats can exist among its participants. In that respect, security regimes differ from security communities where one observes a complete and long-term convergence of interests between members in the avoidance of war.[5]

The study of regimes can be located within the theoretical framework of a neo-liberal understanding of inter-state cooperation. This institutionalist literature is represented by the work of Robert Keohane and others.[6] Regimes are inter-state agreements that aim to enhance common interests in a specific sphere of policies. According to neo-liberal institutionalists, regimes are formed to promote common long-term interests. Keohane and Martin claim that 'institutions are created by states *because of* their anticipated effects on patterns of behavior.'[7] Specific variables enjoy a central position within an institutionalist analysis of regimes. These include the formation of codes of conduct, the level of institutionalization and the existence of common interests. A security regime is expected to enhance security through the application of a code of conduct that influences the behaviour of states, and also through collective measures aimed at conflict management and resolution. Institutionalists do not view security regimes in terms of the balance of power. On the contrary, they refer to the idea of a shift from the traditional concept of the balance of power to long-term security cooperation. They claim that security regimes are formed and persist due to 'the benefits they provide: by facilitating communication, information, transparency; by reducing mutual threat perceptions and worst-case thinking; and by under-cutting the self-fulfilling prophecies that lie at the heart of the security dilemma'.[8] In contrast, realists discuss security regimes as instruments available to states to take part in the play of power politics. According to this perspective, regimes are 'merely arenas for acting out power relationships'.[9] The realist interpretation of security regimes focuses on power politics and tends to minimize issues essential to their understanding, including the importance of norms and principles and the possible long-term convergence of interests.

The institutionalist approach offers an account of ASEAN as a security regime. The Association constitutes a form of cooperation among sovereign states that share common interests. It is based on a set of norms and principles that influence state behaviour and enhance inter-state relations. ASEAN has operated as an instrument to avoid the recurrence of conflict and has improved the climate of regional relations in Southeast Asia. It is considered as a security regime whose operation should not be understood within the framework of the balance of power concept. In comparison, ASEAN was established, according to a realist perspective, during the Second Indochina Conflict as a response to a Vietnamese and Chinese threat. Yet, in contrast to a realist interpretation of security cooperation, ASEAN has never evolved into a formal or tacit alliance despite the presence of external threats since its formation in 1967.

ASEAN is also examined in the academic literature in terms of the 'ASEAN Way', an allegedly distinctive and informal process of interaction.[10] The 'ASEAN Way' is based on standard international norms and various features through which the members reach but also avoid common decisions. This process of interaction should be distinguished from a European model of political and economic integration or from other sub-regional cooperative groupings. Contrary to European integration, the 'ASEAN Way' avoids bureaucratic and supra-national arrangements and reaffirms the principles of national sovereignty and non-interference in the domestic affairs of other states. Hence, the Association is said to offer a unique model of cooperation based on specific cultural attributes.

The 'ASEAN Way' has more recently been considered in light of a constructivist perspective.[11] Constructivism takes a sociological approach to international relations. It looks beyond material factors and rejects the assumption that states are utility-maximizing actors with precise and given interests that can be promoted through cooperation. Instead, its analytic focus includes the role of norms, the importance of ideology and the socialization of relations that may induce identity change and result in the construction of a collective identity among states. Cooperation may thus lead to the formation of a community. When applied to the study of ASEAN and the ARF, this approach concentrates on the formation and spread of identities, ideas and norms.[12] Constructivists view Asian-Pacific multilateralism as promoted by the creation of an emerging collective identity. Attention has been given to the 'ASEAN Way' as a shared identity and its possible extension to the Asia-Pacific through the formation of the ARF.[13] Though it may overemphasize the importance and strength of regional identities, constructivism has a great deal to say on the existence of norms and their influence on security regimes.

ASEAN and the ARF have also been discussed as institutional manifestations of cooperative security. Leifer argues, for instance, that ASEAN 'is best understood as an institutionalized, albeit relatively informal, expression of "cooperative security" which may serve as both a complement and as an alternative to balance-of-power practice'.[14] While introduced as a post-Cold War concept, the principle of cooperative security has been applied to Southeast Asian security relations for a longer period of time through the activities of the Association. This book identifies ASEAN as a regime for cooperative security or as a cooperative security arrangement. The ARF is a multilateral discussion group focusing on dialogue and confidence-building measures as a first step to cooperative security. It should, therefore, be viewed as an embryonic regime for cooperative security. In short, this book examines ASEAN and the ARF as institutions that seek to promote the objectives associated with cooperative security. In particular, they may be understood as aiming to move beyond conventional balance of power practice by improving the environment in which security relations take place.

The principle of cooperative security is the key underlying concept behind Asian-Pacific multilateralism in the post-Cold War. In essence, cooperative security is understood as an alternative to balance of power practice. Acharya explains that it includes the 'rejection of "deterrence mind-sets" associated with great power geopolitics of the Cold War'.[15] Cooperative security operates through dialogue and seeks to address the climate of international relations rather than tackle specific problems. It may be compared to the concept of collective security as embodied in the League of Nations Covenant because it is intended to be comprehensive in membership with security arrangements obtaining on an intra-mural basis. The fundamental difference, however, is that cooperative security, unlike collective security, lacks the vehicles of economic and military sanctions.[16] In fact, it deliberately eschews sanctions. Cooperative security relies on promoting standard international norms, principles and codes of conduct among regional partners in order to decrease regional tensions. Focusing primarily on reassurance, it aims to develop a dialogue amongst the participants and to promote confidence building and possibly preventive diplomacy measures. As will be discussed in Chapter 1, the ARF has not yet progressed from promoting confidence-building measures to preventive diplomacy and conflict resolution, except in a declaratory sense.

Cooperative security was preceded by the concept of common security. The latter was first developed in the 1982 report of the Independent Commission on Disarmament and Security Issues headed by the late Swedish Prime Minister Olof Palme. Written during a period of severe East–West tensions, the Palme Commission Report called on the adversaries to cooperate in an attempt to maintain stability and peace. Wiseman explains that 'common security offers a basis for a cooperative model of international security, in contrast to the competitive model of power politics.'[17] Mikhael Gorbachev and others later introduced the notion of common security to an Asian-Pacific setting. Several similarities exist between common and cooperative security. These include a common rejection of deterrence strategies and balance of power tactics and a broader definition of security that includes military and non-military issues.[18] Both approaches are also based on the principle of inclusiveness, meaning that they do not exclude any political or economic systems or adversaries. In contrast to common security, cooperative security favours a more gradual approach to the institutionalization of relations and recognizes the necessity of maintaining, at least at first, existing bilateral alliances. Cooperative security stresses also the importance of flexibility, consensus building and consultation.

When applied to the Asia-Pacific, cooperative security is based on four central principles.[19] First, it assumes that the institutionalization of security relations in the Asia-Pacific should be seen as a slow and gradual process. Second, the institutionalization of security relations is at first not aimed at replacing existing regional alliances but rather at coexisting and working with them in the promotion of security. Cooperative security regimes, such as ASEAN and the ARF, can be complementary to an existing security architecture. Ultimately, cooperative security is expected to replace bilateral alliances and their narrow focus on military security. Third, cooperative security regimes are based on the principle of inclusiveness as they aim to promote a 'habit of dialogue' among all regional states. Finally, the principle includes an informal level of diplomacy, referred to as 'track-two diplomacy'. It consists of communication between academics, non-governmental organizations and other non-state actors in some dialogue with governments through for example the ASEAN Institutes of Strategic and International Studies (ASEAN-ISIS) and the Council for Security Cooperation in the Asia-Pacific (CSCAP).

Despite a tendency in the current IR literature to study ASEAN and the ARF in terms of an institutionalist or constructivist approach, this book adopts a different angle. It focuses on the relevance of the balance of power factor within and beyond both cooperative security regimes. It claims that the balance of power dimension needs to be addressed when examining ASEAN and the ARF despite a recent inclination in the discipline to ignore it. The academic literature has traditionally found all kinds of reasons to criticize the balance of power. Schroeder writes, for instance, that scholars of international politics 'do not need to be told of the unsatisfactory state of the balance of power theory'.[20] Without a doubt, the concept contains shortcomings that complicate its analysis. The term is often used loosely, which leads to confusion and vagueness. In addition to being ill defined, the balance of power is based on a narrow comprehension of the notions of power and security and fails to take into account domestic issues. Moreover, it tends to exaggerate the potential danger resulting from emerging hegemons and accepts war as the traditional instrument of the balance. Yet, the concept is at the core of the realist paradigm. Thanks to its simplicity and explanatory qualities, the balance of power remains a valuable tool of analysis in the study of international politics attracting constant academic use and interest.

The relevance of the balance of power to an examination of ASEAN and the ARF is indicated in the writings of Michael Leifer.[21] Contrary to the advocates of neo-realism who judge the balance of power entirely in terms of adversarial relations and self-help, Leifer adhered to both a realist and neo-Grotian understanding of the balance of power concept. In that respect, the works of traditional realists and exponents of the English School of International Relations influenced his intellectual framework. The question of the balance of power was explicitly discussed in his 1996 Adelphi Paper on the ARF.[22] In his analysis, Leifer remained pragmatic about the potential role of the Forum and argued that it should be viewed 'as a modest contribution to a viable balance or distribution of power within the Asia-Pacific by other than traditional means'.[23]

The rhetoric of ASEAN and the ARF implicitly reject conventional balance of power politics. Their declarations and statements never mention the phrase and emphasize instead the importance of the 'ASEAN Way'. Nonetheless, the decision to examine the role and relevance of the balance of power factor within both cooperative security regimes has derived from a theoretical and empirical realization. Offering a satisfactory analysis of security regimes, neo-liberals still underestimate the persistence of realist beliefs among political leaders taking part in this kind of inter-state arrangement. Hence, this book contends that close attention needs to be given when examining security regimes to the power considerations involved. In particular, it is the role played by the constraining of power in security regime dynamics that ought to be studied further. This book therefore concentrates on the balance of power factor and examines how it may influence the workings of such institutions and the underlying calculations made by the participants. Hence, rather than discrediting an associative interpretation of security regimes, the monograph raises the point that the underlying calculations made by the participants include considerations that are alien to such an analysis and which need therefore to be addressed.

At an empirical level, it has been found that the balance of power concept, rather than being a Euro-centric approach which loses most of its significance outside of a Western context, has been very much in existence and applied in post-colonial Southeast Asia. Despite long-term cooperation, intra-ASEAN relations have continued to be affected by persistent feelings of mistrust, bilateral disputes and contradictory strategic perspectives. Most ASEAN states have been dependent on external guarantees to ensure their individual security. In particular, Singapore, Thailand and the Philippines have relied on the United States to operate as a conventional source of countervailing power in the region. Keeping in mind that most members of the Association have relied on realist practices to guarantee their security, the book explores whether the formation and later development of ASEAN and the ARF may have been influenced by power balancing considerations.

Having introduced the motives to investigate the role of the balance of power factor within regimes for cooperative security, an explanation needs to be given of the various meanings of the term that are adopted in this monograph. Essential differences exist between balance of power in its conventional interpretation and practice and the balance of power factor within cooperative security. This factor may aim to contain a disposition to hegemony on the part of a member by enmeshing it within a rule-based regime that includes sufficient incentive to constrain any hegemonic ambitions. Traditional realist motives may thus be achieved at an intra-mural level through non-military constraints to hegemony. Indeed, the constraining of power within cooperative security could become dependent on political means. Beyond the denial of intra-mural hegemony, the balance of power factor may also involve the promotion of countervailing responses to external military threats. The participants to a cooperative security regime could join external states through diplomatic alignment to engage in conventional balance of power practices. In sum, the balance of power factor may be applied differently in an intra- and extra-mural context.

Chapter 1 examines the establishment and institutional evolution of ASEAN and the ARF. In particular, it analyses the associative experience of both institutions. Chapter 2 introduces the balance of power mode of analysis. Rather than accept a dichotomy of interpretations, it argues that a cooperative security model depends upon and cannot preclude a balance of power factor. Most of the chapter discusses the balance of power concept and addresses theoretically its significance as a factor within and beyond regimes for cooperative security. The role of the balance of power factor is first observed at the end of Chapter 2 by illustrating one specific aspect of ASEAN's founding moments. The practical relevance of the balance of power to cooperative security regimes is then examined in four separate case studies. Except for the discussion on the ARF, they are all analysed in a similar way. They are considered by first focusing on the associative perspective involved before trying to determine how the balance of power factor played a role. This analysis is then followed by a discussion on how each perspective interacted with the other.

Chapter 3 deals with ASEAN's early years from 1967 until 1975 and with its enlargement to include Brunei in 1984. It offers an illustration of the balance of power factor within cooperative security and its interaction with the more well-known associative aspect of ASEAN. The motivations that led the Sultanate to enter a regime for cooperative security are analysed. In particular, the chapter determines why Brunei expected to increase its security by joining the Association. In addition to the security advantages associated with the cooperative process, Brunei's decision may have resulted from the benefits linked to an intra-mural balance of power factor, which denies hegemonic actions. ASEAN may have been perceived as a form of political defence for constraining threatening neighbours. At issue was a common understanding of the benefit of Brunei's membership by Malaysia's Prime Minister Hussein Onn and Indonesia's President Suharto, neither of whom saw profit in threatening the Sultanate. The chapter also focuses on the role of Singapore in convincing Brunei to take part in ASEAN. Singapore's Prime Minister Lee Kuan Yew may have persuaded Sultan Hassanal Bolkiah that membership would enhance his country's security because any threat to a member would rebound adversely on the cohesion of the Association.

Chapter 4 examines the balance of power factor beyond cooperative security by focusing on ASEAN's response to the Third Indochina Conflict (1978–91). The chapter begins with ASEAN's corporate stand and analyses what was at issue. The member states cooperated closely to isolate Vietnam on the international scene and deny legitimacy to its puppet government in Phnom Penh. Yet, the associative principles may have been bypassed by the source of threat, which was extra- rather than intra-mural. The study of the balance of power factor consists of a conventional analysis of the term as the constraining of power occurred through military rather than political means. Hence, the concept is interpreted differently than in the former case study. Thailand, as a front-line state to the conflict, required external geopolitical partners to oppose a Vietnamese hegemony in Indochina. Endorsing a strategy of attrition, the ASEAN states may have played a diplomatic role in a countervailing arrangement against Vietnam. Yet, the security interests of the member states were influenced differently by the Vietnamese invasion leading to divergent strategic perspectives on how to tackle the Cambodian issue. The practice of traditional balance of power tactics may therefore have affected intra-mural cooperation.

Chapter 5 studies the role of the balance of power factor in the formation of the ARF. While the Forum can be seen as an ASEAN attempt to expand to the wider region its approach to cooperative security, the chapter argues that its establishment also involved power-balancing considerations. ASEAN's changing security environment at the end of the Cold War is first discussed. It is then asserted that the Association took into account the distribution of power when creating the ARF. Indeed, the ARF may have been conceived as an instrument for ensuring a continued US involvement in the region and for including China in a rule-based arrangement. Beyond the ARF's founding moments, the relevance of the balance of power factor is also examined through the workings of the Forum and the existence among some participants of alternative views on the role of the institution.

Chapter 6 evaluates ASEAN's involvement in the South China Sea dispute. The nature of the conflict is first reviewed by discussing the relevance of international law, the conflicting territorial claims and the economic and geo-strategic interests involved. ASEAN's part is then analysed through an associative and balance of power dimension. It is indicated that ASEAN's involvement may be characterized by the absence of an associative perspective and an inability to promote countervailing arrangements. It is argued that the member states have failed so far in an attempt to establish a code of conduct for the South China Sea and have adopted contrasting positions vis-à-vis the People's Republic of China

(PRC). The study of the balance of power concentrates on ASEAN's incapacity to practise conventional balance of power politics due to the limitations associated with cooperative security and the lack of access to an external source of countervailing power. It is also pointed out that China's participation in the ARF may not contain sufficient incentive to constrain its hegemonic dispositions in the South China Sea.

The methodological approach adopted in this monograph aims to combine a theoretical and factual understanding of ASEAN and the ARF. The methodology is based on a historical narrative. As a research practice, historical narration concentrates on the description and interpretation of events. The historical narrative has as a central subject a specific aspect of the history of ASEAN and the ARF and covers a period from the few years that preceded the formation of the Association until the end of 2002. A historical approach is required due to the fact that the balance of power factor has been significant at different periods of ASEAN and the ARF. It is demonstrated that the balance of power has influenced most of their crucial moments and developments. Consequently, the use of a historical narrative provides the reader with a complete understanding of the role of this factor within both cooperative security regimes. The objective of this study is not, however, to quantify the significance of the balance of power factor simply because it is impossible to measure the relative importance of this specific dimension on the cooperative process.

1 Regimes for cooperative security

The formation and institutional evolution of ASEAN and the ARF

Introduction

This chapter examines the formation and institutional evolution of ASEAN and the ARF. In particular, it analyses the associative experience of both institutions. In discussing multilateralism[1] in Southeast Asia and the Asia-Pacific, ASEAN and the ARF are referred to as inter-state arrangements that seek to address the climate of international relations through the vehicle of dialogue as opposed to problem solving. As examples of cooperative security, both institutions are promoting the notion of security cooperation 'with others' as opposed to 'against others'.[2] ASEAN is a diplomatic association for political and security cooperation that concentrates on conflict avoidance and management, driven initially by the goal of regional reconciliation. The ARF is a more extensive inter-governmental grouping, which focuses on dialogue and confidence-building measures as a first step in promoting cooperative security. As examples of the latter, both cooperative security regimes may be viewed as regional attempts to move beyond the traditional concept of the balance of power despite the fact that cooperative security was developed with the object of complementing existing bilateral alliances of Cold War provenance.

ASEAN and the ARF are examined separately despite the leading role of the Association in the creation and institutional evolution of the Forum. This chapter consists of two sections. The first discusses ASEAN as a co-operative security arrangement by reviewing its origins and institutional experience and considering its allegedly distinctive process of interaction, the so-called 'ASEAN Way'. This section also discusses the weakening of the Association since 1997 and its achievements and limitations as a cooperative security regime. The second section studies the ARF with special reference to its establishment and institutional evolution. Furthermore, the Forum is compared and contrasted to the Association and its principal achievements and weaknesses are pointed out.

ASEAN's institutional evolution as a regime for cooperative security

ASEAN's origins: confrontation and regional reconciliation

The few years that preceded the creation of ASEAN were distinguished by regional conflict and disrupted regional relationships. The main source of inter-state antagonism resulted from the formation in September 1963 of the Federation of Malaysia, which consisted of Malaya, Singapore, Sabah and Sarawak. Sukarno, the first president of Indonesia, opposed the establishment of Malaysia, which he viewed as a British neo-colonial design. Sukarno started a campaign of Confrontation to oppose the new federation. A similar policy over West Irian, which had remained under Dutch authority since Indonesia's independence in December 1949, had led to a diplomatic settlement in August 1962 by which Jakarta gained control over the territory. Indonesia's new policy of Confrontation challenged the legitimacy of the newly established Federation of Malaysia. Confrontation was based on coercive diplomacy and made use of small-scale armed activities. This military and ideological campaign reinforced an outburst of Indonesian nationalism. Confrontation amplified sub-regional tensions, making any kind of neighbourly amity impossible.[3]

A second source of regional antagonism resulted from the Philippines' claim to the British colony of North Borneo (Sabah). In June 1962, the Philippines indicated to the British government that it disputed Britain's control and sovereignty over the territory.[4] Though the Philippine government had initially supported the proposal by Malaya's Prime Minister Tunku Abdul Rahman to establish Malaysia, the integration of Sabah in the new federation strained diplomatic relations between Manila and Kuala Lumpur. Diasdado Macapagal, who served as president of the Philippines from 1961 until 1965, pressed the Philippines' territorial claim to Sabah and challenged with Sukarno the legitimacy of Malaysia. The election of Ferdinand Marcos as president of the Philippines in November 1965 led to the normalization of bilateral relations in June 1966. This started a new phase that improved Philippine–Malaysian relations but only up to a point. Indeed, Manila never abandoned but only decreased the vigour with which it would pursue its claim to Sabah.

The eventual establishment of ASEAN first required a transformation in the regional political environment. Specifically, it was dependent on an Indonesian–Malaysian reconciliation. The regional alteration resulted from a change in political leadership in Indonesia. An abortive coup in October 1965, mounted allegedly by the Indonesian Communist Party (PKI), was followed by Sukarno's gradual political downfall and the massacre of suspected PKI members. Lt General Suharto assumed executive powers on 11 March 1966, which initiated a new era in Indonesian politics known as the New Order. This transformation arose partly from the regional and domestic costs involved over Confrontation.[5] Similar to the neighbouring conservative governments, the new military leadership in Indonesia preferred to focus on domestic stability and economic development and to adopt a pro-Western and anti-communist political orientation.

Suharto saw the end of Confrontation as a first necessity.[6] The new Indonesian Foreign Minister Adam Malik tried to reach reconciliation with Malaysia and to gain access to external assistance, which the country desperately needed in order to stabilize and consolidate its economy. To attain international rehabilitation, particularly with regard to the United States, Indonesia had first to be accepted by its neighbours and to be viewed as a responsible regional actor.[7] A starting process of reconciliation between Jakarta and Kuala Lumpur made regional cooperation possible and desirable as a means to avoid future confrontation. Regional cooperation was first discussed in the spring of 1966 when Malaysia's Deputy Prime Minister Tun Abdul Razak, Malik and the Thai Foreign Minister Thanat Khoman held talks in Bangkok on the normalization of Indonesian–Malaysian relations. Though not directly involved, Suharto decisively influenced the negotiations by supporting a pragmatic foreign policy based on regional cooperation and domestic economic development.

Regional attempts had already been made in the early 1960s to establish inter-state cooperation. The Association of Southeast Asia (ASA) had been created in Bangkok in July 1961 as an instrument to advance dialogue between Thailand, Malaya and the Philippines.[8] Indonesia had refused to take part because it viewed ASA as a Western-aligned organization. Although officially focusing on economic and cultural cooperation, ASA had been primarily designed to promote regional consultation and intra-mural stability in the interest of domestic regime security. At the foreign ministers' meeting of April 1963, Abdul Rahman had declared that 'we believe sincerely that the best possible way of preventing the Communists from trying to destroy the lives and souls of our nations is by improving the lot of our people.'[9] ASA's structure had included an annual meeting of foreign ministers, a Joint Working Party that preceded the ministerial session and a Standing Committee led by the foreign minister of the host country and attended by the ambassadors of the other member states.[10] ASA had been severely affected by the steady deterioration of Malayan–Philippine relations over Sabah and its operations were interrupted in mid-1963. A second sub-regional attempt was even more short-lived. Consisting of Malaya, the Philippines and Indonesia, Maphilindo was a loose confederation based ostensibly on Malay brotherhood, which had been created through the Manila Agreements of 1963. Maphilindo was a device for both undermining Malaysia and reconciling Indonesia, Malaya and the Philippines. Its viability was destroyed due to Confrontation.

As the primary regional actor and keen to avoid domestic political embarrassment, Indonesia refused to join ASA, which had renewed its activities through its third foreign ministers' meeting held in Bangkok in August 1966.[11] Despite Malaysia's reluctance to abandon the already existing arrangement, Jakarta proposed a new project for regional cooperation. Diplomatic talks continued supported by a close collaboration between Malik and Khoman who favoured the formation of a new and wider regional grouping. Indonesia affirmed its willingness to engage with its neighbours through regional cooperation based on the notion of equality.[12] It was keen to launch a new start in regional cooperation in order to reconcile national pride and international rehabilitation. Discussing ASEAN, Gordon writes that 'the new group was created *for* Indonesia, since leaders in Djakarta have preferred to view ASA as a "Western-inspired" organization with which they could not associate.'[13] Still, ASEAN adopted in 1967 the inherent cooperative security premises and structure of ASA. ASA's operations and purposes were incorporated into the new diplomatic association. During the inaugural meeting of ASEAN, Tun Abdul Razak declared: 'We, in Malaysia, are extremely happy that the ideals and aspirations which led to the establishment of ASA six years ago have now grown and have gathered another form and wider import in the birth of ASEAN today.'[14] It can therefore be argued that rather than being abandoned, ASA had 'simply been enlarged and given a new name'.[15]

The motivation for ASEAN was based not only on regional reconciliation. The Association should also be viewed as a response to an advancing communist threat in Indochina and a related fear of internal communist insurgencies. Concerns also existed regarding the consequences of the Chinese Cultural Revolution and the future political direction that Beijing might adopt. Nevertheless, the origins of ASEAN were primarily intramural. It was created to locate regional reconciliation within an institutionalized structure of dialogue permitting a concentration of resources on economic development in the interest of domestic regime security.[16] This priority is essential as it helps us define ASEAN as a regime for cooperative security pivoting on domestic security. The process of reconciliation between Indonesia and Malaysia and the need to prevent the recurrence of confrontation through regional cooperation are at the heart of the origins of ASEAN. The full restoration of relations between Jakarta and Kuala Lumpur occurred only after the organization of elections in Sabah and the creation of ASEAN, though bilateral contacts had previously been re-established through the Bangkok Agreement of August 1966.

ASEAN in the Cold War period

ASEAN was established through the Bangkok Declaration of August 1967. Its original members – Indonesia, Malaysia, the Philippines, Singapore and Thailand[17] – came together in the interest of regional cooperation. The emphasis was put on boosting intra-mural stability and peace. Among its declared purposes, the Association would aim to 'accelerate the economic growth, social progress and cultural development in the region' and 'promote regional peace and stability through abiding respect for justice and the rule of law in the relationship among countries of the region and adherence to the principles of the United Nations Charter'.[18] The Bangkok Declaration was a modest and abstract document, as it did not include a programme for transforming objectives into realities; concrete steps to regional cooperation were absent. Moreover, the issue of political cooperation was not mentioned officially in Bangkok as it was considered too soon to address openly such a difficult matter. Instead, the founding document emphasized unexceptional and non-sensitive issues, including social and economic cooperation.

Nevertheless, regional security was the first preoccupation of the founders of the Association. As Malik would later point out, 'considerations of national and regional security have . . . figured largely in the minds of the founders of the ASEAN.'[19] The Association was given an undeclared political and security role as it was expected to provide a framework for negotiation through which troublesome issues could be approached. Significantly, the ASEAN Ministerial Meeting (AMM), consisting of an annual gathering of the five foreign ministers, was introduced as the highest authority. Over the years, the AMM would become the key instrument of dialogue where security matters could commonly be discussed. It was agreed in Bangkok that a Standing Committee would also be established. It would be led by the foreign minister of the host country and attended by the ambassadors of the other member states. In short, ASEAN's structure demonstrated the attention given to regional relations. This focus had been inherited from ASA.

Military cooperation was rejected at the outset due to several factors. The Association hoped to avoid hostile Vietnamese and Chinese reactions by denying an official anti-communist position. During the inaugural meeting, Singapore's Foreign Minister S. Rajaratnam affirmed that 'those who are outside the grouping should not regard this as a grouping against anything, against anybody.'[20] Besides, the participants did not possess the necessary resources to engage in collective defence.[21] That reluctance also resulted from deep intra-mural differences. Feelings of mistrust and territorial disputes affected most bilateral relations and the members did not share a common security perspective or threat perception. Differences existed with regards to the PRC and Vietnam and they disagreed on the role of external powers. With the exception of Indonesia, the member states relied on defence cooperation with foreign actors to preserve their security. Jakarta favoured an autonomous order in which regional players would be responsible for their own defence.

As with most organizations, ASEAN resulted from the fact that it served its members' narrowly defined interests.[22] The new Indonesian leadership wanted to attain rehabilitation at the regional and international level. Jakarta was keen to restore its credibility and persuade its neighbours that it should no longer be viewed as a source of threat. Moreover, Indonesia sought to ensure access to Western capital and wished to see the establishment of a stable environment that would enhance domestic political stability and economic development.[23] Finally, Jakarta hoped that the Association could operate as an autonomous security foundation free from external intervention. During the inaugural meeting, Malik declared: 'Indonesia always wants to see South East Asia developed into a region which can stand on its own feet, strong enough to defend against any negative influence from outside the region.'[24] By no longer acting as an aggressive power, Indonesia also expected its neighbouring states to become less reliant on external actors to ensure their security.

To cooperate with a former aggressor to its newly obtained sovereignty was a calculated risk for Malaysia. ASEAN was viewed in Kuala Lumpur as an opportunity to institutionalize the end of confrontation with Indonesia and improve relations with other neighbouring states. During the inaugural meeting, Tun Abdul Razak also referred to the regional order. He affirmed that the 'vacuum left by the retreat of colonial rule must be filled by the growth and consideration of indigenous powers – otherwise our future, individually and jointly, will remain dangerously threatened'.[25] Singapore wanted to enhance its Southeast Asian identity as well as to register its sovereignty, though intensely suspicious of Indonesia's and Malaysia's motives. Singapore–Malaysian relations had been affected by the separation of Singapore from the Federation of Malaysia in 1965.[26] The newly established city-state, often defined as a Chinese enclave in a Malay world, was left with a great feeling of vulnerability.[27] Singapore's Prime Minister Lee Kuan Yew would later write in his memoirs that 'Singapore sought the understanding and support of its neighbours in enhancing stability and security in the region.'[28] An amelioration of regional relations was also important for Malaysia and Singapore in light of the British policy of military withdrawal East of Suez first announced in 1967. Thailand expected ASEAN to evolve into an additional defence assurance against its communist neighbours and thus complement its reliance on extra-regional powers. Finally, the Philippines wanted to reaffirm its Southeast Asian identity and build better relations with its neighbours in an effort to manage its territorial disputes as well as its ties with the United States.

These national objectives led to the convergence of shared interests. This resulted primarily from a common emphasis on domestic sources of insecurity. The ASEAN states were being challenged domestically by insurgencies, including irredentist and separatist movements. The Association united a group of conservative political regimes that suffered domestically from weak institutions and socio-economic problems. The non-communist and developing members hoped for regional political stability in order to attain individual economic progress.[29] Moreover, they wished to cope with the seeds of revolutionary challenge. The Bangkok Declaration stated that the Southeast Asian countries 'share a primary responsibility for strengthening the economic and social stability of the region and ensuring their peaceful and progressive national development'.[30] By participating in a regional organization, the members expected to gain from increased sub-regional stability, enabling them to pay closer attention to domestic development. The convergence of interests also resulted from similar regional concerns that originated from the fear of the long-term consequences of the American intervention in Vietnam and China's ambitions in Southeast Asia.[31] Most participants were apprehensive of the declining US power in the region. The Bangkok Declaration announced the determination of the member states 'to ensure their stability and security from external interference in any form or manifestation in order to preserve their national identities in accordance with the ideals and aspirations of their people'.[32] Yet, ASEAN did not obtain an extra-mural dimension during its early years due to the absence of the necessary military means, common political will and consensus to confront regional matters collectively. In sum, attention was primarily given to an intra-mural approach to security cooperation that aimed to increase regional consultation and domestic regime security and consolidation.

ASEAN's early years were characterized by troubled bilateral relations and tensions that demonstrated the weakness of the embryonic security regime. Malaysia's discovery in March 1968 that Manila was training Muslim fighters in Corregidor to infiltrate Sabah caused a severe deterioration in bilateral relations.[33] Relations had previously improved as a result of an official visit by President Marcos to Kuala Lumpur in January 1968. The Corregidor Affair gave rise to ASEAN's only example of preventive diplomacy at an intra-mural level.[34] Suharto intervened during the second AMM held in Jakarta in August 1968 and suggested a private meeting that led to the implementation of a cooling-off period between Kuala Lumpur and Manila. These efforts were shattered by a Congressional decision, later endorsed by President Marcos in September 1968, to include Sabah within Philippine territory. Bilateral relations had improved by the time of the ministerial meeting organized in Malaysia in December 1969. Yet, the crisis demonstrated the ongoing significance of the Sabah issue and ASEAN's inability to act as an effective conflict resolver. The territorial dispute has continued to affect Philippine–Malaysian relations and therefore the cohesion of the Association.

Nevertheless, ASEAN's early years led to the formulation of a declaratory principle for regional order. In November 1971, the member states signed in Kuala Lumpur the Zone of Peace, Freedom and Neutrality (ZOPFAN) Declaration. In essence, it registered a call for regional autonomy. The ZOPFAN document stated that the participants 'are determined to exert initially necessary efforts to secure the recognition of, and respect for, Southeast Asia as a Zone of Peace, Freedom and Neutrality, free from any form or manner of interference by outside powers'.[35] It repeated a determination, previously announced in the Bangkok Declaration, to avoid external intervention. Yet, it also denoted deep divisions. ZOPFAN was a reaction to a Malaysian proposal to neutralize Southeast Asia through great power guarantees. This notion had not been well received in Indonesia, which opposed allocating such a role to external powers. ZOPFAN was introduced as a compromise. The principle excluded a specific role for external powers in Southeast Asia and avoided the legal obligations associated with the traditional concept of neutralization. Moreover, lacking any kind of operational relevance, it did not make specific demands on the member states.

Arising from an historical experience of colonialism and Japanese occupation, ZOPFAN has symbolized a suspicion of external intervention and domination. However, it has continued to be controversial among the ASEAN members, as no consensus has ever been reached on its specific meaning or possible application. This derives from the coexistence of contrasting views on the regional role of external powers. Indonesia has traditionally favoured a regional order determined primarily by the Southeast Asian states. The other members have relied on ties with the United States and other actors to ensure their security. Hence, most participants have not perceived the Association as a security arrangement that could replace existing bilateral links with external players. Though ZOPFAN's realization will probably never become possible or uniformly desirable, it still expresses a regional ambition to maintain some form of independence from external interference. The Southeast Asia Nuclear Weapon-Free Zone (SEANWFZ) Treaty, which was introduced in December 1995 in the final declaration of the fifth ASEAN summit, was represented as a building block to ZOPFAN.[36] Still, the creation of the ARF has violated in the post-Cold War the underlying tenet of ZOPFAN.

In short, the early years of the Association should be examined in the context of cooperative security. Based on an inclusive approach to security cooperation, the creation of ASEAN was an attempt to address the climate of regional relations through a mode of conflict avoidance rather than preventive diplomacy or dispute resolution. The Association relied on dialogue and aimed to form a web of bilateral and regional relations.[37] Efforts were made to institutionalize a process of consultation rather than concrete confidence-building measures between states that still held stronger ties with their former colonial masters than with their direct neighbours.[38] Diplomatic interaction was expected to help manage inter-state relations and reduce feelings of suspicion. The 1967 Declaration reaffirmed the sovereignty of the member states and demanded respect for the principles of the United Nations (UN) Charter. Hence, ASEAN was during these early years an informal exercise in confidence building.[39] Of course, it can be asserted that ASEAN reached no tangible achievements during its first decade of existence. It was based only on a modest declaration that lacked concrete and formal steps to regional cooperation. The newly established arrangement missed cohesion and direction.[40] Despite the rhetoric, the early years were still defined by inter-state tensions and disputes. Nevertheless, this period was important for the institutional experience of the Association. In particular, credit needs to be given to the development of dialogue that gradually led to a 'habit of cooperation'. This cooperation later enabled the member states to react collectively and with some confidence to the communist victories in Indochina in 1975 and Vietnam's invasion of Cambodia in December 1978.[41]

The first summit of the ASEAN heads of state and government came in the wake of the new political environment that emanated from the US withdrawal from South Vietnam in 1973 and the communist take-over of Phnom Penh and Saigon in April 1975 and Laos by the end of the same year. The rapid success of revolutionary communism surprised the ASEAN states and shattered hopes of enlarging the Association to all Southeast Asian nations. Jorgensen-Dahl points out, however, that 'the communist victory injected an altogether more compelling sense of urgency into the activities of ASEAN.'[42] As a collective response to external shocks and a sign of unity and cohesion, the Bali Summit of February 1976 led to two statements: the Declaration of ASEAN Concord and the Treaty of Amity and Cooperation (TAC) in Southeast Asia. Previously prepared by senior officials, both documents consolidated the commitment made by each member state to ASEAN and its principles.

The Declaration of ASEAN Concord provided ASEAN with a political identity and acknowledged the indivisibility of security within the Association. It affirmed that the 'stability of each member state and of the ASEAN region is an essential contribution to international peace and security. Each member state resolves to eliminate threats posed by subversion to its stability, thus strengthening national and ASEAN resilience.'[43] The ASEAN Concord provided the cooperative security arrangement with a political influence. It formalized political cooperation within the ASEAN framework and called for a 'strengthening of political solidarity by promoting the harmonization of views, coordinating positions and, where possible and desirable, taking common actions'.[44] The ASEAN Concord also referred to the issue of regional order by endorsing ZOPFAN. The latter was not put forward as a tangible corporate objective but rather as an aspiration dependent on a common approach to socio-economic development and political stability.[45] Finally, the Concord excluded military cooperation on an intra-ASEAN basis, thus denying a move beyond existing extra-ASEAN bilateral collaboration between national defence forces. In short, the Concord demonstrated a willingness to move beyond the initial ambition to institutionalize a process of reconciliation.

The ASEAN Concord formally proposed the principle of resilience as a shared approach to domestic and regional security. At the opening of the Bali Summit, President Suharto had already declared: 'Our concept of security is inward-looking, namely to establish an orderly, peaceful and stable condition within each territory, free from any subversive elements and infiltration, wherever their origins may be.'[46] The concept of national resilience had previously entered the ASEAN vocabulary as a translation of an Indonesian term, *Ketahanan Nasional*.[47] Influenced by Indonesia's struggle for independence and socio-economic vulnerability, the term had been advanced by the new military leadership when it came to power and had been officially endorsed as a national security doctrine in 1973. At a seminar organized in Jakarta in October 1974, Suharto had stated that national resilience 'covers the strengthening of all the component elements in the development of a nation in its entirety, thus consisting of resilience in the ideological, political, economic, social, cultural and military fields'.[48] Rather than focusing on external military threats, the principle of national resilience favoured a non-traditional and inward-looking approach to security. It registered an ambition to underpin domestic and regional stability through the use of economic and social development. By improving the living conditions of local populations, the ASEAN leaders expected to check subversive influences.[49]

It was also anticipated that resilient states would lead to regional resilience, which would constitute in the longer run a collective security foundation against internal and external threats.[50] Indeed, Suharto had also argued in October 1974 that if 'each member-country develops its own "national resilience", gradually a "regional resilience" may emerge, i.e. the ability of member-countries to settle jointly their common problems and look after their future and well-being together'.[51] This bottom-up approach was believed to decrease intra-regional tensions and vulnerabilities that had facilitated external intervention in the past. One should note therefore the underlying premise of the synergy between national and regional resilience; namely, the indivisibility of national and regional political stability enhancing economic development. In short, the principle of resilience represented a consensual approach to security shared by the ASEAN participants. Such a consensus has been central to ASEAN's experience as a regime for cooperative security.

In addition to its focus on intra-mural security and political stability, the Concord set out means to promote cooperation in economic, cultural and social fields. It mentioned the signing of an agreement to create a central ASEAN Secretariat in Jakarta.[52] Established after the Bali Summit, the Secretariat has remained the central organ of ASEAN. Yet, it has never been granted executive power and has only played a limited role in the ASEAN cooperative process.

The TAC sought to establish a norm-based code of conduct for regional inter-state relations.[53] Among others, it enunciated the following principles: 'mutual respect for the independence, sovereignty, equality, territorial integrity and national identity of all nations'; 'the right of every state to lead its national existence free from external interference, subversion or coercion'; 'non-interference in the internal affairs of one another'; 'settlement of differences or disputes by peaceful means'; and 'renunciation of the threat or use of force'.[54] Based on the UN Charter, most of these principles are well known in the study of international relations as they represent the underlying foundations of the traditional European states system constructed on the sovereignty of nation-states. Nonetheless, the adherence to a common set of norms and principles should be viewed as vital to the operation of a cooperative security regime. As a result, the TAC played a crucial role in the institutional experience of ASEAN. The Treaty also included provision for a dispute resolution mechanism, a High Council for establishing techniques of mediation and consultation. Yet, it stipulated that the 'foregoing provision of this Chapter shall not apply to a dispute unless all the parties to the dispute agree to their application to that dispute'.[55] The provision for a High Council, which is at odds with ASEAN's basic norm of non-intervention in the internal affairs of other states, has never been invoked by the members. Instead, members have continued to rely on the code of conduct discussed above. Simon suggests, however, that the provision 'created an expectation, evolving into a norm, that ASEAN members would not resort to force in resolving conflicts among themselves'.[56]

The Treaty was open to accession by all other Southeast Asian nations. ASEAN hoped that this regional code of conduct, based primarily on respect for national sovereignty, would promote peaceful coexistence in Southeast Asia. By adhering to the TAC, the Indochinese states would have accepted the norms and principles promoted by ASEAN. Indeed, the TAC was an implicit attempt to reach some kind of accommodation with Hanoi and to include Vietnam in a stable regional order. In addition, the Treaty was expected to consolidate a common ASEAN identity when dealing with extra-mural relations. Yet, the Indochinese states remained suspicious, viewing ASEAN as an anti-communist arrangement. While wishing to develop good bilateral relations with the different members, Vietnam refused to treat with the Association as a distinct diplomatic grouping. By rejecting the TAC, Hanoi thwarted ASEAN's attempt to promote a new regional order in Southeast Asia.

Nevertheless, the 1976 Bali Summit represents a cornerstone in the institutional evolution of ASEAN. It provided ASEAN with a political identity, a shared approach to security and a code of conduct for regulating intra-mural relations and managing existing or potential disputes. Codified within the TAC, the code of conduct relied on a modest set of international norms and principles that characterized the lowest common denominator among the regional partners. As in the case of the Bangkok Declaration, respect for national sovereignty, in contrast to the notion of political integration, was set forward as the core ASEAN principle. The Association was also explicitly portrayed as a political and security arrangement, though characterized by a low level of institutionalization and lacking mechanisms for concrete confidence-building measures or preventive diplomacy. ASEAN continued to rely on dialogue and to operate through a mode of conflict avoidance and management. The Bali Summit emphasized the need for a peaceful and non-confrontational approach to cooperation and made clear that ASEAN would deal with security matters through political and economic means rather than by conventional military methods. Originally emphasizing domestic regime consolidation and regional consultation, the Association also gained an extra-mural relevance as a response to the events in Indochina. Finally, the Bali Summit strengthened a sense of regionalism amongst the members that further defined the Association as a regional entity. In sum, the Bali Summit was essential for the development of ASEAN as a regime for cooperative security.

Still, the second summit of the ASEAN heads of state and government in Kuala Lumpur in August 1977 was disappointing. It celebrated ASEAN's tenth anniversary but failed to contribute to the institutional evolution of the Association. Attempts to develop peaceful relations with the Indochinese states were repeated. The final communiqué stated that the heads of state and government 'emphasized the desire of ASEAN countries to develop peaceful and mutually beneficial relations with all countries in the region, including Kampuchea, Laos and Vietnam'.[57] The summit led also to the development of the ASEAN Post-Ministerial Conference (PMC). Indeed, it was followed by a series of bilateral meetings with the heads of government of Australia, Japan and New Zealand.

Vietnam's invasion of Cambodia in December 1978 represented a major challenge to the Association and its institutional norms. The aggression violated ASEAN's central principle, namely respect for national sovereignty, and endangered the security interests of some of its members, particularly Thailand which became a front-line state, by affecting the Southeast Asian distribution of power. The Third Indochina Conflict dominated the activities of the organization for the following twelve years during which it showed its capacity to speak with one voice. The conflict also indicated its limitations and weaknesses.

ASEAN's collective response to the Cambodian issue raised the level of political and security cooperation among its member states. Playing an effective diplomatic role, especially at the UN, the Association enhanced its reputation as a regional organization. During a special meeting of the foreign ministers held on 12 January 1979, the members recalled 'the pledge given by Vietnam to the ASEAN member countries to strictly respect the independence, sovereignty and territorial integrity of each country and to cooperate with those countries in maintaining and strengthening regional peace and stability'.[58] ASEAN sponsored in September 1979 a resolution in the United Nations General Assembly (UNGA) that confirmed the legitimacy of the ousted government of Democratic Kampuchea (DK) and one in November of that year that demanded a cease-fire in Cambodia, the withdrawal of all foreign troops and called for the right of self-determination for the Cambodian people. Afterwards, ASEAN lobbied yearly at the UN to ensure the annual condemnation of Vietnam's occupation of Cambodia. It also helped create in June 1982 the coalition government of Democratic Kampuchea which brought together the three Khmer resistance factions as a way of keeping the UN seat.[59] In sum, ASEAN prevented Vietnam's puppet regime in Phnom Penh from gaining international recognition.

Nevertheless, ASEAN's reaction to the Third Indochina Conflict was limited to collective diplomacy owing to its lack of military capabilities and an aversion to intra-ASEAN military cooperation. ASEAN was unable to offer Thailand the means necessary to counter Vietnamese power. This limitation forced Bangkok to rely increasingly on its strategic alignment with the PRC to pressure Vietnam militarily.[60] Besides upholding its legalistic position, the Association was obliged to take part in a tacit alliance with China and the United States to prevent Vietnam from dominating Indochina. ASEAN fulfilled a diplomatic role within this coalition. Divergent security perspectives also distinguished the member states. Thailand and Singapore followed a strong anti-Vietnamese position while supporting China's active involvement in the conflict. In contrast, Indonesia and Malaysia considered the PRC as their prime security concern and remained suspicious of its regional ambitions. Vietnam was thus viewed as a useful buffer against potential northern threats.

The limitations of ASEAN's diplomacy over Cambodia indicate the constraints associated with cooperative security. They display the minimal influence of a cooperative security regime when dealing with military and/or external matters. ASEAN can in such cases only be expected to operate as an instrument for collective diplomacy. Significantly, the Association played only a secondary role in the final diplomatic stages that led to the resolution of the Third Indochina Conflict. As argued before, cooperative security is intended to be comprehensive in membership with security arrangements obtaining on an intra-mural basis. It promotes a preventive approach to security and lacks any kind of cooperative military dimension. In short, a regime for cooperative security is strictly speaking unable to assist beyond collective diplomacy any of its participants when faced with an external security threat. Moreover, cooperative security does not preclude the divergence of security perspectives and interests among the member countries.

The 'ASEAN Way' and the weakening of ASEAN since 1997

The associative dimension of ASEAN has been discussed so far by paying attention to formal agreements. Yet, an informal process of interaction, the so-called 'ASEAN Way', has also influenced its institutional experience. In this part, some of its characteristics are reviewed before analysing its distinctiveness and the extent to which it has been a function of the relative homogeneity of the Association up to 1997. At issue is whether the 'ASEAN Way' is more than a piece of rhetoric designed to register a brand identity. The 'ASEAN Way' may be defined as an allegedly distinctive and informal process of interaction within the ASEAN framework through which the members relate to each other and reach but also avoid common decisions. It has existed as an abstract and ill-defined concept. It consists of various features that include: a high level of informality, the practice of quiet diplomacy, a continuing process of dialogue, a willingness to exercise self-restraint, solidarity, the practice of consensus building and the art of conflict avoidance. The standard norms and principles mentioned earlier, including respect for national sovereignty and non-intervention in the internal affairs of member states, are also integrated into this process of interaction of a quasi-familial kind.

ASEAN negotiations are characterized by informality. At the highest level, private talks, held during golf games, meals or other forms of social gatherings at the periphery of official meetings, are often seen as more appropriate by the participants than formal sessions or multilateral conferences. Thanks to a high level of informality, the members are expected to feel more comfortable when dealing with each other. In addition to the AMMs and the summits of heads of state and government, ASEAN's institutional process is distinguished by a series of ad hoc sessions, including sub-committees and working groups. These additional meetings are an essential part of the framework of cooperation as they advance a sense of security and trust between the member countries.

The 'ASEAN Way' is also defined by a practice of consensus building and conflict avoidance that ensures the sovereign equality of the member states. During the process of consultation, consensus is slowly built up between all the actors involved through the avoidance of stated disagreements. This practice of negotiation is supposed to require a willingness by the various parties involved to compromise on their own self-interests for the sake of the larger group.[61] ASEAN states practise conflict avoidance by not addressing specific problems and disputes. Thus, the Association does not aim to solve differences but rather to promote a peaceful security environment. This approach to conflict management has long been seen as the only way available for weak states to consolidate their domestic legitimacy and promote regional stability. It has been an essential part of the process of regional reconciliation started in 1967.

The 'ASEAN Way' represents an informal style of diplomacy for co-operation and conflict avoidance. It is a process-oriented and network-based model of cooperation that avoids bureaucratic arrangements found in some other organizations such as the European Union (EU). In that respect, ASEAN's process of interaction has often been contrasted to the European model of political and economic integration and is said to have established a kind of familiar and personal atmosphere that offers the Association a particular quality.[62] Indeed, it has been argued that the 'ASEAN Way' offers a distinctive model relying on specific cultural attributes.

This assertion remains questionable. Beyond the rhetoric, the 'ASEAN Way' may be analysed as a traditional inter-governmental approach to cooperation dependent on the narrowly defined interests of the participating states. This process of interaction is based on a decentralized and loosely coordinated framework of cooperation that is supervised by foreign ministers and heads of state and government.[63] In addition to the influence of cultural attributes, the 'ASEAN Way' seems primarily dominated by national interests that take complete precedence in case of disagreements.[64] As a result, the constant search for consensus and solidarity can be observed as a sign of weakness as it prevents discussions on more tangible or sensitive issues. Acharya explains that a 'great deal of what passes for the "ASEAN way" (. . .) is simply a pragmatic and practical response to situations in which multilateralism is being constrained by individual state interests'.[65] The distinctiveness of this process of interaction may be refuted when compared to other sub-regional cooperative groupings equally constrained by national interests and inter-governmental features.[66]

The applicability of the 'ASEAN Way' has been affected since 1997 by an expansion of membership and a series of crises that have decreased the cohesion of the institution. The end of the Cold War and the Cambodian settlement made possible the original hope of uniting the entire sub-region under ASEAN auspices. Confidence existed in ASEAN's ability to increase peace and stability. Though not a direct participant to the eventual resolution of the war, the Association had been transformed by its involvement in the Third Indochina Conflict into a respected and well-known diplomatic arrangement. ASEAN had first been enlarged to include Brunei in January 1984. Its post-Cold War expansion started with Vietnam in July 1995, which symbolized the institutionalization of a process of reconciliation between Hanoi and the ASEAN states.[67] By then, ASEAN had established the ARF and taken the initiative over the Asia–Europe Meeting (ASEM) that was later inaugurated in Bangkok in March 1996. Myanmar (Burma) was the last Southeast Asian state to adhere to the TAC in July 1995. At the fifth ASEAN summit held in Bangkok in December 1995, which was attended for the first time by the ten Southeast Asian heads of state and government, a commitment was made to bring all the Southeast Asian states into the group by the year 2000.[68] Enlargement was expected to lead to an increase in influence at the regional level to counter major powers in the ARF and to a better assimilation of traditionally isolated and isolationist countries. Yet, the entry of Myanmar and Cambodia damaged ASEAN.

Washington and the EU pressured the member states to delay Myanmar's adherence to the Association due to its brutal military regime and human rights record. Western pressure was unpersuasive and even counter-productive. ASEAN had declared its desire to engage Myanmar rather than to isolate it through economic and political sanctions. Having been committed to a policy of 'constructive engagement',[69] the members could not give in without prejudicing their own independence. Moreover, excluding Myanmar on grounds of domestic considerations would have been at odds with ASEAN's basic norm of non-interference in the internal affairs of other members. Differences still existed among the member states. Singapore, Indonesia and Malaysia supported Myanmar's entry into the Association and criticized Western intervention. Thailand and the Philippines were more concerned about the military regime and its lack of domestic reforms. Partly to avoid a hazardous precedent, the decision was taken to accept Myanmar with Laos and Cambodia in July 1997. Myanmar's admission was also influenced by geopolitical calculations; namely the need to reduce China's growing influence on Yangon (Rangoon).

In the case of Cambodia, antagonism between its two prime ministers, Norodom Ranariddh and Hun Sen, resulted in the latter seizing power in

Phnom Penh on 5 July 1997. The outbreak of violence occurred just weeks prior to the AMM expected to celebrate a united Southeast Asia on the occasion of ASEAN's thirtieth anniversary. An ASEAN delegation, led by Indonesia's Foreign Minister Ali Alatas and consisting also of the foreign ministers of Thailand and the Philippines, met Hun Sen, Ranariddh and King Norodom Sihanouk but failed to mediate in the internal conflict. The member states reluctantly decided to delay the Cambodian membership at a special meeting of the foreign ministers held in Kuala Lumpur on 10 July 1997. The joint statement declared that 'in the light of unfortunate circumstances which have resulted from the use of force, the wisest course of action is to delay the admission of Cambodia into ASEAN until a later date.'[70] At the AMM on 24–25 July 1997, the foreign ministers 'expressed regret that Cambodia could not be admitted into ASEAN due to the present circumstances in the country'.[71] Hun Sen's action caused embarrassment and led to discussions on the problems of enlargement and the applicability of the principle of non-intervention.[72] ASEAN's reaction to the Cambodian coup was a direct violation of its non-interference principle as it made Cambodia's entry conditional upon the domestic situation. This contrasted the case of Cambodia to ASEAN's handling of Myanmar's membership.

In response to the events in Cambodia, Malaysia's Deputy Prime Minister Anwar Ibrahim proposed in July 1997 the notion of 'constructive intervention' and argued that 'ASEAN must now move from being a largely reactive organization to one that is proactive. We need to "intervene" before simmering problems erupt into full-blown crises.'[73] Thailand's Foreign Minister Surin Pitsuwan suggested in June 1998 the need to amend the basic principle of non-interference, which caused disagreement between the member states at the annual ministerial meeting of July 1998. Only supported by Thailand and the Philippines, the notion of 'flexible engagement' was strongly rejected by the other members that feared interference in their domestic affairs. Singapore's Foreign Minister Professor S. Jayakumar referred to ASEAN's basic principles, including the concept of non-interference, in his opening statement. He declared that they 'have contributed to ASEAN's success in the past, and will continue to do so in the future. Discarding them will not make ASEAN stronger. To the contrary, to do so may imperil ASEAN's future.'[74] The notion of 'flexible engagement' was eventually softened to the euphemistic compromise of 'enhanced interaction'. The admission of Cambodia was again discussed during the sixth ASEAN summit organized in Hanoi in December 1998. Thailand, Singapore and the Philippines wanted to delay its membership while Vietnam and Indonesia in particular but also Malaysia, Laos and Myanmar favoured its early participation. After its future admission had been announced in Hanoi, Cambodia joined ASEAN in April 1999.

In addition to the problems of expansion, ASEAN was incapable of avoiding and later dealing with the ecological disaster that followed the forest fires in Sumatra and Kalimantan in 1997. The haze, that reached

Malaysia, Singapore and Brunei and parts of Thailand and the Philippines, marked a significant failure in environmental management and intra-mural cooperation that discredited ASEAN as a sub-regional diplomatic player.[75] Subsequently, the member countries experienced an acute economic adversity that started with the collapse of the Thai baht in July 1997. The Association was unable to make a substantial contribution to a potential economic recovery and the member states had to rely on international help, especially from the International Monetary Fund (IMF) and the World Bank, and domestic initiatives. The East Asian financial crisis of 1997–98 confirmed the underdevelopment of ASEAN as an economic institution. Indonesia was most affected by the crisis that severely worsened its socio-economic problems and student-led protests provoked the unexpected downfall of Suharto in May 1998. These events influenced the status and political condition of the Association. The loss of Indonesian leadership, that followed the fall of Suharto and the collapse of Indonesia's economy, further weakened the regime for cooperative security. ASEAN cannot be expected to significantly move forward when its leading member is absorbed by domestic difficulties.

In short, the enlargement process has questioned the application of ASEAN principles. It has weakened the effectiveness of the Association by complicating the process of consultation and the achievement of consensus that governs decision-making. This has resulted in a decline in unity and harmony among the participants. When set in the wider context of the East Asian financial crisis and the loss of Indonesian leadership, it must be said that ASEAN has since 1997 developed into a less influential and cohesive institution. In addition to questioning some of its core principles, all these events have weakened the Association by diminishing its capacity to speak with one voice and enhancing the divergence of interests among the member states. ASEAN has over the past few years been characterized by its inability to act, a lack of common vision and the absence of substantial developments. The successive crises have also demonstrated that the ASEAN process of interaction is more fruitful in a buoyant regional economic climate and that it loses most of its appeal during a period of harsh recession. The relevance of the 'ASEAN Way' seems therefore to depend on specific circumstances; namely, the relative homogeneity of the sub-regional association and the national interests involved.

Nevertheless, as a result of the terror attacks in the United States on 11 September 2001 and the bombings on the Indonesian island of Bali on 12 October 2002 that killed almost 200 people, the threat of terrorism in Southeast Asia has become a new common ground for cooperation within ASEAN.[76] The issue of terrorism dominated the seventh ASEAN summit in Brunei in November 2001, during which the heads of state and government endorsed the ASEAN Declaration on Joint Action to Counter Terrorism.[77] They declared their commitment to counter, prevent and suppress all acts of terrorism, in adherence to international law and the UN Charter, and called for the adoption of counter-terrorist measures. A Special ASEAN Ministerial Meeting on Terrorism was also organized in Kuala Lumpur in May 2002.[78] Following the Bali bombings, the ASEAN heads of state and government signed a Declaration on Terrorism during their summit in Phnom Penh in early November 2002. The leaders pledged to carry out the anti-terror measures adopted previously and declared that the 'ASEAN countries shall continue with practical cooperative measures among ourselves and with the international community.'[79] It is still too soon to say, however, whether these declarations and their non-binding recommendations will ever be implemented or simply remain proclamations of good intentions.

Interestingly, the 'ASEAN Way' is particularly adequate for the exchange of intelligence on terrorism. For instance, discrete discussions can be held through the ASEAN Foreign Ministers' Retreat that first met in July 1999 on militant Islamic groups, such as *Jemaah Islamiah* (*JI*), and on the means available for these extremist groups to organize and fund their operations. Yet, it is impossible to assess the impact of the 'ASEAN Way' on a joint response to terrorism, as the content of these conversations is kept secret. One can therefore only speculate on the role of the 'ASEAN Way' as a means of improving intelligence sharing.

ASEAN's achievements and limitations as a regime for cooperative security

ASEAN's greatest accomplishment as a cooperative security regime is related to its contribution to conflict avoidance and management. It has operated as an instrument to avoid the recurrence of conflict. For example, Singapore's Foreign Minister Professor S. Jayakumar affirmed in 1998 that ASEAN's primary role is 'to manage relationships which have been and could otherwise still, all too easily turn conflictual'.[80] The likelihood of regional states using force to resolve disputes has decreased.[81] ASEAN has improved the climate of regional relations and has generally succeeded in containing peacefully, rather than addressing or solving, differences between its members. Its approach to conflict avoidance and management has been defined by the absence of concrete confidence-building measures and preventive diplomacy. Rejecting formal or legal mechanisms, ASEAN has relied on dialogue and consultation, the practices of self-restraint and consensus building and on the principles of national sovereignty and non-interference in the domestic affairs of other states. External intervention may also have been prevented by the reduction of intra-mural tensions.

Nonetheless, ASEAN's shortcomings as a diplomatic tool to manage intra-regional disputes should be noted. It is unable to solve sources of conflict and is ill equipped to deal with pressing matters or with controversial issues where clashing interests cannot be avoided. The member states have never used their own dispute resolution mechanism, the High Council, to settle tensions or latent conflicts. Their mode of conflict avoidance has been restricted to the management of inter-state tensions. At the domestic level, the Association has been paralysed by its non-interference principle as demonstrated by the crisis in East Timor in 1999. Due to these limitations, regional relations have continued to be influenced by feelings of suspicion, competition and a series of territorial disputes.[82] The members maintain separate national security policies in which other participants are still perceived as potential enemies. This is particularly the case of Singapore. Persisting bilateral disputes have affected ASEAN's contribution to conflict management and are key factors undermining the stability of the cooperative security regime.[83] Moreover, border clashes between Thailand and Myanmar in early 2001 led to an extensive exchange of fire and demonstrated that the use of force between member states could not be excluded. Hence, the Association should be defined as a security regime rather than as a security community due to the persistence of numerous disputes and the ongoing possibility of a clash of arms in Southeast Asia. Bilateral relations have also continued to be troubled by minor matters that can lead to larger diplomatic incidents. For example, the execution of a Filipino maid by the Singaporean authorities in March 1995 led to a surge of nationalism in the Philippines and strained bilateral relations. Singapore–Malaysian ties have also been affected by political comments, including remarks by the Singaporean Senior Minister Lee Kuan Yew on the crime rate in Johor, that demonstrated the continuing complexity and vulnerability of these relations.

ASEAN has integrated within its structure a set of norms and principles and introduced a code of conduct regulating intra-mural relations. Since its creation, the institution has constituted a normative foundation that seeks to persuade its participants to 'pursue "self-inhibiting" and peaceful behaviour in inter-state relations'.[84] This represents an achievement when considering the kind of regional interactions that preceded the establishment of the Association. Hence, ASEAN has been successful in fulfilling some of the objectives associated with security regimes. These include the enhancement of regional security through the application of norms and principles. Relevant to this process has been the TAC, which formally introduced a norm-based code of conduct in the ASEAN framework. The adherence to the TAC has in the post-Cold War gradually been extended to all Southeast Asian states.

Furthermore, ASEAN's inter-state relations have been highly institutionalized, though not in a European sense, by the holding of a considerable number of yearly meetings at formal and informal levels. Relying on an inter-governmental approach to cooperation, the ASEAN states also agreed during the 1992 summit of heads of state and government in Singapore to 'meet formally every three years with informal meetings in between'.[85] ASEAN has developed according to an inter-governmental approach to cooperation. Its Secretariat cannot be compared to the supra-national institutions developed by the EU. For instance, the Secretary-General is only head of the Secretariat rather than a head representative of the Association. This results from the fact that ASEAN has constantly reaffirmed the principles of national sovereignty and non-interference in the domestic affairs of other states and has remained an arrangement with no supra-national power or character. Indeed, it has never promoted political or economic integration.

Finally, ASEAN has succeeded in partly re-defining sub-regional relations with external powers by becoming a diplomatic player of some relevance in the international society. This factor should not be exaggerated though as the participants have neither established an autonomous order nor has ASEAN become an economic or trading grouping of real significance. Still, the Association has given a sense of diplomatic confidence to its members.[86] For instance, the AMM has since 1978 been followed by a PMC with ASEAN's dialogue partners. As such, ASEAN has gained diplomatic influence by establishing regular diplomatic contacts with essential actors including the United States, Japan and the EU. Moreover, the Third Indochina Conflict transformed the institution into a well-known and respected international diplomatic community. More recently, the terror attacks on 11 September have further consolidated ASEAN's relations with its dialogue partners, particularly the United States. The member countries have stipulated that an effective response to the threat of terrorism in Southeast Asia would demand deeper forms of cooperation with their key regional partners. The ten member states signed during their thirty-fifth AMM in Brunei in July 2002 a joint declaration on counter-terrorism with the United States, represented by Secretary of State Colin Powell.[87] The political statement confirmed ASEAN's commitment to the international war on terrorism.

Nevertheless, it is at the extra-mural level that ASEAN has also shown its greatest limitations. The management of regional order is beyond its influence, which is reduced to collective diplomacy. The Third Indochina Conflict demonstrated that its approach to cooperation rapidly becomes inappropriate when applied to external matters and where military coercion is required. Its diplomatic relevance in this case was dependent on special circumstances; namely, its close cooperation with China and the United States. When lacking the support of great powers, as is the case with regard to its involvement in the South China Sea dispute, ASEAN's diplomatic influence on external matters becomes much more limited indeed. These shortcomings may be associated with cooperative security, which excludes military cooperation and relies on an intra-mural basis.

Creation and development of the ARF

Origins and institutional progress of the ARF

With the exception of ASEAN, the East–West ideological rivalry as well as a series of strong bilateral security agreements linking the United States to its regional allies meant that bilateralism had dominated the Cold War regional security architecture. Moreover, the absence of multilateralism in East Asia resulted not only from the region's extreme diversity in economic and political systems but also in strategic perspectives.[88] Western attempts to promote multilateral security cooperation came in the form of multilateral alliances. They included the ANZUS Treaty signed by the United States, Australia and New Zealand in September 1951 and the South-East Asia Collective Defence Treaty, or Manila Pact, of September 1954 and its institutional structure, the South-East Asia Treaty Organization (SEATO), created in February 1955. These multilateral security undertakings were entangled in the East–West confrontation and dominated by a military dimension and by the participation of external powers.

At the end of the Cold War, some regional specialists and policy-makers suggested that traditional bilateral security arrangements would not be sufficient to address a rising regional interdependence and cope with the uncertain security environment in East Asia. This led to a variety of proposals to promote multilateralism. At issue though was the lack of prospect of multilateral security cooperation on any other basis than a variant of ASEAN's model of cooperative security. Mikhael Gorbachev had already called during his Vladivostok speech of July 1986 for the creation of an Asian-Pacific equivalent to the Conference on Security and Cooperation in Europe (CSCE), which had resulted from the Helsinki Final Act of 1975. At the ASEAN-PMC held in Jakarta in July 1990, Gareth Evans and Joe Clark, the foreign ministers of Australia and Canada, suggested separately an Asia-Pacific conference on security and cooperation. This was opposed by the United States that feared the potential weakening of its bilateral security arrangements. In addition, most East Asian leaders felt uncomfortable with a European model for cooperation. Most regional players did not support an overly structured and complex form of multilateralism and preferred instead a flexible and informal manner whereby the level of institutionalization could be kept to a minimum. Post-Cold War multilateral security cooperation in the Asia-Pacific seemed therefore to be dependent on an extension of the ASEAN model to the wider region.

The idea of using the PMC as a forum for a regional security dialogue was officially discussed during the 1991 AMM and confirmed at the highest level during the fourth summit of heads of state and government held in Singapore in January 1992.[89] The first discussions on regional security were held at the ASEAN-PMC in Manila in July 1992. Encouraged by Tokyo and Washington, a first ASEAN-PMC Senior Officials Meeting (SOM) was organized in Singapore in May 1993. The foreign ministers of the ASEAN countries and of the seven dialogue partners – namely Japan, South Korea, Australia, New Zealand, the United States, Canada and the EU – decided at the meeting to invite the foreign ministers of China, Russia, Vietnam, Laos and Papua New Guinea to a special session in Singapore in July 1993 that would coincide with the annual meeting of the ASEAN foreign ministers. The founding dinner of the ARF was held in Singapore on 25 July 1993 and it was agreed that the first working session would take place in Bangkok one year later. An informal process of dialogue was also developed by several research institutes through the establishment in June 1993 of the Council for Security Cooperation in the Asia-Pacific (CSCAP) as a 'track-two' instrument to complement governmental activities and promote security cooperation through non-governmental efforts.

ASEAN's decision to establish the ARF resulted from several motivations. First, changes in the regional strategic environment forced the ASEAN countries to question their sub-regional approach to security. This primarily resulted from the external origins of post-Cold War security challenges and the strategic and economic interdependence linking their sub-region to the rest of the Asia-Pacific.[90] Rather than expanding the PMC, the Association decided to form a new multilateral security dialogue. Second, the ARF was seen by the ASEAN states as an instrument to 'engage Beijing in a comprehensive fashion in a stable regional international system'.[91] Finally, ASEAN hoped to consolidate its diplomatic position in the post-Cold War, particularly since the 1991 International Conference on Cambodia that concluded the Third Indochina Conflict. In an attempt to preserve its post-Cold War relevance, ASEAN sought to develop, or further define, its stabilizing role in Southeast Asian relations through the formation of the ARF. The member states needed to avoid being excluded from a new strategic architecture that was chiefly dependent on a Chinese–Japanese–US triangle.

Most regional actors supported the position of leadership adopted by ASEAN. Its primary role in the formation of the ARF resulted from the fact that no other regional player was in a position to propose the development of a multilateral security dialogue. In addition, Acharya explains that 'ASEAN's own norms and institutional style provided a ready-made foundation upon which the ARF could build itself.'[92] Still, the Forum would never have been realized without the support and participation of the United States, Japan and China. As declared in a speech to the South Korean National Assembly in July 1993, the US President Bill Clinton supported the notion of cooperation through a multilateral security dialogue. Japan also played an important role in the ARF by being an instrument in pioneering its formation. Finally, leaders in Beijing, who had generally perceived multilateralism as an attempt to contain Chinese rising power or to interfere in the Taiwan issue, were reassured by the fact that ASEAN was leading the new cooperative process.

The first ARF meeting took place in Bangkok on 25 July 1994 and had been preceded by the first ARF Senior Officials Meeting (SOM) in Bangkok in May of that year, which had contributed to its organization. The gathering of eighteen foreign ministers to discuss Asian-Pacific security matters was a symbolic achievement. The chairman's statement declared that 'the ARF had enabled the countries in the Asia-Pacific to foster the habit of constructive dialogue and consultation on political and security issues of common interest and concern.'[93] The first meeting led to several tangible successes. It was agreed that the Forum would meet annually and the different participants accepted ASEAN's TAC as a code of conduct for regulating regional relations.[94] By extending the geographical ambit of its treaty, the Association hoped that other ARF participants would reject the use of force as a means to solve disputes with ASEAN states. It had in mind Beijing and its territorial claims in the South China Sea.[95] Reports on security matters, including nuclear non-proliferation, were commissioned for the next ARF session.

The second annual ministerial meeting, which welcomed Cambodia as a participant, took place in Brunei on 1 August 1995 and led to the acceptance of a Concept Paper that outlined the future evolution of the Forum. It stated that the ARF would progress through three stages of security cooperation: confidence building, preventive diplomacy (PD) and conflict resolution mechanisms. As a result of China's demands, the third stage was amended to 'elaboration of approaches to conflicts' in the chairman's statement.[96] This manifested China's influence on the cooperative process. The ARF was said to be in its first stage of development. The Concept Paper affirmed: 'In its initial phase, the ARF should (. . .) concentrate on enhancing the trust and confidence amongst participants and thereby foster a regional environment conductive to maintaining the peace and prosperity of the region.'[97] It also suggested two complementary approaches to security cooperation: one based on ASEAN's experience and practice of cooperation and the other on 'the implementation of concrete confidence-building measures'.[98] Two lists of measures (Annexes A and B) were set out, the first to be implemented in the immediate future and the second in the longer run. Finally, the Concept Paper introduced 'track-two activities' aimed at discussing sensitive security questions, including proposals mentioned in Annex B, through non-governmental institutes and organizations.

Furthermore, the Concept Paper consolidated ASEAN's leading role in the organizational activities of the ARF. It was agreed that all major meetings would be held in ASEAN capitals and hosted by the members of the Association. The Concept Paper also declared that ASEAN would provide the bureaucratic framework to support ARF activities. Finally, it stipulated that the Forum's procedures had to be based: 'on prevailing ASEAN norms and practices. Decisions should be made by consensus and after careful and extensive consultations. No voting will take place.'[99] The Concept Paper provoked resentment among some participants, including South Korea which felt annoyed by ASEAN's managerial position and its own inability to introduce a Northeast Asian security dialogue.

The second ARF meeting led to the establishment of Inter-Sessional Support Groups (ISGs), to be co-chaired by an ASEAN and non-ASEAN participant, which would meet between the annual ministerial sessions. It was agreed to organize an ISG on confidence-building measures (CBMs) to be co-chaired for the first year by Indonesia and Japan. A series of Inter-Sessional Meetings (ISMs) were also set up to deal with cooperative activities, including peacekeeping operations, confidence-building measures, disaster relief and search and rescue missions. The two structures were created to recommend ways of implementing proposals set out in Annex A of the Concept Paper. As explained by the International Institute for Strategic Studies (IISS), the use of 'two different names for two evidently similar bodies was again intended to accommodate China's objections, in this case to any impression of continuous institutionalized activities'.[100]

The third session was held in Jakarta in July 1996 and led to continuing efforts for regional cooperative security. It was decided to organize a new ISM on disaster relief and the Philippines and China proposed co-chairing the following ISG on CBMs in Beijing in March 1997. The idea of 'track-two' sessions on preventive diplomacy and non-proliferation through CSCAP was also introduced. One should note the Singapore conference of September 1997 that followed the initiative. A set of criteria for membership was adopted in Jakarta.[101] Among others, ARF participants needed to be sovereign states, which excluded Taiwan's future involvement. Moreover, the annual session led to the admission of Myanmar and India. India's participation complicated the dialogue by introducing a new set of security matters within the Forum. The ASEAN initiative to enlarge the geographical scope of the ARF was not well received by some participants, including the United States and Japan, which would have preferred a deepening, rather than an enlargement, of the diplomatic process. In contrast, China supported India's involvement, which it considered as an additional means to avoid a US domination of the Forum.[102]

Partly due to the effects of the financial crisis of 1997–98, the more recent annual ministerial meetings have yielded almost no progress. As a result, the ARF has been criticized for being no more than a 'talk shop' that is unable to respond to security developments in the Asia-Pacific. The fourth meeting organized in Subang Jaya in July 1997 was dominated by the entry of Myanmar into ASEAN and the coup in Cambodia. Western criticism over the issue of human rights in Myanmar was brought into the Forum. Initially agreed at the second ARF meeting, the chairman's statement of 1997 reiterated that the ARF would attempt to move towards the second stage of development in cases where preventive diplomacy overlapped with confidence building.[103] Yet, no progress towards a transition was made during the 1998 and 1999 ministerial meetings, held respectively in Manila and Singapore. Although acknowledging the need to discuss the concept of preventive diplomacy, the chairman's statement of 1999 declared: 'The Ministers emphasised the importance of confidence building to the success of the ARF and encouraged the further development of confidence building measures (CBMs).'[104] Progress was hampered due to the lack of agreement over the definition and scope of preventive diplomacy, especially whether it might involve a breach of national sovereignty.

Organized in Hanoi in July 2001, the eighth ARF meeting affirmed that confidence building would remain 'the foundation and main thrust of the whole ARF process'.[105] However, some steps were taken towards preventive diplomacy. The meeting adopted a document on the Concept and Principles of Preventive Diplomacy that defined and outlined eight principles of preventive diplomacy.[106] The foreign ministers also endorsed papers on the Enhanced Role of the ARF Chair and on the Terms of Reference for ARF Experts/Eminent Persons. Following the terror attacks on 11 September, the question of terrorism dominated the ninth ARF meeting held in Brunei in July 2002. The foreign ministers endorsed an ARF Statement on Measures Against Terrorist Financing and announced the establishment of an ISM on counter-terrorism and transnational crime to be co-chaired by Malaysia and the United States. With regard to regional stability, the chairman's statement declared that the ARF 'continues to make significant progress in addressing regional security concerns, implementing confidence building measures and initiating exploratory work on preventive diplomacy'.[107] The foreign ministers also stressed the need for an active participation of defence and military officials, who so far have only played a marginal role in the ARF. Interestingly, the ninth session followed the Asia Security Conference organized by IISS in Singapore in May 2002. The conference was the first gathering of Asia-Pacific defence ministers to discuss regional security concerns.

The ARF as an inter-governmental discussion group for cooperative security

Founded on the principle of inclusiveness, the ARF is a multilateral discussion group focusing on dialogue and confidence-building measures as a first step to cooperative security. It is based on a multilateral perspective that aims to complement a bilateral approach, which has traditionally relied on military deterrence to preserve a stable security environment. The ARF is the first inclusive security arrangement at the level of the Asia-Pacific. Multilateral discussions are for the first time being held on regional problems and security matters. The Forum is an instrument to share information, promote confidence-building measures and enhance the practice of transparency. It helps lessen feelings of suspicion. It also provides a regional opportunity to discuss different views on security and integrate isolated countries into the regional security system.[108] Significantly, ASEAN has institutionalized a multilateral security dialogue in the Asia-Pacific despite America's preference for bilateral structures and China's suspicion of multilateralism. The discussion group also includes Japan and Russia. As pointed out by Singapore's Foreign Minister Professor S. Jayakumar, the ARF has thus become 'a means of encouraging the evolution of a more predictable and constructive pattern of relations between major powers with interests in the region'.[109]

The ARF has been a helpful tool to tackle the climate of regional security relations. In addition to implementing confidence-building measures, it has provided useful opportunities to defuse tensions deriving from specific crises. For instance, the second annual ARF session was influenced by two matters, which had affected regional stability in the first part of the year. The Philippines had discovered in February 1995 the Chinese occupation of the Philippine claimed Mischief Reef, located in the Spratly Islands. The 1992 ASEAN Declaration on the South China Sea, which calls for a peaceful resolution of the dispute, was mentioned in the chairman's statement of 1995. Regional security had also been influenced by a deterioration in Sino-US relations after Taiwanese President Lee Teng Hui had been offered a visa for a private visit to the United States in June 1995. The ARF meeting provided an avenue for Washington and Beijing to initiate a new process of diplomatic *rapprochement*. The ARF has also served as a vehicle to promote dialogue with North Korea. The latter joined the Forum at its seventh ministerial meeting in Bangkok in July 2000. The session included a meeting between US Secretary of State Madeleine Albright and North Korean Foreign Minister Paek Nam-Sun, representing the highest level bilateral talks since the Korean War (1950–53). Paek also held separate discussions with the foreign ministers of South Korea and Japan. The ARF meeting paved the way for Albright's visit to Pyongyang in October 2000 where she met senior North Korean officials, including Chairman Kim Jong-Il. The ARF meeting in July 2002 offered an opportunity to the United States and North Korea to resume a dialogue. Secretary of State Colin Powell met Paek on the sidelines of the gathering in Brunei. Bilateral relations had significantly worsened since the election of US President George W. Bush, particularly after his State of the Union address on 29 January 2002 that had characterized North Korea, Iran and Iraq as an 'Axis of Evil'.

Nonetheless, the shortcomings of the ARF in respect of the main regional security concerns, which are the Korean peninsula, Taiwan and the South China Sea dispute, should be kept in mind. The institution is in no position to tackle these issues. The minimal involvement of the ARF in the South China Sea dispute is examined in Chapter 6. North Korea only joined the Forum in 2000. The Korean question had until then been addressed bilaterally and through the organization of multilateral talks involving the United States, the PRC and the two Koreas. The ARF had also made some general statements on the Korean peninsula. Opposing Taipei's participation in the Forum, the PRC refuses to discuss the Taiwan issue, which it considers a domestic matter. The 1996 events in the Taiwan Straits were also a reminder of the inability of the ARF to confront a major crisis.[110] China's military exercises in March 1996 to intimidate Taiwan and influence its coming presidential election led to a US deployment of two carrier squadrons to deter further Chinese actions. Except for Singapore and Japan, the East Asian states did not respond publicly to China's military exercises. The events demonstrated that the Asia-Pacific security environment has remained dependent on a series of bilateral power relationships, above all that between Washington and Beijing. The ARF meeting succeeded, however, in offering a vehicle for dialogue for the United States and China. In short, the influence of the Forum on inter-state relations has been restrained to the promotion of dialogue and consultation, the implementation of some confidence-building measures and attempts to foster international norms.

Having described the ARF as a multilateral discussion group for co-operative security, let us now analyse it further by comparing it to ASEAN. The Forum is based on an ASEAN model of cooperative security. This has involved transmitting to the Asia-Pacific norms and principles, an informal process of dialogue and consultation and also a mode of conflict avoidance and management developed since 1967. ASEAN has promoted within the ARF its own practices of self-restraint and consensus building and favoured an informal security dialogue over legally binding confidence measures. This tendency has resulted from its resistance to institutionalization. This should not be exaggerated though as ASEAN's political evolution has been dependent on formal agreements, including the TAC and the Concord, and on numerous yearly meetings. Finally, the ARF rejects any form of collective defence. Hence, the Association has tried to extend its 'ASEAN Way' to the rest of the region.[111]

The ARF is also defined by other characteristics that can be contrasted with an ASEAN approach to cooperative security. The Forum is already well developed in some ways given its inter-sessional activity. It has achieved through the Concept Paper a level of institutionalization never attained by the Association. Although an extension of the 'ASEAN Way', the ARF is thus linked to a more structured approach to cooperative security. Still, progress has been slow and limited. The ARF has so far led to the implement-ation of few concrete confidence-building measures. The activities of the ISGs and ISMs have included the publication of defence white papers on a voluntary basis, the promotion of dialogue on security perceptions, the exchange of views on defence policies and the organization of meetings of heads of defence colleges and institutions.

The Concept Paper emphasizes a gradual approach to security co-operation and conflict management. The ambition to move beyond confidence building by aiming, at least in the longer run, to prevent and/or solve specific disputes has been introduced through the three stages of development. As mentioned above, the participants reiterated in 1997 that the ARF would attempt to move towards preventive diplomacy where it overlapped with confidence building. Yet, until recently, the notion of preventive diplomacy was not defined in the context of the ARF beyond the imprecise definition given by the UN Secretary-General Boutros Boutros-

Ghali in 1992.[112] Discussions on a definition have been characterized by controversy and disagreement.[113] The overlap between preventive diplomacy and confidence-building measures has been debated. A working definition of preventive diplomacy was agreed upon at a workshop held by the CSCAP Working Group on Confidence- and Security-Building Measures (CSBMs) in Bangkok in early 1999 and discussed at the following ISG on CBMs.[114] After much debate, the eighth ARF meeting finally adopted in July 2001 a document on Concept and Principles of Preventive Diplomacy.

The initiative to move beyond the promotion of confidence-building measures has not been well received by some participants, especially China. In contrast to CBMs, preventive diplomacy focuses on specific security issues and has been understood by some as a more threatening form of cooperative security. The PRC rejects constraining measures and wants the ARF to remain a diplomatic instrument focusing on dialogue and consultation. Refusing to discuss the question of Taiwan, it is also unlikely that Beijing will ever accept the implementation of preventive diplomacy measures for the South China Sea. In addition, such measures contradict ASEAN's preference for conflict avoidance, which further complicates their application within an ARF framework. Though the Forum should be viewed as a long-term project, it is still legitimate to question if it will ever succeed to move towards its next stage of development.

The ARF is also defined by attributes that weaken its influence as a cooperative security arrangement. It was created despite the persistence of several security issues resulting from the Cold War, including the Korean peninsula and the Taiwan question. Hence, the ARF sought to establish a security dialogue despite the presence of regional flashpoints and can therefore be contrasted to ASEAN, which was created after the resolution of Confrontation and left with no substantial *casus belli* among its members.[115] Indeed, ASEAN post-dated conflict and conflict resolution as there were no significant problems left to address. This point distinguishes both arrangements in their approach to cooperative security and questions the applicability of the 'ASEAN Way' to an Asian-Pacific security environment. Moreover, no consensual approach to security exists among the most influential ARF participants. The joint US–Japanese Declaration of April 1996 on regional security, which revised but also reconfirmed their strategic alliance, demonstrated their persisting reliance on bilateral security structures. In comparison, Beijing supports a multipolar perspective and has criticized bilateralism as hiding a form of US unilateralism in the Asia-Pacific and an attempt to encircle the PRC as a rising power and potential threat. Contrary to the ARF, the ASEAN states adopted informally the principle of national and regional resilience as a shared security doctrine. This approach to security was a function of the relative homogeneity that existed within the sub-regional association up to 1997.

The ARF also suffers from structural limitations that affect its development. It has a large membership that confines its capacity to maintain internal coherence and develop a code of conduct. The Concept Paper stipulates that the ARF will progress based on consensus and 'at a pace comfortable to all participants'.[116] Yet, finding a general agreement on common objectives is a troubling matter, as deep divisions exist between the participants. While China and the ASEAN members favour general discussions as a way to avoid disagreements, other states, including the United States and Japan, prefer a more rapid implementation of CBMs.[117] Moreover, Canada and Australia, which are commonly viewed within the region as external players with a limited stake in East Asia, have been pressing actively for the implementation of preventive diplomacy measures. Such measures are strongly opposed by China, partly due to the fear of external interference in its domestic affairs, and are perceived with some ambivalence by the United States that prefers its regional policy and bilateral ties not to be constrained by formal measures.

The applicability of the ASEAN approach to regional security relations is another central issue. The US, Japan and China have different expectations and strategic perspectives that cannot implicitly be ignored in an 'ASEAN Way'.[118] While Washington and Tokyo see the ARF as a means of complementing existing bilateral security structures, Beijing wishes to promote multipolarity that can be regarded as a code for constraining US unilateralism. In addition, ASEAN's mode of conflict avoidance is not applicable to the Taiwan question and the Korean peninsula, which require tangible solutions. Crucial differences also contrast North from Southeast Asian security relations. With the exception of the South China Sea, the territorial disputes in Southeast Asia cannot be compared to the complex security problems that persist in the Northeast. The two sub-regions can also be differentiated with regard to the involvement of the great powers.[119] Northeast Asian relations are dominated by the security interests of the United States, China, Japan and to a lesser extent Russia. In contrast, external intervention has been reduced in post-Cold War Southeast Asia, particularly since the end of the Third Indochina Conflict.

Finally, some participants may not appreciate ASEAN's leading position in the ARF in the longer run. The diplomatic centrality and managerial role of the Association was essential to ensure an initial Chinese participation and is still supported by the PRC, Russia and India as a way to avoid a US domination of the arrangement. Yet, ASEAN's leadership has led to a concentration on Southeast Asian issues. A continued ASEAN sponsorship may cast doubt upon the relevance of the ARF with reference to Northeast Asian security issues. While these limitations do not question the usefulness of the Forum as an instrument for regional dialogue, they force us to remain realistic regarding its actual potential. No dramatic achievements should be expected to result from its activities.

Conclusion

This chapter has examined the associative experience of both ASEAN and the ARF. The Association should be regarded as a regime for cooperative security due to several factors. It has promoted norms and principles leading to an intra-mural code of conduct and established a mechanism for conflict management based on conflict avoidance rather than resolution. Additionally, ASEAN has set up an institutional framework consisting of: a structure for multilateral discussions that relies on summits of heads of state and government, ministerial meetings and ad hoc sessions; institutional arrangements, including the Concord, the TAC and ZOPFAN, and an informal process of interaction, the so-called 'ASEAN Way'. Yet, one should define the kind of security regime that has evolved in Southeast Asia since 1967. In light of the limitations addressed throughout the chapter, it can be argued that ASEAN has remained a rather weak security regime, especially since 1997. For example, its approach to cooperative security has not substantially evolved since the Bali Summit of 1976.

Despite its limitations, the ARF presents most of the characteristics of an embryonic regime for cooperative security. While an extension of the 'ASEAN Way', the Forum is linked to a more structured approach of cooperative security. It has achieved a level of institutionalization through inter-sessional activity never attained by the Association. Moreover, the ARF provides to its participants some of the advantages mentioned by a neo-liberal perspective, namely the establishment of a multilateral dialogue, an increase in transparency and the implementation of confidence-building measures. It is still uncertain, however, whether the ARF will succeed in developing a set of norms and principles respected by its many participants.

2 The role of the balance of power factor within and beyond regimes for cooperative security

Introduction

ASEAN and the ARF may be considered as regional attempts to provide for security by moving beyond conventional balance of power politics. Through their underlying premises and functions as well as their focus on long-term cooperation, both associative arrangements exclude the balance of power in principle. Nonetheless, this book argues that the institutional experience of ASEAN and the ARF was informed with some reference to the balance of power. The purpose of this chapter is to further discuss this traditional concept and to examine how it could be relevant to such inter-state arrangements, which have been conceived primarily as alternatives to its core assumptions. To that end, it addresses the balance of power factor within the study of regional regimes for cooperative security.

This chapter consists of three sections. The first examines the conventional understanding of the balance of power by reviewing its meanings, premises, objectives and modes of operation. The second section describes how the balance of power has operated as a policy over time with special reference to its military dimension. It also points out the shortcomings of balance of power politics and different alternatives that have been advocated by theorists and practitioners. The final section discusses the balance of power as a factor within cooperative security. Its possible relevance is considered before analysing the part played by this factor during ASEAN's founding moments.

Balance of power theory

No real consensus exists regarding a precise definition of the term 'balance of power' or on the actual functioning of the power balancing process in the international system. The term is often used loosely, which leads to confusion and vagueness. Martin Wight has argued, for example, that it could have nine different meanings.[1] Among many others, Inis Claude has largely contributed to a better comprehension of the term by giving it four definitions. These are: a *situation,* referring to the distribution of power; a *policy,* associated with policies taking the power situation into account and seeking to revise its pattern; a *symbol*, seen as a sign of realistic concern with the power issue; and as a *system*.[2] As a system, the phrase refers to 'a certain kind of arrangement for the operation of international relations in a world of many states'.[3]

Michael Sheehan has further described the distinction between balance of power as a policy and as a system.[4] As a policy, it involves 'the creation and preservation of equilibrium, the confrontation of power with countervailing power to prevent a single power laying down the law to all others'.[5] As a system, the balance of power has often been used as a point of reference for studying the working of the states system. As pointed out by Sheehan, the central element regarding 'the systemic approach to the balance of power is that it posits a direct structure of the state system and the behavior of states within the system'.[6] Therefore, the focus is on the interdependence and interaction existing between the states part of the system. In this book, the balance of power is studied and expressed as a policy rather than as a system.

Despite the imprecision, theorists of balance of power agree on some central principles. In its most conventional form, the balance of power theory assumes that as soon as a state's position within the anarchical state system becomes a threat to the survival of others, a countervailing initiative, based on one or more actors, is created to restrain the rising state and ensure the preservation of the states system. States need to counterbalance any potential hegemon to ensure their survival and to prevent their being dictated to. Security is approached in unilateral, competitive and zero-sum terms. Security is only possible in the system when states attempt to achieve a balanced distribution of power amongst themselves between periods of tension and conflict. Claude writes:

> If there is an orthodox position among theorists, it is that the stability and order of a multistate system, and the security of its constituent parts, are endangered by the rise of any state to preponderance, and that the essential task of the balance of power system is therefore to maintain or restore a situation of approximate equilibrium.[7]

The underlying assumptions of the balance of power theory are based on realist suppositions. As a theory, the balance of power has been at the core of classical and modern realism, the most dominant school of International Relations (IR). Historically linked with the notions of *Realpolitik* and *raison d'état,* the balance of power received a central position in the writings of Machiavelli, Hobbes and other classical realists. In modern IR theory, the concept has remained at the core of the realist paradigm and was introduced by Kenneth Waltz as the central principle of neo-realism.[8] Modern realists start with the Peace of Westphalia in 1648, which they see as creating an international states system. Realists depict this system as based on anarchy where states, the only relevant actors, focus on their survival and security.

Cooperation is limited and temporary and the emphasis is put on the distribution of power. War plays a natural role within the system as the instrument of the balance.

Balance of power theory rests on the centrality and constant pursuit of power, implicitly understood as military power, in international relations. Power is the most essential concept in realist theory. The realist tradition relies on a coercive understanding of the concept and focuses on its strategic dimension. Yet, definitions of the term have traditionally been vague.[9] Morgenthau defines political power as a person's capacity to control some of another person's actions through influencing that person's mind.[10] Power is the result of the sum of different components that include military, economic, political and ideological attributes. The notion of power is therefore impossible to measure precisely and is examined in a relational context rather than in absolute terms. A state's capabilities are measured in relation to the attributes of one or more other countries. Moreover, power is not only the result of aggregate capabilities as it also depends on a state's willingness and intention to implement its will. Morgenthau claims that 'International politics, like all politics, is a struggle for power.'[11] The notion of a constant struggle for power is problematic, as states do not limit their actions to a permanent accumulation of capabilities. Waltz addresses this limitation. He explains that 'neo-realism sees power as a possibly useful means, with states running risks if they have either too little or too much of it.'[12] States are not searching to maximize power but security. In addition, Waltz insists that structural constraints rather than a pure struggle for power characterizes international politics.

Yet, it would be incorrect to assume that the balance of power should exclusively be associated with realism. Richard Little has emphasized the existence of a second tradition of thought. He refers to an 'adversarial' and an 'associative' balance of power tradition. The former, namely the realist perspective, remains the most well-known interpretation of the concept. In contrast, the associative tradition is based on the idea that rather than using power competitively to enhance narrow self-interests, it may be used 'communally to sustain a just equilibrium which would reflect the interests of all the members of the system'.[13] In modern IR literature, the associative approach to the balance of power is mainly represented in the English School, particularly in the works of Martin Wight and Hedley Bull.[14]

Having introduced the various meanings and theoretical foundations of the balance of power, let us further discuss its objectives. In essence, the fundamental purpose of balance of power is to deny hegemony either regionally or globally. It aims at ensuring the survival of individual states by preventing the dominance of any one state. By providing such countervailing measures, the balance of power is indirectly expected to provide stability and peace in the international system. Many theorists have discussed the objectives of the balance of power. Let us mention some of these arguments by considering two realist thinkers, Hans Morgenthau and Henry Kissinger, and an English School approach through the writings of Hedley Bull. When dealing with the balance of power, Morgenthau refers to a 'stabilizing factor in a society of sovereign nations'[15] necessary to preserve the stability of the system and the independence of states from the domination of one hegemon. Yet, he points out that the balance of power offers dangers linked to the uncertainty of power calculations. He suggests that a state wishing to preserve a margin of safety needs to 'aim not at a balance, that is, equality of power, but at superiority of power in their own behalf'.[16] To that end, a state needs to seek the summit of power available. In *Diplomacy*, Kissinger explains that the term 'balance of power' refers to a system that rarely occurs in history. He indicates that such a system does not aim to avoid war but to 'limit the ability of states to dominate others and the scope of conflicts'.[17]

Hedley Bull was a leading theorist of the English School of International Relations, which is associated with the international society perspective. Bull asserts that an international society: 'exists when a group of states (. . .), form a society in the sense that they conceive themselves to be bound by a common set of rules in their relations with one another, and share in the working of common institutions.'[18] Bull focuses on the balance of power as part of the larger context of international order defined as 'a pattern of activity that sustains the elementary or primary goals of the society of states, or international society'.[19] The institutions that sustain international order are the states themselves, as well as other rules and mechanisms such as the balance of power, international law, diplomacy, a system of great powers and war. In an institutionalized sense, the balance of power presents three essential objectives.[20] First, a balance of power in the international system aids in preventing the states system from becoming a universal empire. Second, local balances of power help in preserving the independence of states that may otherwise be absorbed or dominated by regional hegemonic states. Third, the existence of balances of power, at the global and local level, makes the operation of other institutions feasible.

Let us conclude this review of the balance of power theory by stating its various forms and modes of operation. Regarding forms of operation, Organski argues that two types of balances can be distinguished. A simple balance involves two groups, each consisting of one or more states, opposing each other with a roughly equal amount of power while a multiple balance includes several groups balancing each other on a unilateral and multilateral basis.[21] The same distinction has also been referred to as bipolar and multi-polar balances of power. While most theorists agree on the complex forms taken by the balance of power, no consensus exists regarding the functioning of the balancing process within the system. This is said to be automatic, comparable to physical laws, semi-automatic, through a balancer, or manual, through states' actions.[22] Let us clarify this point further by comparing how Kissinger and Waltz discuss the operation of the balance of power.

Kissinger considers the balance of power to be dependent on states' actions. Stability, an underlying objective of balance of power, is examined as a product of legitimacy, which needs to be created by statesmen. He defines 'legitimacy' as an 'international arrangement about the nature of workable arrangements and about the permissible aims and methods of foreign policy'.[23] Kissinger refers to two models that have maintained the operation of a balance of power system: the British and the Bismarck model.[24] The British model consists of waiting for the balance of power to be under direct threat before joining the weaker side to restore the balance. This position of balancer, which was traditionally followed by Britain vis-à-vis the European distribution of power, is often understood as involving a semi-automatic balancing process. The Bismarck model avoids the creation of challenges to the balance by maintaining 'close relations with as many parties as possible, by building overlapping alliance systems, and by using the resulting influence to moderate the claims of the contenders'.[25] Hence, its operation may be seen as primarily manual.

Opposing most traditional realists, Waltz rejects the belief that a balance of power needs to be promoted by states' policies, thus implying that its operation is automatic. He argues that balance of power politics 'prevail wherever two, and only two, requirements are met: that the order be anarchic and that it be populated by units wishing to survive'.[26] Through a systemic interpretation of the balance of power theory, Waltz makes predictions about states' actions.[27] First, he foresees states as practising balancing behaviour even when balancing power is not the objective of their policies. Second, he expects the existence of a balanced power distribution within the system. Finally, Waltz does not predict that a balance of power will be held over time. Rather, he argues that once a balance is disturbed, it will be re-established.

There is a degree of consensus in the prevailing literature that the balance of power remains one of the most valuable tools of analysis in the study of international politics. Schroeder writes: 'the concept of balance of power seems indispensable. There is hardly a discussion of current international politics in serious journals or newspapers which does not use it or rest on it.'[28] At the same time, IR scholars in general and balance of power theorists in particular are aware of its limitations. As any theoretical concept employed in the study of social sciences, the balance of power contains shortcomings that complicate its analysis. Let us mention some of its limitations aware that others exist as well. The theory has been the target of several criticisms that include its unsophisticated analysis of the concept of power, its narrow understanding of the term security and its failure to include domestic issues. Security has primarily been limited to conventional inter-state military relations while political, economic, social and environmental matters have been mostly ignored. Regarding its level of analysis, the balance of power theory does not take into consideration domestic aspects including internal threats and political systems. The balance of power perspective also exaggerates the potential danger resulting from emerging hegemons. This view often limits the intentions of rising states to aggressive and expanding policies and fails to consider great powers as possible benign states that contribute to regional stability. Finally, the theory focuses excessively on relative gains, underestimating the existence of common interests and the prospect of long-term cooperation.

Balance of power politics

Military dimension

While the balance of power has been discussed so far in a descriptive fashion, the concept has also been applied as a policy prescription. As a policy, the balance of power has most commonly been expressed through a military dimension. The distinguishing feature of the policy of balance is a disposition to mobilize and employ military force, often in coalition, in order to affect the distribution of power. It may be observed in history as an old-fashioned exercise of military power. Though the principle was already applied as a military doctrine in Renaissance Italy, the eighteenth century was the golden age for balance of power politics. It became legitimate to prevent a state from expanding its territory and power excessively to maintain stability and peace. The nineteenth century experienced a long period of stability resulting from the Vienna settlement of 1814–15 and the Concert of Europe. Thinkers and practitioners of the balance of power concurred that the aims of the principle had been achieved.

Yet, the outbreak of the First World War symbolized the failure of balance of power strategy in the attempt to preserve stability and peace in the international system. Critics later argued that the system of alliances, which had dominated European security relations, had fuelled antagonism and rivalries and provoked an arms race between the opposing camps. The balance of power was said to have made war on the continent unavoidable. Wilsonian liberalism was introduced as an alternative approach to security. It originated from US President Woodrow Wilson's Fourteen Points speech to the US Senate on 8 January 1918 in which he described a European peace based on moral, legal and economic principles and interests. Contrary to the origins of the First World War, it was argued that the Second World War was caused by a policy of appeasement adopted by Britain and France, as for instance at the Munich Conference held on 29 September 1938, and that it could have been prevented by balance of power politics. Osgood asserts that the 'ascent of Hitler's Germany showed that a peacetime deterrent coalition, whatever its effects in other circumstances might be, was essential to peace and order in the face of the most dangerous bid for hegemony since Napoleon'.[29] In partial consequence, the Cold War was again a period of balance of power arrangements whereby states committed themselves to undertake military obligations to one another against an external threat. Moreover, some military obligations concluded at its height still obtain, especially in the Asia-Pacific.

Based on the simple notion that unbalanced power may be dangerous to the security of individual states and that it needs to be confronted through countervailing measures, the balance of power has often been considered as an attractive concept to foreign policy-makers. States have traditionally followed three fundamental strategies, which may be identified as a balancing perspective. First, a state pays close attention to the power distribution; that is, it measures its own capacities in relation to those of other significant players. This may force a state to regard even current friends as potential enemies. Second, a state can follow a strategy of unilateral balancing which includes actions to strengthen its own capabilities. This strategy is characterized by a relative and competitive understanding of power. Finally, a state may consider unilateral balancing as insufficient to fulfil its sense of relative security. Consequently, it may follow a policy of balancing through external association which involves strengthening its own relative position through diplomatic or military alignments or even formal alliance.

More specifically, states possess a variety of methods through which to affect the distribution of power, which are aimed at expanding their absolute power and/or affecting negatively the power of their enemies. Morgenthau refers to five tactics: to divide and rule, to offer compensations based on territories, to arm, to enter alliances with other states and to hold the balance.[30] Organski introduces some additional methods including the creation of buffer zones and intervention in the domestic affairs of other states.[31] Of course, these various military approaches may also be used to establish hegemonies or other military objectives. The balance of power as a military policy has most often been expressed through an alliance, taking either a formal or tacit form.[32]

Governments enter alliances so as to enhance their power positions and to react to rising hegemonies in the international system. Alliances may affect the distribution of power by maintaining the territorial status quo in a specific region. States will conventionally align themselves with the weaker side in order to restrain the rising power. Such alliances present a defensive character. States may also enter offensive alliances in the interest of hegemony, as was the case for example of the Nazi–Soviet Non-Aggression Pact of August 1939 and the Tripartite Pact signed by Germany, Italy and Japan in September 1940. Wight explains that political alliances 'are always contracted with third parties in view; unlike friendships, they are necessarily, so to speak, self-conscious; their purpose is to enhance the security of the allies or to advance their interests, against the outer world'.[33] To maximize their function, alliances should operate as flexible and temporary security arrangements; implying that their participants must be willing to enter rapidly new alliances to preserve a balanced distribution of power. However, alliances can be influenced by ideological factors that limit the flexibility of alliance formation. As a classical example of balance of power politics, the North Atlantic Treaty was concluded during the Cold War intended to preserve the territorial status quo in Europe in an attempt to defend Western European security from Soviet Communism. One should note also the French unease with the 'benign' hegemony of the United States, which was expressed in France's withdrawal from the military structure of the North Atlantic Treaty Organization (NATO).[34]

The study of alliances, as an expression of balance of power politics, has been influenced by the work of Stephen Walt. In *Origins of Alliances*, he examines their formation as a reaction to threats rather than power. Walt points out that instead of studying balancing or 'bandwagoning' as reactions to rising external threats defined exclusively in terms of capabilities (aggregate power), it is 'more accurate to say that states tend to ally with or against the foreign power that poses the greatest threat'.[35] He argues that the level of threat needs to be determined not only by considering aggregate power but also by including three other essential factors: geographic proximity, offensive power and aggressive intentions.[36] As a result, he manages to separate the traditional balance of power theory from his own balance of threat perspective. Walt deals with some limitations of the traditional balance of power theory by refining to a large extent the notion of a threatening state. Walt therefore transforms the balance of power into a more context dependent concept. For instance, his approach makes it possible to distinguish benign from hostile hegemons. This benefits our analysis of the ARF that is viewed in Chapter 5 as a tool to deal with China as a rising power. The PRC is regarded regionally as a menacing actor while the United States, which remains the regional hegemonic power, inspires confidence among most regional players.[37]

Shortcomings and alternatives

As seen above, balance of power has theoretical limitations, which affect its application to international politics and diplomacy. The balance of power suffers not only from deficiencies when examined in a descriptive form but also similar weaknesses arise when it is applied as a policy prescription. Due to its ambiguities and inconsistencies, the concept is often less serviceable than anticipated by policy-makers who might expect too much from its predictability and appealing simplicity.[38] For instance, how should aggregate power and changes in the power distribution be predicted or analysed? While a strong supporter of the balance of power principle, Morgenthau refers to its main weaknesses as being 'its uncertainty, its unreality, and its inadequacy'.[39] In particular, he considers the uncertainty associated with balance of power policies as responsible for failing to prevent the First World War.[40] Wight also argues that balance of power is 'inherently unstable, because powers are not static societies, but are constantly growing or declining in relation to one another'.[41]

Yet, the most serious shortcoming of the balance of power relates to its relationship with war and conflict. As a military doctrine, it accepts war implicitly as a means to pursue other objectives. Many factors, including the costs of modern warfare and the importance of domestic matters in the formulation of foreign policies, explain why most states are no longer ready or capable to use war as an instrument of the balance. Moreover, the balance of power has often been described as promoting rather than limiting the chances of conflict. In his book, *The Transformation of European Politics, 1763–1848*, Paul W. Schroeder asserts that the balance of power 'blocked the peaceful resolution of conflicts (. . .) directly prompted conflict, and made the periodic escalation of particular conflicts into general systemic wars more likely'.[42] The same conclusions are reached by John Vasquez who points out that war is more likely to occur among states concerned with territorial disputes and following balance of power tactics.[43] States relying on the latter are left in a competitive security environment where no real attention is given to the possible existence of long-term compatible objectives. As such, seeking a power equilibrium may not naturally lead, as is often argued, to stability and peace. Wight writes that the balance of power 'is essentially competitive: it leads to rivalry of power, which leads to war, as a consequence of which one side is temporarily eliminated and the other has a temporary monopoly of power'.[44] Considering these limitations, it is not surprising that alternatives have been developed and applied in foreign policy.

Schroeder has discussed strategies followed by states to ensure their security in the international system. In his article 'Historical Reality vs. Neo-realist Theory', the historian opposes Waltz's assumption that states automatically rely on self-help when confronted with a threat and that this strategy systematically evolves into a balance of power situation.[45] Instead, he examines other strategies that were in his view more often adopted by states in European history. These include: 'hiding' from threats for instance by declaring neutrality; 'transcending' which consists of states reaching consensus on norms, values and objectives as a means of defending themselves from conflictual threats; and 'bandwagoning' which involves states joining the strongest nation or group of nations to ensure their security.[46]

In addition to these tactics, conceptual ideas on security have been developed as alternatives to the balance of power and its shortcomings. Let us mention four specific perspectives, namely collective, comprehensive, common and cooperative security. The tragedy of the First World War led to the emergence of collective security. Charles and Clifford Kupchan explain that under collective security, 'states agree to abide by certain norms and rules to maintain stability and, when necessary, band together to stop aggression'.[47] As its strongest supporter, Wilson was convinced that this approach to security would provide the means to prevent future conflicts. Collective security was formally integrated in the League of Nations as one of its underlying principles.[48] The League resulted from the Versailles Peace Conference and was conceived as a collective security arrangement to enhance cooperation and maintain peace and security. In the event, its operative premises were shown to be flawed, hence the post-Second World War interest in balance of power.

Many theorists and practitioners have commented on the similarities between balance of power and collective security. For instance, Vose Gulick explains that collective security, 'far from being alien to the "age-old tradition of the balance of power", not only derives from the latter, but also must be regarded as the logical end of the balance-of-power system'.[49] Differences should be indicated though. In the case of balance of power, the balancing policies occur in an anarchical system where states are responsible for their own security. The balancing under collective security is regulated by moral and legal justifications and is 'predicated upon the notion of all against one'.[50] An institutionalized balance of power is still based on anarchy but one in which there is a sense of international governance as opposed to world government. Thus, rather than dependent on individual political and military considerations, it leads, in principle after the violation of international obligations, to an immediate and common response by all the participants of a collective security arrangement.[51] This security perspective offers two main advantages, in principle, vis-à-vis the balance of power: 'it provides for more effective balancing against aggressors, and it promotes trust and cooperation.'[52] In practice, however, governments have generally opposed or abdicated the obligations associated with the principle of collective security. In effect, examples of operational collective security are limited and require the active role of a hegemon. The experience of the League of Nations and the United States role during the Gulf War of 1991 for instance should be noted.

The notion of comprehensive security was first formulated in Japan in the 1970s. It focuses on political, economic and social problems at different levels of analysis and therefore offers an alternative to traditional concepts of security that concentrate exclusively on national defence and external military threats. It assumes that broadening the definition of the term beyond military issues can enhance security. Comprehensive security has also been recognized by some ASEAN states, primarily Indonesia, Malaysia and Singapore, and included in their security doctrines.[53] In contrast to the Japanese interpretation of the concept, the approach taken by the ASEAN states has primarily been inward looking. When discussing ASEAN's comprehensive approach, Lizée and Peou explain that it 'is based on the proposition that national security does not only reside in the absence of external military hostility but also in the presence of socio-economic development within national boundaries'.[54] The inward-looking approach to domestic regime security and regional stability has been illustrated through the principles of national and regional resilience. The principles, advanced by the New Order in Indonesia, register an ambition to underpin domestic and regional stability through the use of economic and social development. At issue is domestic regime security and consolidation.

Contrary to collective security, which is based on a collective reaction to aggression, common security seeks primarily to offer an alternative to the use of force.[55] This principle, as defined by the Independent Commission on Disarmament and Security Issues under the leadership of Olof Palme, needs to be located in the context of the Cold War. It should primarily be seen as an attempt to move beyond the strategy of nuclear deterrence. A key factor in common security is the mutual possession of nuclear weapons and expectation of mutually assured destruction. Leading to a balance of terror, the Palme Report stressed that the nuclear deterrence doctrine could no longer be seen as appropriate to avoid an East–West nuclear conflict. Offering common security as an alternative, it argued that the two nuclear sides: 'must achieve security not against the adversary but together with him. International security must rest on a commitment to joint survival rather than on a threat of mutual destruction.'[56] The Report proposed various criteria for security policies including that they 'should be in the interest of both opponents'; that they 'should be pursued by both opponents together'; and that they 'favour activities where the possibilities for and advantages of deception are limited'.[57]

As the concept of cooperative security was discussed in the Introduction, let us now compare and contrast it with two other alternatives to the balance of power. It may be identified with the concept of collective security, as embodied in the League of Nations Covenant, because it is intended to be comprehensive in membership with security arrangements functioning on an intra-mural basis. The fundamental difference, however, is that cooperative security, unlike collective security, lacks the vehicle of economic or military sanctions. It operates, at least in the Asia-Pacific, through dialogue and seeks to address the climate of international relations rather than tackle specific problems. Cooperative security relies on the promotion of standard international norms and principles to be adhered to by the various participants. Focusing on reassurance, cooperative security arrangements aim to develop a 'habit of dialogue' amongst the participants and to promote confidence-building and possibly preventive diplomacy measures. Therefore, while collective security primarily takes a reactive approach to rising sources of unrest, cooperative security focuses on confidence building and a preventive dimension, albeit not through problem solving.

Cooperative security is even more similar to the principle of common security. Rejecting the perspective of the security dilemma, cooperative security supports the notion developed in the Palme Commission Report that security should be promoted 'with others' as opposed to 'against others'. Both concepts are inclusive in their understanding of security, implying that they aim to engage all regional players without excluding political and economic systems or adversaries. They also seek to offer alternatives to the strategy of deterrence and focus on broadening the analysis of security by integrating non-military factors. Yet, predicting a more gradual institutionalization of relations in the Asia-Pacific, cooperative security is a more adaptable notion. It acknowledges the importance of current 'bilateral and balance-of-power arrangements in contributing to regional security and retaining them – indeed, for working with and through them – allowing multilateralism to develop from more ad hoc, and flexible processes until the conditions for institutionalized multilateralism become more favourable'.[58] Moreover, while common security is a notion that was developed in a context of nuclear weapons, this has not been the case with cooperative security.

Relevance of the balance of power factor to regimes for cooperative security

Relevance of the balance of power

Bearing in mind its weaknesses and alternatives, this section discusses the balance of power as a factor within and beyond cooperative security. Regional security cooperation does not lead generally to a lessening of realist convictions among policy-makers. On the contrary, these views, resulting from military competition, latent conflicts and feelings of mistrust, often remain influential within cooperative security regimes. Hence, attention ought to be given to the constraining of power in security regime dynamics. While inter-state arrangements for cooperative security are often said to have been conceived as alternatives to the traditional concept of the balance of power, this book aims to determine how its central principles can still be relevant to ASEAN and the ARF. Thus, it is suspected that both these regimes for cooperative security were informed with some reference to balance of power practice.

The interpretation of the balance of power factor is based on the general principles and assumptions found in the conventional understanding of the concept. In accordance with balance of power theories, its purpose is to keep a cooperative security arrangement and its participants secure from intra- or extra-mural hegemony. Hence, the conventional logic and objectives of the balance of power, namely the denial of regional and global hegemony through containing any hegemonic disposition, are left unchanged. The participants of a security regime continue playing close attention to the power distribution within and beyond the associative arrangement and to react in cases of rising disequilibria. The term hegemony should be analysed as involving more than a traditional understanding of military expansion and domination by including political forms of hegemonic disposition as well. By preserving its central logic, the notion of a balance of power factor within cooperative security thus holds the core simplicity and explanatory qualities of the traditional concept.

Yet, attention needs to be given to the differences between balance of power in its conventional interpretation and practice and the balance of power factor within cooperative security regimes. This factor is defined as the disposition to promote countervailing arrangements to deny hegemony within and beyond cooperative security even if devoid of direct military content. The balance of power is examined in this book as a policy consideration, rather than as a system, that influences the modalities of regimes for cooperative security. The interpretation of the balance of power factor within cooperative security is defined by two specific assumptions. First, the constraining of power is seen as one element in the operation of a larger security arrangement. Other features pointed out by an associative approach to cooperation include: the presence of norms and principles, the promotion of a code of conduct, the level of institutionalization and the existence of common interests. The balance of power factor can therefore coexist with or even complement other aspects involved in the cooperative process. Second, the constraining of power within a cooperative security regime is dependent on political rather than military means. The necessity to focus on the restraining of power through political channels results from the fact that security regimes remain by definition diplomatic associations lacking any form of common military power. Thus, the method by which power is constrained within cooperative security distinguishes the balance of power factor from a more conventional application of the concept.

The relevance of balance of power politics to security regimes needs to be examined. When doing so, it is essential to keep in mind the likely divergence of security interests among the participants. Whereas one expects a shared strategic perspective within an alliance or collective defence arrangement, the same is not necessarily true in the case of security regimes. Instead, contradictory strategic perspectives and competing security interests are likely to obtain among the member states. It is in that context that balance of power practice becomes particularly relevant.

Having said that, let us focus on two specific aspects. First, the balance of power factor within cooperative security involves a denial of intra-mural hegemony. This consideration aims to contain a disposition to hegemony on the part of a rising power by integrating it within a rule-based regime that includes sufficient incentive to constrain any hegemonic ambitions. The premises of confidence building and trust on which a cooperative security regime is based serve as a constraint on larger member states. Through their stake in the associative arrangement, these participants can be expected to restrain their actions. The modalities of ASEAN and the ARF, which depend on the extent to which participants have a stake in these institutions, serve as a system of checks and balances. Yet, the constraining of power within cooperative security can still have a military dimension. The denial of hegemony need not be limited to intra-mural restraints as it can also depend on security links with outside actors. In that sense, externally supported distributions of power can influence intra-mural relations.

Second, the balance of power factor involves the promotion of countervailing arrangements beyond the walls of a diplomatic association. For example, the participants to a cooperative security regime may join an external power through tacit diplomatic alignment to respond to a rising threat. The specific role adopted by a cooperative security regime and its participants within a countervailing arrangement would be limited to a diplomatic dimension due to the lack of collective military power. However, because of contending strategic perspectives, the promotion of countervailing arrangements beyond the walls of a regime can be expected to impact adversely on intra-mural cooperation. It is in that respect that extra-mural balance of power tactics can play a part within regimes for cooperative security and influence intra-mural relations.

The two aspects mentioned, a denial of intra-mural hegemony and the promotion of countervailing responses to external threats, are not innovative to the study of security regimes. They are part of a realist perspective on cooperation in which regimes are discussed as instruments available to states to engage in the play of power politics. As such, a security regime should be judged as an attempt to restrain a possible hegemon from dominating a region and/or as a reaction to an external challenge. Thus, realists compare regime dynamics with the formation of other security alignments, including alliances. In contrast, this approach is associated in this book with one consideration only, the balance of power factor, which influences, together with an associative dimension, the operation of a cooperative security regime.

If one assumes that the balance of power factor is relevant to regimes for cooperative security, it is important to determine the means by which it may be employed in fulfilling its role. Members of a cooperative security regime can depend on political mechanisms to contain hegemonic dispositions. These countervailing arrangements involve institutional processes, namely agreements, treaties and other forms of institutional checks and balances applied among the member states. In particular, the balance of power factor within cooperative security should be identified in the context of norms and principles promoted by a regime. A collective code of conduct based on standard international norms and principles and respected by all the member states can constrain the larger participants and ensure that they do not threaten their smaller cooperative partners. Any aggressive action or act of hegemony would undermine these norms and rebound adversely on the political cohesion of a cooperative security regime as well as on the interest of larger participants with a stake in the viability of the arrangement. In short, the restraint from political association can have a power balancing relevance.

Serving as a means to constrain hegemonic dispositions, the norms and principles promoted by a security regime should not be viewed as an attempt to move beyond balance of power considerations. They may be seen as a step beyond conventional balance of power tactics but not as an effort to move beyond the core objective of the balance of power, namely the denial of hegemony through containing hegemonic dispositions. These norms and principles only codify and formalize the kind of bilateral and regional power relationships that exist. In short, one should refer to the institutionalization of a power balancing strategy that restrains potential hegemons through their participation within a rule-based security arrangement.

The interpretation of the balance of power factor within cooperative security must be contrasted with the views of the advocates of neo-realism who examine the balance of power concept entirely in terms of adversarial relations and self-help. Regimes for cooperative security are not expected to embrace conventional balance of power politics to contain an intra-mural rising power but rather to restrain its potential hegemonic dispositions through diplomatic and institutional means. At an intra-mural level, traditional realist motivations can thus be fulfilled through the use of non-military restraints on hegemony. In contrast, the containing of power beyond cooperative security is reliant on a conventional practice of countervailing power, namely the formation of a tacit alliance with external states, rather than on a denial of hegemony through political means. Outside of cooperative security, the restraining of power through political and institutional channels has no relevance. Indeed, external actors have no stake in the norms promoted by a cooperative security arrangement that operates exclusively on an intra-mural basis. This differentiates an intra- and extra-mural application of the balance of power factor. In short, the interpretation of this factor must be associated with both an adversarial and associative understanding of the balance of power concept. The use of both traditions has often characterized the works of traditional realists, including Morgenthau,[59] and exponents of the English School of International Relations.

Having compared and contrasted the balance of power factor within and beyond cooperative security to a conventional application of the concept, it is important to repeat the central question addressed in this book. It concerns the extent to which the balance of power factor plays a part in the operation of cooperative security regimes and in the calculations of their participants. The hypothesis is tested that the balance of power factor operates within and beyond regimes for cooperative security. The membership and external links of such groupings may indeed be constructed with the denial of hegemony in mind. It is in that respect that the balance of power factor may coexist with and complement the cooperative security process.

Balance of power and the founding moments of ASEAN

This final part observes the relevance of the balance of power in empirical terms. It illustrates one specific aspect of the founding moments of ASEAN, namely the influence of the balance of power factor on the calculations of the member states. As explained in Chapter 1, the Association was established to locate regional reconciliation within an institutionalized structure of dialogue. It is in that respect that ASEAN was defined as a regime for cooperative security. The object now is not to question how these founding moments were described previously but rather to complement this analysis by examining a consideration not mentioned so far. These events may best be understood by acknowledging the influence of different, and possibly contradictory, factors. In addition to the associative principles included in the creation of ASEAN, let us emphasize how balance of power practice was relevant to its founding moments by involving an intra-mural denial of hegemony.

Though the establishment of the Association symbolized the end of the period of Confrontation between some of its participants, intra-mural relations were characterized by mistrust and sources of tension. Despite the political reconciliation between Kuala Lumpur and Jakarta, Malaysia remained fearful of Indonesia. In addition to these apprehensions, which were a direct result of the policy of Confrontation, the intra-mural security environment was distinguished by a multitude of bilateral issues. The latter included the Philippine claim to Sabah, Thai-Malaysian tensions over the Muslim Malay community within Thailand and Singapore's mistrust of Malaysia and Indonesia, which arose from the sense of vulnerability of a newly created ethnic-Chinese state surrounded by Malay neighbours. Singapore's traumatic separation from the Federation of Malaysia in 1965 would also continue to affect its bilateral relations with Kuala Lumpur. In short, regardless of the shared cooperative efforts, persistent inter-state distrust led to the maintenance of contradictory strategic perspectives and security interests.

The primary relevance of balance of power politics within cooperative security resulted from Malaysia and Singapore needing to address a concern essential to their individual security, namely Indonesian power and influence. ASEAN was partly and implicitly about coping with Indonesia just as the original European Economic Community (EEC) had been about managing German power. Hurrell has pointed out that many 'would see the position of Germany within the European Community as the classic illustration of this "regionalist entrapment", designed to mitigate and manage the unavoidable impact of German preponderance'.[60] A corresponding analogy can be made with Indonesia and its position within ASEAN when it was first established. As in the European example, how to deal with the largest regional actor was a core question to be addressed in maritime Southeast Asia. Various members of the Association were anxious in 1967 to constrain any disposition towards hegemony by Indonesia but were in no position to contain their neighbouring state through conventional methods.[61] Instead, they were forced to rely on institutional and political channels. Hence, some participants perceived ASEAN as a form of political defence for constraining a potential menacing neighbour.

Indonesia is a natural hegemon in Southeast Asia because of its scale and population. Indonesia's foreign policy has been defined by a feeling of both vulnerability, due to domestic weaknesses and fragmentation, and regional entitlement that has emanated from its military struggle for independence, geographical dimensions, large population, strategic position and natural resources.[62] Indonesia in 1967 had not yet shaken off a reputation for being volatile and unpredictable, previously demonstrated through Confrontation over West Irian and Malaysia. Regional leaders remembered the Sukarno period, with its flamboyant, expansionist and aggressive foreign policy. Moreover, Suharto was only acting president in 1967 and Sukarno was not yet completely toppled. Mainly due to domestic politics, Sukarno had opposed the formation of the Federation of Malaysia through the threat of force.[63] Having experienced Confrontation, Malaysia and Singapore were conscious of a potential Indonesian threat. Most participants perceived ASEAN as an instrument through which to 'domesticate' Indonesia, so ensuring that it would adopt a responsible and peaceful foreign policy.[64]

The new leadership in Jakarta was aware of the mistrust that persisted in other ASEAN capitals in respect of Indonesia's position in Southeast Asia. Though actively involved in the creation of the Association, Suharto's approach to ASEAN during its formative period was characterized by self-restraint, thus distinguishing his policies from those of the Sukarno regime.[65] Indonesia did refuse to join ASA, which was Malaysia's initial preference, and insisted on a new start in regional cooperation to avoid domestic political embarrassment. Suharto was willing to follow a policy of self-constraint in order to promote domestic economic development within a framework of regional stability. By eschewing any position of assertive leadership, the new Indonesian president sought to reassure his partners and build trust. His policy decisively influenced the formation and later success of the Association. Indonesia's change in approach was a self-conscious choice required because of urgent domestic needs.[66] For instance, Luhulima refers to 'the domestication of Indonesia' as arising from internal transformations and problems and the coming to power of General Suharto.[67]

There was an awareness in Jakarta that ASEAN would operate as a constraining factor on Indonesia's foreign policy. The willingness to follow a policy of self-restraint should be contrasted to the Sukarno period that had led to the failure of Maphilindo, and also to the position adopted by India within the South Asian Association for Regional Cooperation (SAARC) that has been distinguished by some form of regional dominance.[68] In short, while the different ASEAN leaders acknowledged Indonesia's natural primacy in the region, Jakarta embraced a policy of political self-abnegation and up to a point self-imposed containment. Leifer claims that 'regional cooperation with Indonesia's enthusiastic participation (. . .) was envisaged both as a means to satisfy its natural ambition and also to contain its more objectionable hegemonic disposition.'[69] This aspect indicates that ASEAN was informed with some reference to balance of power practice. A potential disposition towards hegemony by Indonesia was constrained politically through its integration within an embryonic regime for cooperative security.

Nonetheless, Indonesia felt that it was entitled to a position of natural leadership within the Association. It was commonly accepted that the ASEAN states would have to respect Indonesia's interests and natural regional ambitions. Djiwandono explains that Indonesia's 'membership in ASEAN may accord it, implicitly, the status of first among equals without resort to an aggressive confrontation policy. This may be regarded as something in return for its "domestication" within ASEAN'.[70] Indonesia's regional vision had not changed, in principle. The traditional ambitions central to Sukarno's regional policies influenced the Suharto regime when it, for instance, requested that specific security matters and interests, as expressed in the Manila Agreements of 1963 and formally integrated in Maphilindo, be included in the ASEAN Declaration.[71] These demands, which questioned the future of foreign military bases in Southeast Asia, had been called for by Sukarno himself. After long and tedious negotiations, a paragraph was added to the Declaration that read:

> Affirming that all foreign bases are temporary and remain only with the expressed concurrence of the countries concerned and are not intended to be used directly or indirectly to subvert the national independence and freedom of States in the area or prejudice the orderly processes of their national development.[72]

Hoping for an autonomous regional order unaffected by external intervention, Indonesia emphasized in Bangkok that regional security could only be obtained through full independence and the avoidance of external domination. Jakarta's preference for a regional order based on the exclusive managerial role of Southeast Asian states was therefore registered in the ASEAN Declaration. Jakarta hoped that the Association could operate as an autonomous security foundation free from external intervention. Central to that vision was Indonesia's ambition to play a managerial role in regional relations.[73] In addition, its expectations were later further incorporated in the associative framework through ZOPFAN and the principles of national and regional resilience. Yet, this does not imply that Jakarta ignored the associative principles contained in the cooperative process. On the contrary, rather than revert to former military tactics, Suharto's New Order expected to attain its natural regional position through membership of the Association. Indonesia hoped to demonstrate its significance and influence as a regional actor.[74] Some ASEAN members perceived Jakarta's claim to a natural position of regional leadership, despite its policy of self-containment, as a persistent threat. This was for example the case of Singapore.

In 1971, the city-state was disturbed by the common Indonesian and Malaysian policy over the straits of Malacca and Singapore. Malaysia, Indonesia and Singapore had issued a statement in November 1971 on their exclusive responsibility over the safety of navigation in the straits. However, the city-state did not agree with a section of the declaration introduced by the two other governments that asserted that 'the Straits of Malacca and Singapore are not international straits, while fully recognizing their use for international shipping in accordance with the principle of innocent passage'.[75] Indonesia and Malaysia therefore challenged the right of free passage through the straits. However, the collusion disappeared with differences over Malaysia's proposal to neutralize Southeast Asia and Indonesia's archipelago policy, from which Singapore benefited. It was only in 1973 after a private meeting with President Suharto that Singapore's Prime Minister Lee Kuan Yew saw security in ASEAN. Anxious to preserve the newly obtained sovereignty and independence of Singapore, Lee Kuan Yew became aware that the Association could function as an effective instrument for constraining its threatening neighbours. In addition to the obvious advantages linked to regional consultation and cooperation, the city-state came to appreciate ASEAN's potential in unconventional power balancing terms. The fear of the effect of acting in a hegemonic fashion may have partly persuaded Malaysia and Indonesia to constrain their conduct in their dealings with the ethnic-Chinese state. The formation of a diplomatic association could be expected to encourage its members to contain contentious ambitions or claims. It is in that context of suspicion that the constraining of power by political means would continue to be relevant.

It has been asserted so far that ASEAN was constructed partly with the constraint of Indonesia's power and influence in mind. It is also interesting to question whether the participants had extra-mural power balancing in mind, primarily vis-à-vis China and Vietnam. Communist ideology was feared at domestic and international levels. The advancing communist threat in Indochina, the problem of internal insurgencies but also the potential consequences of the Chinese Cultural Revolution were matters that influenced the security and defence agendas of most ASEAN states. To claim that the Association was established to contain China and Vietnam would be in accord with a realist interpretation of security cooperation. Yet, the balance of power factor had no extra-mural dimension. The Association was not formed as a direct response to an external adversary and has never evolved into a formal or a tacit alliance. In the absence of joint military capabilities and a common threat perception, ASEAN could not act as a source of countervailing power to contain extra-mural threats. In short, the cooperative security regime precluded the conventional practice of the balance of power. Not a collective security arrangement and lacking the same kind of ideological underpinnings, ASEAN was thus no substitute for the South-East Collective Defence Treaty, or Manila Pact, of September 1954 which was a classical example of a Cold War alliance. Ironically, Beijing still viewed the Association as part of a US policy of containment against the PRC.

Most ASEAN members relied on external guarantees to ensure their individual security. In 1967, Thailand and the Philippines were signatories to the Manila Treaty and members of the South-East Asia Treaty Organization (SEATO) and the United States had military bases in both states. Malaysia and Singapore were part of the Anglo-Malaysian Defence Agreement that also included Australia and New Zealand and which was replaced in 1971 by consultative Five Power Defence Arrangements. With the exception of Indonesia, that proclaimed a non-aligned policy, member governments rejected the notion of a regional order based exclusively on the managerial role of regional states and perceived the United States as the primary source of countervailing power to contain external aggression. In addition, the majority of the ASEAN states supported the US commitment in Indochina, with Thailand and the Philippines directly involved in the conflict. Only Indonesia maintained diplomatic relations with the Democratic Republic of Vietnam (DRV).

Even so, the establishment of the Association was influenced by a combination of intra- and extra-mural considerations that varied from one member state to another.[76] The need to constrain intra-mural hegemonic dispositions strongly influenced the calculations of Malaysia, Singapore and later Brunei. Indonesia wished to promote a stable regional environment that would benefit its own domestic regime consolidation and socio-economic development. For these members ASEAN had primarily an intra-mural significance. Due to their geographic location, Thailand and the Philippines had less to fear from Indonesia. Thailand was concerned about the communist threat in continental Southeast Asia. The conventional practice of countervailing power had always been a core ingredient in its foreign policy and it only viewed ASEAN as supplementary to its alliance with the United States. Bangkok wanted to organize a regional arrangement with an anti-communist threat in mind. Hence, Thailand, but also Indonesia, perceived the Association as a collective political defence against Chinese infiltration and influence. Still, ASEAN only obtained an extra-mural dimension after the communist victories in Indochina. This was indicated by ASEAN's attempt, which was thwarted by Vietnam, to promote a new regional order in Southeast Asia through the Treaty of Amity and Cooperation (TAC).[77] Even then, the Declaration of ASEAN Concord explicitly excluded military cooperation on a formal intra-ASEAN basis.

Conclusion

The founding moments of ASEAN have until now been examined through an associative and balance of power perspective. In Chapter 1, it was argued that the associative dimension was symbolized by the institutionalization of a process of reconciliation within a structure of dialogue. In the final section of this chapter, it has been claimed that ASEAN was partly about coping with Indonesia's power and influence in Southeast Asia. Rather than entering an associative arrangement with Indonesia based on a strategy of bandwagoning, some members viewed ASEAN as a form of political defence for constraining hegemonic dispositions. The participants agreed to cooperate because of narrowly defined interests and the convergence of shared benefits but some also to restrain a potential menacing neighbour. The coexistence of associative and balance of power dimensions has therefore been demonstrated.

This book seeks also to analyse how each perspective may have interacted with the other. The cooperative principles and the constraining of power were closely intermingled in the formation of ASEAN. The cooperative security regime was partly constructed with the denial of hegemony in mind but not in a conventional sense. Hence, the membership in cooperative security was not an attempt to move beyond balance of power considerations as such calculations were part of the initial framework. The constraining of power should also be seen in the context of the associative dimension. The political constraint imposed on the larger members was dependent on their stake in the new diplomatic association. Any act of hegemony would have undermined ASEAN's emerging norms, that is primarily the respect for national sovereignty, and the premises of confidence building and trust on which ASEAN was based. This consideration served as a source of constraint on Indonesian power. In short, the constraining of Indonesian power was a primary and implicit aspect of the creation of ASEAN and this important consideration was intermingled with the associative principles.

Neo-liberal institutionalists may agree that realist persuasions can dominate the early years of a security regime but they would expect these considerations to diminish or even disappear once the institution reaches a level of maturity. For example, Hurrell proposes a 'stage-theory' course for the study of regionalism whereby the use of realism would be limited to its initial phase, while other approaches, including the institutionalist one, would be seen as more appropriate to the analysis of its later developments.[78] The aim of this book, however, is to investigate the balance of power as a factor within and beyond cooperative security that outlasts the actual creation of a security regime. Hence, the following four chapters deal with events that took place after the formation of ASEAN and the ARF, including the South China Sea issue that has become, in the post-Cold War, central to the security interests of some members of the Association.

3   The balance of power factor and the denial of intra-mural hegemony

ASEAN's early years and its
enlargement to include
Brunei in 1984

Introduction

The balance of power factor within cooperative security regimes is analysed in this chapter by examining ASEAN's early years from 1967 until 1975 and its expansion of membership to include Brunei. It was previously argued that the concept of the balance of power could be relevant in two respects in explaining the modalities of a regime for cooperative security: it could contribute to a denial of intra-mural hegemony; and it may also include the promotion of countervailing arrangements beyond the walls of a diplomatic association in response to a rising threat. It is the first relevance of the balance of power factor that is mainly addressed in this chapter. Beyond the associative benefits associated with cooperative security, the enlargement process had a geo-strategic significance. Brunei's decision to join ASEAN was influenced by calculations about the balance of power factor. At issue was the constraint imposed on larger member states through their stake in the Association from which Brunei could benefit to promote its own security. To that extent, the intra-mural distribution of power was held in check by the regime for cooperative security.

This chapter consists of three sections. The first examines the influence of the balance of power factor and of a conventional understanding of the concept on the early years of the Association. The second focuses on ASEAN's initial enlargement process by first emphasizing Brunei's strained relations with Malaysia and Indonesia during the 1960s and 1970s. The expansion of membership is then discussed by noting the coexistence of associative and balance of power perspectives. The final section determines how the balance of power factor complemented the associative dimension involved in ASEAN's early years and its enlargement to include Brunei.

The influence of balance of power on ASEAN's early years, 1967–75

This first section follows on the hypothesis that ASEAN was established with some reference to balance of power practice. It suggests that the balance of power factor played a part in the initial period of the Association. The influence of power balancing considerations is discussed through the examination of illustrations. These include the study of two events in Singapore–Indonesian relations – the 1968 crisis over the hanging of two Indonesian marines and Singapore's response to Indonesia's annexation of East Timor in 1975 – and the diplomacy that led to the formulation of the ZOPFAN principle. The 1968 crisis is interpreted as an example of the constraining of power through political means. In contrast, the rejection of a proposal for regional neutralization is said to have been influenced by contending views on regional order and conventional balance of power practices, namely the preservation of defence ties with external powers outside an ASEAN framework. This first section thus applies an interpretation of the balance of power factor within cooperative security as well as a conventional understanding of the concept.

The constraining of a disposition to hegemony by Indonesia, as displayed by its former policy of Confrontation, played a critical role in the formation of ASEAN. The primary relevance of the balance of power factor resulted from the fact that some participants needed to deal with one issue essential to their individual security: how to handle Indonesian power and influence in Southeast Asia. ASEAN was partly about coping with Indonesia just as the original European Economic Community (EEC) had been about managing German power. Hence, some members perceived the Association as a form of political defence for constraining a menacing neighbour. Indonesia was a willing party to such constraint through its active integration in the cooperative security arrangement. There was a conscious restraint in its actions and behaviour within ASEAN that could be noticed even at the lowest level of diplomatic interaction.[1] Jakarta eschewed any position of assertive leadership and followed a policy of political self-abnegation and at least to a point self-imposed containment. Suharto's policy towards the Association was influenced by a desire to reassure his partners and diminish their fears of a potential hegemony in the wider interest of Indonesia's international rehabilitation.

Nevertheless, the New Order did not assign itself an insignificant role in the political evolution of the Association. The initial cooperative process was influenced by Indonesia's expectation of a regional order based on the exclusive managerial role of Southeast Asian states. This was indicated in 1967 in the Bangkok Declaration. In addition, Indonesia's preference for a regional security zone free from outside intervention was later put forward through the principles of national and regional resilience. Indonesia's Foreign Minister Adam Malik declared at a seminar held in Jakarta in October 1974:

> we believe that the way most effective and satisfactory in the long run would be if the nations of Southeast Asia, jointly and separately, are able to build up their own, indigenous ideological, political, economic

and socio-cultural strength, which, *together*, constitute a nation's real capacity to endure, to develop and to defend itself against any negative influences, from within or from without.[2]

The ambition to organize Southeast Asian relations independently from external interference was central to Indonesia's nationalism and foreign policy. Its introduction within the ASEAN framework symbolized a continuing sense of regional entitlement. In that respect, a structural tension existed within the cooperative security regime between the notions of Indonesian self-denial and its managerial disposition. The other members were aware of the risk of an Indonesian dominance. This awareness partly explains the lack of institutional progress during ASEAN's early years. For instance, the common preference for National Secretariats over a centralized body can be interpreted as a way of ignoring the issue of leadership and so ensuring the equal status of the participants.[3]

To examine the relevance of the balance of power factor, attention needs to be given to the smaller members and their concern to counteract any hegemonic disposition within ASEAN. Such states are inclined to take account of power balancing considerations when cooperating with their partners. For example, Singapore suffered from an acute sense of vulnerability, which resulted from its road to independence, limited size, ethnic-Chinese identity and confined geographic location.[4] Despite its participation in ASEAN from the outset, it was particularly suspicious of Indonesia's and Malaysia's intentions. As a result, Singapore's position in the Association had 'to be viewed not just as an aspect of its foreign policy but also against a wider background of its approach to the crucial or fundamental issue of viability'.[5] Let us now illustrate the influence of the balance of power on ASEAN's early years by first examining two incidents in Singapore-Indonesian relations.

On 17 October 1968, Singapore's government hanged two Indonesian marines found guilty of having bombed a bank on the island during the period of Confrontation. Suharto had pleaded personally for clemency, but the city-state decided to carry out the sentence to register its sovereignty and newly obtained independence. The president felt insulted by Singapore's unwillingness to accommodate his request. Lee Kuan Yew's intransigence was not understood in Jakarta because Suharto had previously terminated the policy of Confrontation and sought regional reconciliation.[6] Indonesia's political elite was also less familiar with judicial procedures in Commonwealth countries, which are traditionally separated from the executive and legislative powers. Public opinion called for a fierce governmental response and demonstrations in Jakarta led to the sacking of Singapore's embassy. Under the New Order, Indonesia's leadership was dominated by the military, which regarded Singapore with suspicion due to its ethnic Chinese identity. Some generals were keen to punish the city-state for its action. Yet, Suharto's reaction was constrained. The role of Foreign Minister Adam Malik should be noted here. He wished to play down the issue and maintain relations with Singapore. Though the political influence of the foreign ministry was limited, Malik succeeded in convincing Suharto of the advantages of self-restraint. Hence, the president and his foreign minister avoided a new period of bilateral tensions and demonstrated their belief in regional cooperation. In contrast, Leifer explains when discussing Singapore's conduct that 'the whole episode indicated the absence of any serious recognition that the Association might serve the security interests of Singapore through providing a regional structure of consultation and co-operation'.[7] Relations between Singapore and Indonesia cooled but were not disrupted.

The Association did not address the 1968 crisis and its management remained limited to a bilateral context. Still, it represented a first critical test for the new military administration in Indonesia and for ASEAN itself. Indeed, a military reaction would have destroyed the viability of the Association. Indonesia's policy of self-restraint towards Singapore should be examined in the context of not only its economic priorities and bilateral relations with the city-state but also of its participation in a political association. Suharto was influenced by domestic priorities, especially the need to promote economic development.[8] He had to further legitimize his domestic position of leadership through socio-economic progress and consolidate ties with regional and Western states. The relevance of the balance of power factor is also central to an analysis of the events. In addition to manifesting its strong commitment to regional cooperation, Jakarta was constrained by the potential consequences of responding in an hegemonic fashion. An aggressive reaction towards Singapore would have undermined the premises of confidence building and trust on which ASEAN was based and which served as a constraint on Indonesian power. Suharto and Malik showed their acceptance of the notion of self-imposed containment within the framework of the cooperative security arrangement. In short, the policy of self-constraint adopted by Jakarta in 1968 benefited Indonesia's interests and ensured the survival of the embryonic security regime. Singapore had not yet come to appreciate ASEAN's potential in power balancing terms, namely as a political means for constraining its menacing neighbours. Instead, it relied on a self-help policy that rejected any kind of accommodation.

Singapore–Indonesian relations remained strained until May 1973 when Lee Kuan Yew paid an official visit to Jakarta and honoured the two marines' graves in the Kalibata Heroes' cemetery. Suggested by Singapore's ambassador to Indonesia, Lee Khoon Choy, this gesture was perceived in Jakarta as a sign of conciliation and led to a new beginning in bilateral relations.[9] The official visit reduced feelings of suspicion. Lee Kuan Yew's perception of the role of ASEAN also changed after his private meeting with the Indonesian leader. The prime minister was convinced by Suharto's commitment to regional cooperation and became aware that the Association could function as a political instrument for constraining regional partners.

Furthermore, both leaders agreed that ASEAN would operate as a form of collective political defence with a political rather than a military role against Chinese influence. Bilateral relations were further enhanced when Indonesia's president visited Singapore in August 1974. The personal links that were gradually developed between Lee Kuan Yew and Suharto helped strengthen bilateral ties as well as the cohesion of the Association itself.[10]

Indonesia's annexation of East Timor in December 1975 was another issue that complicated Singapore–Indonesian relations during ASEAN's early years. While the example of East Timor is compared to the case of Brunei in the next section, let us now focus briefly on the relevance of power balancing considerations in an illustration of a lack of ASEAN solidarity. At issue was Singapore's decision to abstain on a resolution in the General Assembly of the United Nations that condemned Indonesia's actions in East Timor. The city-state was most vocal in its opposition to the annexation and the only ASEAN member that failed to support Indonesia in the UN vote in December 1975. This decision angered Suharto and temporarily cooled bilateral relations. Eager to oppose any kind of violation of the principle of national sovereignty and the non-use of force, it should be noted that Singapore took corresponding positions on the annexation of Western Sahara and on Grenada and subsequently on Kuwait.[11]

While Singapore could not accept a blatant violation of national sovereignty, it was primarily concerned about Indonesia's potential expansionist policies. The city-state was in 1975 still fearful of Jakarta's regional intentions and potential hegemonic ambitions. Singapore's diplomatic stance in the UN should therefore be examined as a refusal to endorse an Indonesian act of hegemony. Its initial reaction in the General Assembly resulted from a perception of threat that took precedence over the obligation of ASEAN solidarity. Due to its geo-strategic situation, the city-state needed to demonstrate its opposition to the annexation, as it was itself 'afraid of being "Timorized" by Indonesia or Malaysia'.[12] Thus, its response was influenced by power balancing considerations. Singapore eventually closed ranks with all other ASEAN members by voting against the resolution during the second vote in the General Assembly held in 1976. Having sent a diplomatic signal to Jakarta, the city-state was keen afterwards to show its continuing commitment to ASEAN and to preserve its relationship with Indonesia. The TAC had been signed in the meantime during the Bali Summit of February 1976. The TAC had established a norm-based code of conduct for regional inter-state relations and introduced respect for national sovereignty as ASEAN's central principle. The city-state felt partly reassured by Indonesia's adherence to a code of conduct that offered a system of checks and balances within the regime for cooperative security.

The relevance of the balance of power has so far been illustrated by focusing on two events that affected a specific bilateral relationship. The 1968 crisis was viewed as an example of the intra-mural constraining of power through political and institutional means. In contrast, Indonesia's annexation of East Timor was a hegemonic action towards an extra-mural territory that provoked a diplomatic response from Singapore. Attention will now be given to the ZOPFAN principle, which was described in Chapter 1 as an associative attempt to register a call for regional autonomy. Conflicting strategic perspectives influenced the diplomacy that led to the formulation of the declaratory principle. At stake was the existence of contending approaches within the Association regarding how to manage regional order and preserve a satisfactory distribution of power. The negotiations over the merits of neutralization also indicated the importance of conventional balance of power practices in the foreign policy calculations of Thailand, Singapore and the Philippines.

ZOPFAN originated from the need to react to two interrelated and extra-mural strategic modifications that occurred in 1971. A rapprochement had begun in Sino-US relations and was kept secret until after Dr Henry Kissinger's visit to Beijing in July 1971. The US national security adviser made a second journey in October during which a formal visit by US President Richard Nixon to China was discussed. It was feared in Southeast Asia that Washington had granted the PRC a regional sphere of influence in return for its support for 'Peace with Honor' in Vietnam. During that month, the vote on the representation of China in the UN also took place. On 25 October 1971, Beijing replaced Taipei as the representative of China in the organization and hence joined the United Nations Security Council. These surprising developments upset America's allies and friends in Southeast Asia. The need to react to these external changes was felt in most ASEAN capitals. Yet, the persistence of contradictory security perspectives complicated any attempt at a common response.

Malaysia had already put forward without prior consultation with its ASEAN partners a plan for neutralizing Southeast Asia at the Lusaka Non-Alignment Conference in September 1970. It proposed neutralizing the region by using external powers as a guarantee to a regional application of this legal condition. Koh explains that neutralization 'is a process of international law whereby a state assumes the status of permanent or perpetual neutrality, both in times of peace and of war; a status which is recognized as such and guaranteed by certain other states'.[13] The Malaysian initiative, which emanated from the new prime ministership of Tun Abdul Razak, was partly an attempt to accommodate the United States, China and the Soviet Union by recognizing their regional influence.[14] The proposal had resulted from regional changes in the political environment and domestic considerations. The former included the onset of the gradual US withdrawal from South Vietnam following the election of President Nixon and the implementation of the so-called Nixon Doctrine. Introduced at a press conference in Guam in July 1969, the Nixon Doctrine called for Asian nations to play a more active part in their defence against communism. Implying a partial US disengagement from Asia, the doctrine led to a US policy of Vietnamization in Indochina.[15] The Malaysian initiative also reflected concern about growing Soviet influence in Vietnam, as Moscow had become Hanoi's principal ally, and about the implications of a British decision to accelerate its policy of military withdrawal East of Suez first announced in 1967. Originally expected for the mid-1970s, the military disengagement was moved to the end of 1971. This decision surprised Singapore and Malaysia, as both were dependent on their military ties with London. In addition to its regional character, the proposal was influenced by domestic factors. It was a means put forward by Kuala Lumpur to ease tension with the ethnic Chinese community in Malaysia by acknowledging the PRC and possibly normalizing relations with Beijing in light of the post-May 1969 racial riots.[16] Despite Malaysian diplomatic efforts in 1970–71 to promote the proposal, the latter only received a cold response from the other ASEAN states.[17] The United States, China and the Soviet Union were also not keen to commit themselves to the demands of neutralization.

The events of the autumn of 1971 persuaded ASEAN's foreign ministers to reconsider the Malaysian neutralization plan during an unofficial meeting held in Kuala Lumpur in November. The proposal met with opposition due to clashing perspectives on the regional distribution of power. Malaysia's initiative to neutralize Southeast Asia was unacceptable, above all, to Indonesia as it questioned its natural position of regional leadership. The proposal went against its expectations of a future intra-mural distribution of power determined by regional actors. It opened the door to increased external interference, primarily from China, and contradicted the preferences laid down in the Bangkok Declaration. Hence, the Malaysian initiative reinforced Indonesia's threat perception and challenged its managerial ambitions in Southeast Asia. In addition, Jakarta was pressing for its own principle of national resilience. Rather than be reliant on foreign guarantees, Indonesia supported an active and independent foreign policy and believed in the development of domestic and regional capabilities to reduce external intervention. Malik had expressed reservations regarding the neutralization initiative in September 1971. He had stated:

> I strongly believe that it is only through developing among ourselves an area of internal cohesion and stability, based on indigenous socio-political and economic strength, that we can ever hope to assist in the early stabilization of a new equilibrium in the region that would not be the exclusive 'diktat' of the major powers.[18]

While advocating an autonomous regional order, the military administration in Indonesia still tacitly supported the US presence in Southeast Asia and benefited from the financial and military assistance it received from the United States.

Singapore, Thailand and the Philippines subscribed to a realist tradition of International Relations and viewed the conventional practice of counter-vailing power as a crucial ingredient to their foreign policy. Manila was dependent on its links with Washington to ensure its security. Bangkok had traditionally relied on external ties and was keen to preserve a policy of independence of manoeuvre with the great powers. The Philippines and Thailand were also indirectly involved in the Vietnam War as allies of the United States and faced internal communist insurgencies supported by the PRC. Singapore remained fearful of absorption by Malaysia or Indonesia and perceived the US involvement in the region as vital to its security.[19] S. Rajaratnam, Singapore's foreign minister from 1965 until 1980, declared that the city-state was 'under no illusion that it could single-handedly cope with the many larger predators stalking in the jungle of international politics'.[20]

Consequently, Thailand, the Philippines and Singapore opposed the neutralization plan and argued for the involvement of external powers, primarily the United States, to maintain regional stability.[21] The implementation of the Malaysian proposal would have involved the removal of foreign bases and a reduced reliance on external security relations.[22] The three ASEAN states were concerned about rising Chinese influence. For instance during a visit to Malaysia in June 1971, the Thai Prime Minister Thanom Kittikachorn had criticized a neutralization scheme guaranteed among others by the PRC. Yet, in contrast to Indonesia, the opposition of Thailand, the Philippines and Singapore resulted from power-balancing considerations rather than any hegemonic disposition. They feared that the neutralization plan would hasten America's military withdrawal from the region leaving a 'power vacuum' to be filled by increasing Chinese or even Indonesian influence. The three member states were keen not to restrict their policy options and to preserve their external security ties in balance of power terms. They viewed the regional denial of hegemony as dependent on a military dimension, namely the existence of defence ties with external actors outside an ASEAN framework. Conventional balance of power calculations thus influenced their approach to the proposal for neutralization.

ZOPFAN was a formulation that accommodated these different security outlooks. Leifer explains that 'the outcome of the meeting in Kuala Lumpur represented an intra-mural accommodation of views rather than any assertion of corporate will.'[23] ZOPFAN was a political declaration that avoided the legal rights and obligations associated with the concept of neutralization. It merely stated that the ASEAN foreign ministers agreed that 'the neutralization of South-East Asia is a desirable objective and that we should explore ways and means of bringing about its realization'.[24] As a declaratory principle, ZOPFAN represented continuity with the Bangkok Declaration and did not impose any duties or limitations on the member states.[25] While the regional states acknowledged the legitimate interests of the great powers in the region, the ZOPFAN principle was about opposing external military intervention and domination in Southeast Asia.[26] Indeed, the ASEAN foreign ministers recognized 'the right of every state, large or small, to lead its national existence free from outside interference in its internal affairs as this interference will adversely affect its freedom, independence and integrity'.[27]

Hence, ZOPFAN reflected Indonesia's expectation of a regional order based on the managerial role of Southeast Asian states. It should also be associated with the wider priority of reinforcing regional resilience in Southeast Asia. In return, it did not restrict the right of member states to host foreign bases on their territory and/or rely on defence links with external powers to ensure their security. The document did not mention these issues. Indonesia thus accepted the preservation of ties with foreign powers, including the Five Power Defence Arrangements of April 1971 that had replaced the Anglo-Malaysian Defence Agreement on 1 November 1971 and linked the security of Singapore and Malaysia to a defence cooperation with Britain, Australia and New Zealand.[28] Interestingly, Malaysia had not found its call for the neutralization of Southeast Asia incompatible with its participation in this defence arrangement.[29]

ZOPFAN has never gained operational relevance as a security doctrine and differences in its interpretation have persisted among the member states. Indonesia, and particularly its foreign ministry, became a strong supporter of the principle, which was introduced as part of its foreign policy objective to establish an autonomous regional order. Jakarta has since then repeatedly called for the regional management of differences free from outside interference and based on security cooperation in Southeast Asia. In the post-Cold War, Indonesia has actively supported the Southeast Asia Nuclear Weapon-Free Zone (SEANWFZ) Treaty.[30] In contrast to Indonesia, Singapore has never endorsed the preference for regional autonomy and Thailand has at no time interpreted the principle as leading to a policy of non-alignment or to the termination of its defence links with external players.

ASEAN's enlargement to include Brunei

Brunei's bilateral relations with Malaysia and Indonesia before 1984

The first part of this section concentrates on Brunei's strained ties with Malaysia and Indonesia during the 1960s and 1970s that resulted from persisting antagonisms and challenges to its international legitimacy. These bilateral matters are contrasted with ASEAN's intra-mural relations by focusing particularly on Malaysia's unrestrained and menacing foreign policy towards the Sultanate during the mid-1970s. In addition, it is pointed out that Brunei developed a close relationship with Singapore mainly because both states shared a similar sense of vulnerability vis-à-vis Malaysia and Indonesia. Yet, in contrast to the city-state, the Sultanate could not use the Association before its membership as an instrument to constrain its threatening neighbours. In that respect, an analogy is drawn between the predicament of Brunei and Indonesia's annexation of East Timor.

Brunei's historical survival as a separate entity cannot be detached from its links with Britain.[31] A treaty relationship was first established in 1847.

London extended its protection over the Sultanate in 1888 when it took charge of Brunei's defence and external affairs. While never a colony, Brunei came under British Residency in 1906. Bilateral ties were redefined in 1959 when a Resident was replaced by a High Commissioner. It was then agreed that London would only be responsible for Brunei's defence, including internal security, and foreign affairs. The international status of the Sultanate remained unclear to most regional states due to its peculiar relations with the United Kingdom.

Brunei's ambiguous status, limited territory and formidable wealth complicated its relations with its neighbours. Despite its very small territory, which is also divided in two parts by the Limbang River valley that became part of Sawarak in 1890, the Sultanate's economy has been exceptionally prosperous thanks to its large oil and natural gas reserves. The production of oil first started in 1929. To understand Brunei's distrust of Malaysia and Indonesia, it is essential to review the revolt that took place in the Sultanate in 1962 as well as the failed negotiations regarding its inclusion in the Federation of Malaysia. These events worsened Brunei's ties with its neighbours as they distorted any kind of trust until the end of the 1970s and early 1980s. With reference to Malaysia, they also represented the beginning of a menacing foreign policy towards the Sultanate.

In May 1961, Malaya's Prime Minister Tunku Abdul Rahman officially announced his proposal to establish a wider federation that would unite Malaya, Singapore, Sarawak, Sabah and Brunei. Sir Omar Ali Saifuddin, the Sultan of Brunei, showed an initial enthusiasm for the project and suggested in July 1962 that the Sultanate would take part in the federation.[32] Brunei's small territory and wealth made it vulnerable to external aggression and independence was not perceived as a viable possibility. Rahman's proposal still divided domestic politics in Brunei. The *Partai Ra'ayat Brunei* (People's Party of Brunei), which had been created in 1956 by A.M. Azahari, opposed the notion of a Malaysian federation and supported instead the creation of an independent state of North Borneo consisting of Brunei, Sarawak and Sabah. The People's Party demonstrated its large popular support in the first partial legislative elections held in August 1962.[33]

Domestic divisions led in December 1962 to a revolt organized by the military wing of the People's Party. The rebellion was rapidly crushed by British troops brought in from Singapore. Attention must be given though to the part played by Indonesia as its support, perhaps even during the preparation of the revolt, created distrust and animosity in future bilateral relations. To the disappointment of the People's Party, Sukarno offered no real practical help to the rebels.[34] His assistance was primarily rhetorical as the revolt was portrayed in Jakarta as a fight for independence against British colonialism.[35] The uprising provided the Indonesian leader with an excuse to oppose the establishment of Malaysia, viewed only as a neo-colonial design, and to launch his policy of Confrontation. Brunei was later also the victim of small-scale Indonesian attacks during the period of

Confrontation.[36] In sum, Sukarno's support for the People's Party and its call for an independent state in northern Borneo led to Brunei's deep mistrust of Indonesia until the late 1970s and early 1980s.

The first round of negotiations for Brunei's entry in the Federation of Malaysia occurred in February 1963 and ended with high hopes on the future inclusion of the Sultanate. Owing to its size and domestic vulnerability after the rebellion, Kuala Lumpur was convinced that Brunei had no choice but to enter the Federation of Malaysia.[37] Taking place in June, the second round revealed that serious differences remained. These included disagreements on the distribution of oil revenues and the question of the sultan's order of royal precedence among the rulers of Malaysia that would determine the king of the federation on a five-year rotating period. It resulted also from the sultan's perception that the population of Brunei opposed the new federation.[38] Moreover, after the events of December 1962 Omar Ali Saifuddin wished to preserve his feudal control and avoid the organization of new elections in the Sultanate, which most likely would have resulted in victory for the People's Party.[39] The negotiations were eventually interrupted and Malaysia was established on 16 September 1963 without the participation of Brunei, which preserved its political and defence links with Britain. The failure to reach an agreement affected relations with Kuala Lumpur and enhanced Brunei's regional sense of vulnerability. Saunders explains that 'Tunku Abdul Rahman never forgave the Sultan for his intransigence and early in 1964 recalled the hundreds of teachers and government officers seconded to Brunei.'[40]

Brunei–Malaysian ties worsened significantly after the formation of ASEAN. Tun Abdul Razak succeeded Tunku Abdul Rahman in 1970. The new Malaysian prime minister conducted an adventurous and coercive policy towards Brunei, which was perceived in the Sultanate as designed to undermine its aristocratic regime and international legitimacy and ensure its annexation into the Malaysian federation. Ties were complicated in 1970 when Sultan Hassanal Bolkiah, who had been enthroned in August 1968 after the abdication of his father Omar Ali Saifuddin, revived in a public statement a historical claim to Limbang. Brunei had never recognized the annexation of the territory by Sarawak in 1890 and the sovereignty issue remained a source of bitterness and tension. Malaysia later questioned Brunei's international status by supporting the claims and activities of the People's Party. Kuala Lumpur had strongly opposed that political party and its demands before the establishment of the federation. In July 1973, some of the leaders of the People's Party, who had remained under arrest in Brunei since the 1962 revolt, were helped to escape and received asylum in Malaysia. This aggravated Brunei's mistrust of its neighbour. Allowed to open a political branch in the capital, it was presumably from these facilities that the People's Party sent a new manifesto to the sultan in April 1975.[41] Malaysia was also said to have arranged military training for students who opposed Brunei's feudal political regime.[42]

Malaysia's antagonism towards the Sultanate was demonstrated in the United Nations. In 1975 Malaysia funded the visit of a delegation of the People's Party to the UN Committee on Decolonization where it demanded Brunei's independence. Malaysia also sponsored a resolution in the General Assembly that challenged Brunei's international status by questioning its colonial links with Britain. Adopted in November 1977, the resolution demanded the holding of free elections and the introduction of a democratic political system. It was supported, among others, by Indonesia, the Philippines and Thailand but not by Singapore and provoked political embarrassment in London.

Malaysia's unrestrained foreign policy towards Brunei resulted from several factors. Kuala Lumpur had territorial ambitions in northern Borneo, as it was keen to include the Sultanate in the federation. It was interested in Brunei's oil and gas revenues, which it had failed to take under its control after the 1963 negotiations. Greed thus played an important part in its policy calculations. In addition, bilateral ties were affected by a struggle for cultural leadership. Introduced as the state ideology to establish Brunei's separate identity, the Sultanate defined itself as the last Malay Islamic Monarchy, which complicated relations with Kuala Lumpur.[43] Finally, Malaysia's actions were influenced by domestic security considerations. These involved separatist tendencies in Sarawak and Sabah, the possible revival of North Borneo nationalism that could have been exacerbated by the example of Brunei,[44] and the fear that Brunei could as a result of external intervention become a base of instability. A rapid integration of the Sultanate was perceived as a solution to these concerns. At a seminar organized in Jakarta in October 1974, Tan Sri Mohamad Ghazali Shafie, Malaysia's minister for home affairs, drew attention to 'a set of security issues that cannot be neatly categorized, but which has the potential for upsetting the best security calculations of several Southeast Asian states'.[45] He referred to:

> the security issues that resolve around the continuing existence of vestigial colonial territories in our region. Their existence besides being historically anomalous, also make them the foci of local discontent and foreign intrigue. The security issues that they pose may be peripheral to the ambit of our concern here, but they are nevertheless potential areas of instability.[46]

Ghazali Shafie was here referring to the Sultanate but also to the case of East Timor. In short, Malaysia's diplomatic behaviour was influenced by the need to ensure its defence in light of the potential consequences associated with Brunei's survival as a separate entity.

Arising from its difficult relations with Malaysia, Brunei had gradually established from the mid-1960s close political and military ties with Singapore. The relationship reflected a mutual recognition that they did not represent a threat to each other's survival. Though links remained particularly discreet,

Singapore and Brunei shared a common strategic perspective, comparable security interests and a similar mistrust of their neighbours. Doubtlessly, they had a comparable sense of vulnerability vis-à-vis Malaysia and to a lesser extent Indonesia – Malaysia was perceived as a potential challenge to their individual security while Indonesia had to be coped with as the most influential regional power. Close personal links were developed between Lee Kuan Yew and Omar Ali Saifuddin who would continue to have great political influence even after his abdication in 1968.[47] From the early 1970s, bilateral relations started to involve military contacts, including defence agreements, joint exercises and the presence of troops of the Singapore Armed Forces (SAF) in Brunei.[48] Diplomatic assistance was also strengthened. In contrast to all other ASEAN members, Singapore failed to support Malaysia's actions in the UN against Brunei's international legitimacy. Yet, their respective response to a similar sense of vulnerability should be distinguished. Singapore was active on the world scene and sought recognition and legitimacy through its participation in international organizations while Brunei focused nearly exclusively on the preservation of its links with Britain.

Malaysia was provided with a possible script for its dealings with Brunei by Indonesia's invasion of East Timor in December 1975.[49] Contrary to the Sukarno period, the aggressive military operation took place without the prior formulation of irredentist claims or strong nationalist rhetoric. Jakarta intervened to ensure its own security due to the fear of an independent East Timor under the control of the Revolutionary Front for an Independent East Timor (Fretilin) and communist influence in the Territory.[50] The fear of communism was at its peak as the episode during 1975 coincided with the closing phase of the Vietnam War and the communist takeover of Phnom Penh and Laos. The annexation of East Timor was viewed in the context of the containment of China. Most Western states, including the United States and Australia, tacitly accepted the Indonesian action which was regarded to have eliminated a possible threat of communist intervention.[51] Through an act of military aggression, Jakarta had also terminated the so-called security dangers posed by a colonial vestige. Jakarta received strong Malaysian diplomatic backing, as some of the concerns that led to its action were felt in Kuala Lumpur vis-à-vis the Sultanate. Moreover, Fretilin later argued that Malaysia had provided Indonesia the armament necessary for the invasion. Indonesia's military could not make use of US equipment.

Indonesia's annexation of East Timor was a direct denial of self-determination and a violation of international law. East Timor was formally incorporated on 17 July 1976 as the twenty-seventh province of the Republic of Indonesia. The annexation still had negative international repercussions for Indonesia, especially within the UN. Endless resistance in East Timor to Indonesia's occupation would also lead over the next twenty-four years to a constant policy of repression and severe violations of human rights. Indonesia only renounced its sovereignty over East Timor in 1999. The UN managed the Territory until it gained its independence on 20 May 2002.

The annexation of East Timor had dramatic implications for Brunei. It fuelled its sense of vulnerability. In addition to enhancing its suspicion towards Indonesia, it increased the apprehension of a comparable Malaysian intervention.[52] The invasion also strengthened the ties that existed between Brunei and Singapore, which perceived the example of East Timor as a threat to their own security. In contrast to the city-state, Brunei could not use ASEAN as a political instrument to constrain its ominous neighbours. Yet, Singapore's initial reaction to Indonesia's invasion sent a message to the member states regarding its refusal to endorse a similar solution in northern Borneo.[53]

In response to its menacing environment and the need to avoid annexation by a neighbouring state, Brunei had continued to rely primarily on its military and political links with the United Kingdom. A battalion of British Gurkha Rifles had been stationed in the Sultanate since 1962, ostensibly in a training role and to deter external military intervention.[54] However, Britain was eager to break with its colonial past and wished for Brunei's return to full sovereignty. It was also anxious to complete its military disengagement East of Suez. Desperate to preserve the status quo, the Sultanate aimed to 'delay independence as long as possible and resisted British attempts to withdraw the Gurkha garrison'.[55] An additional step was reached in 1971 when it was agreed that the High Commissioner would no longer advise the sultan on internal matters. Brunei was granted full control of its domestic affairs while external affairs stayed under the supervision of the United Kingdom. The British defence role was amended to match Five Power Defence obligations, namely to consult in the case of an external attack. The British desire to amend relations with Brunei was further enhanced by the election of a Labour government in 1974, which announced its decision to withdraw the Gurkha troops. It subsequently postponed and finally renounced that withdrawal. Still, Brunei's ability to ensure its long-term defence through its special links with Britain had become increasingly uncertain.

In addition to its external ties, the Sultanate developed a limited military capability independent of the Gurhka battalion. The Royal Brunei Malay Regiment was established in 1962 and slowly evolved over the next two decades into a small but well-equipped military force.[56] Large increases in military spending occurred from the mid-1970s until the early 1980s that provided the regiment with helicopters, communication equipment and other supplies. Huxley writes that extensive military budgets were required in that period for 'the acquisition of increasingly sophisticated and expensive weaponry suitable for deterring and defending against external threats'.[57] Brunei's military build-up was connected to the British desire to revise bilateral relations but also to a rise in governmental oil revenues. Nevertheless, it is questionable whether Brunei's military forces ever deterred Malaysia or Indonesia. It was unlikely, for instance, that the Royal Brunei Regiment could have responded to an invasion or faced a guerrilla infiltration.

In sum, Malaysia showed no restraint in its foreign policy and behaved in a menacing fashion towards the Sultanate. Its policy lacked the element of self-constraint that characterized ASEAN's intra-mural relations. Kuala Lumpur sought to undermine Brunei's international legitimacy and acted in an hegemonic fashion in northern Borneo. In addition, Indonesia's annexation of East Timor and its implications for Brunei demonstrated that the practice of self-denial did not apply outside the walls of the Association. Indonesia's invasion of the Territory should be contrasted to its intra-mural policy of political self-abnegation and, at least to a point, self-imposed containment. Consequently, Brunei could hardly rely on ASEAN as a form of political defence for constraining a similar Malaysian intervention. On the contrary, the Sultanate distrusted and kept a diplomatic distance from the Association mainly due to its suspicion of Indonesia and Malaysia.[58] Brunei was reliant on conventional balance of power tactics, namely a policy of balancing through external association and to a much lesser extent the strengthening of its own military power, to ensure its security. Except for its military links with Britain, which were uncertain in the long run, the Sultanate did not possess the capabilities to deter any potential aggression.

Motives for Brunei to join ASEAN

The second part of this section deals with the circumstances that led to ASEAN's initial enlargement to include Brunei in 1984. The motives included a desire to locate a process of reconciliation between the Sultanate and Malaysia and Indonesia within an already existing structure of dialogue. Accordingly, the expansion of membership is described as a replication of the original associative *raison d'être* of ASEAN. Moreover, the enlargement process involved a calculation of the balance of power factor. The benefits linked to the constraint from political association had a power balancing relevance. ASEAN provided Brunei with a vehicle through which to constrain its neighbours by political rather than military means. The expansion of the Association is analysed by first focusing on its associative dimension before indicating how a balance of power perspective played a role in this specific case.

Associative dimension

The motives for a state to join a regime for cooperative security should be examined in light of the advantages the original members already receive. Brunei's willingness to take part in the cooperative process can partly be understood by focusing on how the Association served its participants' narrowly defined objectives and enhanced the convergence of common interests. By the early 1980s, ASEAN had developed a political identity and a shared approach to security and had increased stability in intra-mural relations. It had also evolved into an internationally respected institution that gave some sense of diplomatic confidence to its participants. As a tiny state, Brunei could greatly benefit from a diplomatic platform that disposed of some regional and international relevance. Finally, the Association had established a code of conduct based on a set of standard international norms and principles. The TAC had enunciated the respect for national sovereignty as ASEAN's central principle. ASEAN's reaction to Vietnam's invasion and occupation of Cambodia and its respect for Cambodia's national sovereignty should for instance be noted. In accordance with a neo-liberal interpretation of security regimes, these institutional achievements influenced Brunei's decision to participate in the Association despite the membership of former and potential enemies to its security.

Nevertheless, ASEAN's enlargement was first dependent on a diplomatic rapprochement between Brunei and Malaysia and Indonesia. The rapprochement was initiated by political change in Malaysia that led in 1976 to the new prime ministership of Tun Hussein Onn. Though still pressing for decolonization, Hussein Onn was keen to introduce moderation and cooperation in his government's policy towards the Sultanate. Changes in perception vis-à-vis Brunei were first officially expressed in May 1978 when Suharto and Hussein Onn agreed during the course of a bilateral meeting in Labuan on the need to reach an accommodation with the Sultanate.[59] The shift was a recognition of the new political realities in northern Borneo. Malaysia and Indonesia realized by 1978 that the forthcoming independence of Brunei had become a fait accompli. The issue of sovereignty needed therefore to be addressed. Their new foreign policy also resulted from economic pragmatism. The Sultanate was a tiny entity with great wealth that could provide financial aid and free of interest loans. During a meeting between Suharto and Lee Kuan Yew in June 1978, Singapore's prime minister was asked to inform the sultan that after its return to independence Brunei was welcome to join the Association.[60]

This initial reduction of tension influenced Brunei's negotiations with the United Kingdom on the schedule of its proclamation of independence. A Treaty of Friendship and Cooperation was signed with Britain on 7 January 1979 in which it was agreed that it would take effect and that the Sultanate would gain full sovereignty on 1 January 1984. Brunei's international status, which had complicated its ties with neighbouring states, would thus soon be clarified. Its coming independence made a future participation in the Association possible. Yet, Brunei remained aware of its vulnerability and was eager to preserve its security links with Britain even after its reversion to sovereignty. This was promoted in Britain by the return to power of a Conservative government in 1979, which favoured continuing military ties with the Sultanate. A private defence cooperation agreement was eventually reached in 1983 that ensured the presence of a rotating battalion of the Gurkha Rifles under British command in Brunei.

Bilateral contacts with Malaysia and Indonesia were slowly developed, initially through informal social gatherings that were soon replaced by official visits. In March 1980, the Malaysian king came to Brunei while Sultan Hassanal Bolkiah made his first official trip to Malaysia in September 1981. Tensions in inter-Borneo relations were reduced in March 1981 by the visit of Tan Sri Adbul Rahman Yakub, the Sarawak chief minister, to Brunei. Malaysia's Deputy Prime Minister Datuk Musa Hitam travelled to the Sultanate in March 1982 and announced that Kuala Lumpur would sponsor Brunei's membership in ASEAN. Indonesia's Foreign Minister Professor Mochtar Kusumaatmadja later expressed the same support when he visited Brunei in August 1982. He also declared that there would be no return to the past policies of hostility.[61] The sultan had previously paid an unofficial visit to Jakarta in April 1981. Finally, Dr Mahathir Mohamad, who became prime minister of Malaysia on the retirement of Tun Hussein Onn in 1981, travelled to Brunei in March 1983.

These bilateral contacts were linked to Brunei's informal participation in the Association that started before it reached independence. Its gradual involvement in the cooperative security regime needs to be mentioned. Leifer explains that the 'five years grace period from January 1979 before the resumption of sovereignty was employed to secure familiarity with the working practice of the Association through attendance at its committees'.[62] Prince Mohamed Bolkiah, the future minister for foreign affairs, first attended as an observer the ASEAN ministerial meeting in Manila in June 1981 and was subsequently present at the following ministerial sessions organized respectively in Singapore and Bangkok. This time offered a learning period that preceded Brunei's membership. The Sultanate officially joined the Association during a ceremony of admission held in Jakarta on 7 January 1984.[63] In his speech, Prince Mohamed Bolkiah declared:

> We are confident (. . .) that in this new era based on relations between equals and on the basis of mutual respect for our independence, sovereignty and territorial integrity, Brunei Darussalam will be able to continue to pursue the economic progress and happiness of its people in a wider family of nations.[64]

Brunei's motives for taking part in ASEAN also derived from the existence of a code of conduct regulating intra-mural relations. At the ministerial meeting of July 1984, Brunei's minister for foreign affairs declared that he had observed the important part played by the Association 'in the promotion of regional peace and stability, through abiding respect for justice and the rule of law in the relationship among countries of the region, and the adherence to the principles of the United Nations Charter'.[65] Of particular significance to Brunei's security was the practical registration of respect for national sovereignty. The latter had been enunciated in the TAC in 1976 and demonstrated by ASEAN's common position vis-à-vis the Third Indochina Conflict. Brunei's independence coincided with ASEAN's diplomatic involvement in the Cambodian issue. The violation of Cambodian national sovereignty greatly concerned the Sultanate. Besides ASEAN, Brunei joined in 1984 the United Nations, the Commonwealth and the Organization of the Islamic Conference. By 1992, it had also become a member to the Non-Aligned Movement. Membership in these organizations strengthened and secured, at least to some extent, its international recognition and newly obtained independence.

Brunei is geographically part of Southeast Asia and its participation in ASEAN could thus be examined as a natural and logical consequence of its reversion to sovereignty. The *New Straits Times* wrote in January 1984 that 'Brunei's admission is the most logical, given the factors of geography, history and contemporary policy disposition.'[66] The first expansion in membership should be associated with the original hope stated in the Bangkok Declaration of uniting the entire sub-region under ASEAN auspices. If it had decided not to join, the Sultanate would have been regarded as a regional anomaly, fuelling suspicion among regional states.[67] Brunei had no real alternative but to become a member. An integration in the Malaysian federation was not viewed as an option in the Sultanate and a policy of isolation or the development of close ties with one of the great powers were unlikely alternatives to membership of ASEAN.

In sum, ASEAN's enlargement to include Brunei was influenced by an associative dimension. It resulted from a situation of mutual benefits. In accordance with the concept of cooperative security, the Sultanate joined a multilateral security regime that operated on an intra-mural basis. The institutionalization of a process of reconciliation within an already existing structure of dialogue contributed to improving the climate of regional relations. An analogy should be made between the first expansion of membership and the associative origins of ASEAN, which primarily resulted from an act of reconciliation between Indonesia and Malaysia and the need to prevent the recurrence of regional confrontation.[68] Brunei's membership was expected to build trust and promote confidence building in specific bilateral relations. Moreover, it extended the respect and application of a code of conduct to an additional regional actor.

Balance of power dimension

The associative dimension involved in ASEAN's enlargement to include Brunei has so far been discussed. Keeping this analysis in mind, it is now argued that balance of power politics, resulting in part from enduring feelings of mistrust, played a role in the expansion of membership. Let us begin with how the enlargement process was regarded within ASEAN, with special reference to Malaysia and Indonesia. At issue was a common understanding of the benefits of Brunei's membership by Hussein Onn and Suharto when they met in 1978, as neither saw profit in threatening the Sultanate.[69] These views on the need to maintain stability in inter-state relations should be related to the establishment of the Association. ASEAN was formed to deny intra-mural hegemony, ensure the sovereignty of individual members and promote stability, primarily in Indonesian–Malaysian relations. By asking the Sultanate to join the Association, both leaders agreed to contain potential hegemonic ambitions towards the future state. Acting in an aggressive fashion towards Brunei once it was a member would otherwise disturb the cooperative premises and credibility of ASEAN.

This shared understanding of Brunei's membership is an example of associative, rather than competitive, power balancing. The associative balance of power tradition is based on the notion that instead of using power competitively to enhance narrow self-interests, it may be used collectively to ensure an equilibrium that may serve the interests of the states part of the system.[70] In accordance with our approach to the balance of power concept, defined in political terms, the practice of employing balancing power can take an associative form. It is in that respect that this specific illustration should be considered. Both leaders agreed on the need to constrain their potential hegemonic disposition in northern Borneo in order to secure an intra-mural political equilibrium. Constrained by their stake in the political association, they were eager to preserve ASEAN's cohesion and stability. This interpretation helps us to elaborate upon the operation of the balance of power within ASEAN. This factor most easily interacts with the cooperative perspective when represented in an associative form.

In addition to an intra-mural denial of hegemony, an expansion of membership was in accordance with Indonesia's preference for an autonomous management of regional order within Southeast Asia. Though not enthusiastic about its domestic political regime, Suharto was keen to integrate the Sultanate into the Association to remove an opportunity for external intervention and communist manipulation. The tiny state needed to be part of ASEAN as it might otherwise become a base of instability where subversive actions could be organized against Indonesia. Weatherbee rightly pointed out in 1983 that a 'vulnerable Brunei will to some extent be insulated from the currents of competition through its absorption into the established pattern of ASEAN orientations, and its potential for becoming a venue for new conflict will be reduced'.[71] Subsequently, the new membership consolidated ASEAN's operation as a collective political defence to reduce vulnerabilities with Chinese influence in mind. Indeed, it was feared in Southeast Asia that Beijing had the capacity to damage internal order by exploiting domestic vulnerabilities. While this motivation was influenced by countervailing tactics against a menacing external power, it also indicated Indonesia's ambitions within ASEAN.

Let us now further discuss Brunei's motives for joining the Association. Its participation was linked to an attempt to enhance its national security in light of its constant vulnerability. Except for its military links with Britain, the Sultanate did not possess the capabilities to deter any potential Malaysian aggression. The act of reconciliation and its location within a structure of dialogue did not eliminate Brunei's mistrust of Malaysia and to a lesser extent Indonesia. Sukarno's support for the 1962 rebellion and Malaysia's coercive foreign policy during the mid-1970s were vividly remembered in the Sultanate. Brunei's relations with its neighbours could again deteriorate in the future and it was therefore willing to cooperate with new partners that remained potential enemies. Bilateral relations with Malaysia would remain difficult even after the Sultanate joined the Association, partly due to the unresolved issue of sovereignty over Limbang. For example, this question affected relations in 1987 after it had been reported that Sultan Hassanal Bolkiah had discussed with Prime Minister Dr Mahathir Mohamad the possibility of purchasing the disputed territory. This was denied in Malaysia. In sum, it is in that context of suspicion that an unconventional practice of countervailing power played a part in Brunei's calculations.

Brunei's decision to join ASEAN was influenced by the benefits linked to an intra-mural denial of hegemony. The Sultanate perceived the arrangement as a diplomatic instrument to constrain potential hegemonic ambitions in northern Borneo. ASEAN offered some form of political guarantee that neither Malaysia nor Indonesia would in the future threaten or seek to annex the tiny state. An aggressive action towards the Sultanate would undermine the norms and principles promoted by the Association; above all, the respect for national sovereignty. Leifer writes that: 'The nature of the political evolution of ASEAN had enabled the government of Brunei to regard the Association as a collective security organisation whose members were constrained by self-denying ordinance from behaving in a threatening manner towards one another'.[72] The constraint imposed on Indonesia and Malaysia through their political stake in ASEAN thus had a power balancing relevance. It should be repeated, however, that the enlargement had first been dependent on a willingness by Suharto and Hussein Onn, initially expressed in May 1978, to include Brunei as a member of the Association.

Besides ASEAN and its intra-mural denial of hegemony, Brunei continued to rely on a conventional practice of countervailing power through the preservation of defence ties with Britain. Despite its membership of ASEAN, in 1984 Brunei did not terminate a private agreement reached with Britain in 1983 and open for review after five years that ensured the continuing presence of a 1,000-man battalion of the Gurkha Rifles in the Sultanate. The agreement was renewed in December 1994 in the light of the withdrawal of the Gurkha Brigade from Hong Kong by June 1997. These troops, which remain under British command, have been regarded as a means to deter external intervention or annexation by a neighbouring state. The SAF also maintained in Brunei after its reversion to sovereignty several hundred soldiers under training in a military jungle camp first made available by the sultan in the late 1960s.

To complete this analysis, one should focus on the role of Singapore in convincing the Sultanate to take part in the Association. As seen before, strong but discreet links existed between both states, which shared a common sense of vulnerability vis-à-vis their neighbours. It is therefore not surprising that Suharto asked Lee Kuan Yew to convey a welcoming message in 1978. Singapore's prime minister was best suited to persuade Sultan Hassanal Bolkiah of the change in regional attitude towards Brunei. Lee personally informed the sultan during a visit to Brunei in March 1979.[73] He also discussed the issue with Omar Ali Saifuddin. In his memoirs, Lee refers to his private meeting with Sir Omar and writes that:

> He agreed to consider seeking observer status for Brunei in Asean, but nothing came of it. I explained to him how the world had changed. Sir Omar held on to his implicit faith in the British, that they would always be there to back him. He did not want to recognise Britain's changed circumstances, that there were no British naval or air task forces to come to Brunei's rescue.[74]

Sultan Hassanal Bolkiah travelled to the city-state in January 1980. Singapore made clear to the Sultanate that it had no option but to join the Association as it united Brunei's neighbours but also its potential enemies.[75] During a one-to-one meeting, Singapore's prime minister explicitly asked Sultan Hassanal Bolkiah to look beyond a traditional reliance on Britain and to view ASEAN, as well as other international organizations, as a means to secure Brunei's security.[76] Lee Kuan Yew may have succeeded in persuading the sultan that joining ASEAN would enhance Brunei's defence because any threat by a participant would rebound adversely on the cohesion and credibility of the Association. The city-state was well aware by the early 1980s that ASEAN was an asset for protecting its own national sovereignty. Consequently, Brunei gained from Singapore's experience and expected to achieve similar security objectives through its membership of the Association.

Intra-mural denial of hegemony: balance of power factor meets associative perspective

This final section discusses how a balance of power perspective complemented the associative dimension involved in ASEAN's early years and its enlargement to include Brunei in 1984. Attention needs to be given to the relevance of conventional balance of power tactics before discussing the constraining of power within cooperative security through political means. Most individual members regarded the regional denial of hegemony as dependent on a traditional military dimension, namely the existence of defence ties with external actors. Singapore, Thailand and the Philippines considered the conventional practice of countervailing power outside an ASEAN framework as vital to their individual survival. Defence relationships linked Thailand and the Philippines to the United States and

Singapore participated in the Five Power Defence Arrangements. Despite its proposal for neutralizing Southeast Asia, Malaysia took part in the defence group when it superseded the Anglo-Malaysian Defence Agreement in 1971. Finally, Brunei was eager to maintain a British military presence in the Sultanate after its return to independence. Indonesia was thus the only ASEAN state not to rely on formal defence ties with external powers during the historical period discussed in this chapter.

It is important to examine whether the conventional practice of countervailing power by individual members influenced the institutional experience of ASEAN. Traditional balance of power tactics set a limit to the application of an associative dimension. The reliance on defence ties with external powers negatively affected the operational relevance of ZOPFAN as a declaratory principle. In the case of Brunei, a continuation of the British military connection reflected its feelings of suspicion and mistrust towards Malaysia and Indonesia. These enduring views were introduced in the Association and limited Brunei's future involvement and confidence in the cooperative process. Nonetheless, a regional distribution of power supported by outside powers promoted security in Southeast Asia and positively influenced the functioning of the Association. In particular, the US involvement in Southeast Asia and its operation as a conventional source of countervailing power contributed to regional stability, which was crucial for the development of the cooperative security regime. Hence, intra-mural cooperation was reliant on a specific regional context supported by external powers, primarily the United States.[77]

The constraining of power within cooperative security complemented the associative dimension involved in ASEAN's early years and in its expansion to include Brunei. The need to deal with Indonesia's power and influence in Southeast Asia was an important dimension of ASEAN's institutional experience between 1967 and 1975. In that context, the balance of power factor played a critical part in ASEAN's early years and in the calculations of some participants. Its primary relevance resulted from a denial of intra-mural hegemony imposed on Indonesia through its integration within an embryonic security regime. The practice of countervailing power, though not in a conventional sense, was best illustrated through the 1968 crisis. Beyond showing its strong commitment to ASEAN, Indonesia's understanding of the denial of intra-mural hegemony positively influenced the associative dimension. Jakarta was restrained, among other factors, by its political stake in the Association, and Singapore benefited from this in 1968. Suharto preserved the viability of the associative arrangement by demonstrating his acceptance of the notion of self-imposed containment. Some core principles had been laid down in the Bangkok Declaration, including commitments to the peaceful resolution of disputes, respect for national sovereignty and non-intervention in the internal affairs of other states. An aggressive reaction to the hanging of the two marines would have undermined these norms and rebounded adversely on the emerging political association. The result was to preserve stability in Singapore–Indonesian relations.

Other illustrations revealed the influence of balance of power on intra-mural relations and the early institutional experience of ASEAN. Yet, these cases should be contrasted with our discussion on the constraining of power through political means. Singapore's eagerness to respond to an Indonesian act of hegemony in East Timor was considered. While acting in an aggressive fashion, Indonesia's actions were conducted towards an extra-mural territory. Hence, the intra-mural denial of hegemony through political association was not violated. Nevertheless, Singapore registered its opposition to the violation of UN principles. In the case of ZOPFAN, contradictory views on the regional order and conventional balance of power calculations played a counter-productive part in cooperation and restricted the institutional development of ASEAN. The fear of a potential hegemon in Southeast Asia influenced the reactions of Singapore, Thailand and the Philippines to the Malaysian neutralization plan. With China, but perhaps also Indonesia in mind, the three states indicated their persistent reliance on conventional balance of power practices to ensure their individual security. These member states perceived the regional denial of hegemony to be dependent on a distribution of power supported by external actors.

In the case of Brunei, the focus of the analysis has been to indicate the presence of associative and balance of power factors that influenced the enlargement process and the calculations of the different actors involved. Balance of power practice played an implicit role in the rationale for the enlargement and overlapped with the process of reconciliation. ASEAN's expansion to include Brunei involved the restraining of Indonesian and Malaysian power through political and institutional means. The constraint imposed on these members directly benefited Brunei's security interests and consolidated its position vis-à-vis its neighbours. A practice of counter-vailing power by political means was thus a central element in the institutionalization of the act of reconciliation. As a result, the notion that the expansion of membership should be analysed as an additional example of a radical shift from balance of power politics to inter-state cooperation must be questioned. Some may insist that an enlargement process reduces regional power struggles by expanding geographically the influence of a cooperative security arrangement defined as an alternative to the balance of power concept. In contrast, this book asserts that ASEAN's enlargement to include Brunei was constructed with the denial of hegemony in mind, the key objective of the balance of power.

The balance of power factor was dependent on the political evolution of the Association. The constraint was imposed on the larger members through their growing stake in ASEAN. Once Brunei became a member, Indonesia and Malaysia were in no position to interfere in its domestic affairs or threaten its survival without undermining the political cohesion of the Association. Of particular importance were the standard international norms enunciated in the TAC that established a code of conduct regulating intra-mural relations. The fact that all the members adhered to these norms secured the national sovereignty of Brunei and Singapore. To that extent, the intra-mural distribution of power was held in check.

The constraining of power through political means positively influenced ASEAN's enlargement to include Brunei. The balance of power factor promoted the associative principles by offering the Sultanate a form of political defence for containing hegemonic dispositions. The intra-mural denial of hegemony provided the tiny state with a prime incentive to take part in the regime for cooperative security. In addition, the expansion of membership initially resulted from a willingness by Hussein Onn and Suharto to constrain their potential hegemonic dispositions in northern Borneo and to include Brunei within the political association. Both perceived Brunei's membership as beneficial for domestic and regional stability. Doubtlessly, the enlargement would not have taken place if Malaysia and to a lesser extent Indonesia had not first endorsed a policy of self-imposed containment towards the Sultanate.

Finally, ASEAN's enlargement to include Brunei needs to be compared to the formation of the Association in 1967. In Chapter 2, it was claimed that these founding moments involved the coexistence and interaction of associative and balance of power perspectives. It was argued that the membership of cooperative security was constructed with a reference to the balance of power factor. The similarities with the first expansion process demonstrate the continuing relevance of the balance of power as an intra-mural factor that outlasts the simple creation of a cooperative security regime. In that respect, the enlargement to include Brunei questions neo-liberal expectations that realist persuasions diminish or even disappear once an institution reaches maturity. Though a code of conduct had been established, conventional as well as unconventional power balancing practices still influenced the Association and the calculations of its members. Resulting from contradictory security perspectives, their persistence helps to understand why ASEAN was still a weak security regime after more than fifteen years of existence.

4 The balance of power and extra-mural hegemony

ASEAN's response to the Third Indochina Conflict

Introduction

The Third Indochina Conflict (1978–91) posed an immense political challenge for the ASEAN states. Vietnam's invasion and occupation of Cambodia was a blatant case of aggression that altered the strategic environment in mainland Southeast Asia. This matter became the centre of ASEAN's activities for a period of twelve years. One may wonder why the Cambodian question was such an important issue for the Association. No comparable apprehension had been demonstrated with Indonesia's invasion of East Timor in 1975 or during the mid-1970s when Malaysia challenged Brunei's international legitimacy. In contrast to these cases, a member state, namely Thailand, faced an unprecedented direct external threat to its national security as indicated by the presence of Vietnamese military troops on its border and repeated incursions into its territory.

This chapter discusses ASEAN's response to Vietnam's invasion and occupation of Cambodia by analysing its actions through both associative and balance of power perspectives. The common standpoint adopted by the member states vis-à-vis a case of aggression is first examined. A collective reaction to the events in Indochina brought significant diplomatic achievements and enhanced the international standing of the Association. Yet, unable to evolve into a defence arrangement, ASEAN failed ultimately to manage the problem of regional order. The balance of power is addressed in the conventional use of the term because the power balancing did not occur through political means but through a combination of military, economic and diplomatic ones. By joining a tacit alliance with China, amongst others, the ASEAN states engaged in traditional balance of power practice. Imposed by Bangkok, that policy had a negative effect on intra-mural relations.

The chapter consists of three sections. The first considers ASEAN's relations with Hanoi from the communist victories in 1975 until the invasion of Cambodia in December 1978. The second section offers a brief account of the Third Indochina Conflict, including the motives for the invasion and the international response that it provoked. Finally, ASEAN's reaction to

Vietnam's policy in Cambodia is studied by analysing its role and influence in the war. In addition to reviewing the coexistence of associative and balance of power dimensions, it is examined how the latter influenced the cooperative aspects involved in ASEAN's response to the Third Indochina Conflict.

ASEAN–Vietnamese relations and changes in the regional power distribution, 1975–78

A new political environment resulted in Indochina from the communist takeover of Phnom Penh and Saigon in April 1975 and Laos by the end of the year. The rapid success of revolutionary communism, after the US withdrawal from South Vietnam in 1973, alarmed the ASEAN members. Southeast Asia was polarized ideologically into two groups of communist and non-communist states. Vietnam represented a potential threat to some ASEAN nations. Its communist leadership disposed of the largest armed forces in the region and had demonstrated its military capabilities by uniting the country despite the successive intervention of external powers. Some feared an adventurous Vietnamese foreign policy in Indochina that could affect the stability of Southeast Asia. Moreover, Hanoi was perceived as an indirect threat due to the material and rhetorical support it could provide to communist insurgencies operating within the ASEAN states.

The strategic modifications in Indochina dominated the annual meeting of the foreign ministers held in Kuala Lumpur in May 1975. The joint press statement 'expressed their readiness to enter into friendly and harmonious relationship with each nation in Indochina'.[1] Still, the initial reaction portrayed a sense of consternation and lacked the formulation of a collective response. Differences in perception divided the ASEAN members. The Malaysian Prime Minister Tun Abdul Razak expressed optimism on the end of the Second Indochina War and suggested an enlargement of the Association to include the other Southeast Asian states.[2] In contrast, Bangkok was alarmed by these events and displayed a great feeling of vulnerability exemplified in establishing, along with the Philippines, diplomatic relations with China in 1975 and expelling US bases the following year. Thailand did not dispose of the military capability to deter Vietnam and lacked access to a reliable external source of countervailing power to oppose its potential hegemony in Indochina. In addition to a divergence in the strategic outlook, which will be discussed below, the member states were in no position to influence events in Indochina. Their control over the security environment was severely limited by the nature of their association. Hence, ASEAN would focus until 1978 on a policy of accommodation with Vietnam.

The changes in Indochina eventually led to the first summit of the ASEAN heads of state and government in Bali in February 1976. As their collective response to external shocks, the Bali Summit led to the signing of the Declaration of ASEAN Concord and the Treaty of Amity and Cooperation (TAC). Both documents consolidated the commitment made by each member state to the Association. They provided ASEAN with a political identity, a shared approach to security and a code of conduct for regulating intra-mural relations. Specifically, the TAC was a collective attempt to regulate the regional order by aiming to apply a code of conduct to the whole of Southeast Asia. It was therefore a diplomatic instrument for managing relations with a reunited Vietnam. The attempt to develop peaceful relations with the Indochinese states was later repeated during the second meeting of the ASEAN heads of state and government in Kuala Lumpur in August 1977 that celebrated the tenth anniversary of the Association.

Nevertheless, the Bali Summit indicated important limitations. The events of 1975 did not lead to the transformation of the Association into a formal or tacit alliance. Despite the existence of external adversity, no military dimension was included in the Bali declarations. Bilateral collaboration against border insurgencies had developed between some member states. The ASEAN Concord called for the 'continuation of cooperation on a non-ASEAN basis between member states in security matters in accordance with their mutual needs and interests'.[3] In contrast to a military dimension, the principles of national and regional resilience were introduced in Bali as a shared security doctrine. Sources of instability were regarded as associated with internal threats that could be manipulated by foreign subversive influences. The exclusion of military cooperation within an ASEAN framework should be examined as a collective effort not to alienate or provoke Vietnam and the PRC and as resulting from a lack of military capabilities. Yet, it also indicated the persistence of suspicion and contradictory security perspectives among the member states. These disagreements revolved primarily around divergent threat perceptions with reference to China and Vietnam.

Two major strategic outlooks coexisted within the Association. Thailand perceived a reunited Vietnam as the most immediate danger to its security environment as it feared the creation of an Indochinese federation that would border its territory. Thailand had in its recent history competed with Vietnam over influence in mainland Southeast Asia. Bangkok had developed ties with the PRC since the 1969 Nixon Doctrine. However, fearful of China's potential menace in both domestic and regional affairs, it waited until July 1975 before opening diplomatic relations with Beijing.[4] Thailand followed the lead of Malaysia, which had been the first ASEAN state to establish relations with the PRC in May 1974. Eager to preserve a policy of equidistance with the great powers, Thailand wished to improve its relations with the Soviet Union and to preserve its links with the United States despite the closure of US bases in 1976. The latter had resulted from domestic pressure in Thailand as well as the need to develop peaceful relations with neighbouring communist states.[5] The rapid communist victories in

Indochina after the Paris Peace Agreements of January 1973 had questioned the US commitment to regional security. Evans and Rowley explain that 'Thailand was seeking to balance Moscow and Beijing against each other – though Bangkok's aim was to bring as much restraining influence as possible to bear on a reunited Vietnam.'[6] Sharing the Thai threat perception, Singapore feared Vietnam's aspirations in Indochina and the growing Soviet influence in Southeast Asia. Consequently, it supported a US presence in the region to deter Soviet and Vietnamese hegemonic ambitions.

By contrast, Indonesia perceived the PRC as its primary source of external threat, partly due to the PRC's involvement in the abortive *coup d'état* of 1965, and regarded Vietnam as a useful buffer state against China's regional expansion. Hein explains that it is 'almost axiomatic in Jakarta that an independent and secure Vietnam can make a positive contribution to overall regional security and resilience in the face of the external threat posed by Beijing'.[7] In addition, Indonesia shared with Vietnam the experience of a military struggle for independence and considered its domestic political regime to be primarily nationalistic rather than communist. The TAC reflected Indonesia's preference for an autonomous management of the regional order that would include Vietnam and thus reduce its reliance on external powers. Malaysia viewed the PRC, though to a lesser extent than Indonesia, as a primary danger to its security and wished for Vietnam to be integrated within the region. Malaysia's threat perception was dominated by fears of internal subversion due to China's past assistance to the Communist Party of Malaya (CPM), its interference in domestic affairs and the existence of a large ethnic Chinese minority in the federation.[8] Thanks to its geographic location and military links with the United States, the Philippines did not feel acutely threatened by either Vietnam or the PRC. The Philippines was the third ASEAN state to establish relations with the PRC in July 1975. Indonesia and Singapore – which had pledged to be the last member to recognize China – only normalized relations with Beijing in 1990.

Regardless of its initiatives to regulate regional relations, Vietnam did not recognize ASEAN as a diplomatic entity and regarded the arrangement with hostility due to its conservative and anti-communist ideology. Seen as a reformulation of the South-East Asia Treaty Organization (SEATO), ASEAN was considered as part of a US policy of containment. Vietnam also expected the Association to be short lived. By rejecting the TAC, Hanoi thwarted ASEAN's attempt to apply a code of conduct to the whole of Southeast Asia and demonstrated its limited influence in dealing with extra-mural affairs. Moreover, Vietnam and Laos prevented the inclusion of the ZOPFAN principle in the final resolution of the Fifth Non-Aligned Conference held in Colombo in August 1976 in spite of its inclusion in Algiers in 1973. Hanoi had formerly criticized existing ties with external powers by referring to the promotion of 'independence, peace and genuine neutrality in Southeast Asia'. Vietnam was willing to open bilateral relations with individual participants. Relations were established with Malaysia and the Philippines in 1976 and Thailand in 1978. Indonesia had maintained diplomatic ties with Hanoi throughout the Second Indochina Conflict. Hanoi's refusal to confer at a multilateral level was aimed at weakening ASEAN by dividing its member states and to avoid Vietnam being subject to collective pressure.

Despite the contradictory strategic perspectives and Vietnam's hostility towards the Association, the Indochinese question was not yet a source of tension among the member states. Intra-mural differences and contrasting threat perceptions were kept latent by the emergence of a xenophobic regime in Cambodia, which was keen to preserve its independence from Vietnam.[9] Laos came under Vietnamese influence after the communist victory and Hanoi imposed a relationship of dependency on Vientiane through a Treaty of Friendship and Cooperation signed in July 1977.[10] In contrast, Pol Pot's government of Democratic Kampuchea (DK) opposed such external control and relations with Hanoi soon worsened. Between 1975 and 1978, Vietnamese–Cambodian relations were strained by traditional feelings of animosity, border disputes and ideological quarrels.[11] These divisions favoured the Thai interest as they secured Cambodia's traditional role as a buffer state against Vietnam. Leifer writes that for 'Thailand, in particular, the prospect of an inter-Communist balance of power was attractive politically, while ASEAN as a corporate entity could contemplate the prospect of a structure of regional relations based on a limitation of Vietnamese dominance within Indochina'.[12] Indonesia's interests were also enhanced by a deterioration of Sino-Vietnamese relations in 1975–76. A revival of hostility had started to appear by the end of the Second Indochina War. Matters that led to a worsening of bilateral ties included territorial disputes, ideological disagreements, overseas Chinese living in Vietnam as well as Hanoi's relations with Moscow.[13] In short, the emergence of a power equilibrium in Indochina and renewed Sino-Vietnamese antagonism accommodated intra-mural differences and reduced fears of a Vietnamese or Chinese hegemony.

This acceptable situation in Indochina quickly changed for the worse. A series of clashes on the Vietnamese–Cambodian border led to a Vietnamese military incursion in December 1977 and the suspension of diplomatic relations. The escalation of tension convinced Hanoi and Phnom Penh of the need to reinforce their links with external powers, respectively the Soviet Union and the PRC. Vietnam joined the COMECON on 29 June 1978 and its relations with China continued to deteriorate. The gradual involvement of the Soviet Union and the PRC lessened the advantages of a satisfactory distribution of power in Indochina and led the ASEAN states to fear new external intervention in the region.[14] Due to the nature of their association, the members were incapable of reacting to these events. However, ASEAN became involved in the emerging conflict when the opposite sides lobbied for its support. During official visits to the ASEAN capitals in September–

October 1978, including a five-day trip to Bangkok, Vietnam's Prime Minister Pham Van Dong offered a Treaty of Friendship and Non-Aggression to his hosts. He pledged that Vietnam would not interfere in internal affairs or assist domestic communist parties. Thayer points out that as 'a sign of its growing political maturity, ASEAN co-ordinated its response to Dong's visit, presented a united front, and collectively agreed to individually decline the offer of a non-aggression treaty'.[15] Chinese Vice Premier Deng Xiaoping visited Thailand, Malaysia and Singapore later that year. General Kriangsak Chomanan, Thailand's prime minister between November 1977 and February 1980, had previously strengthened relations with the PRC during an official visit to Beijing in April 1978.

While consolidating the diplomatic image of the Association, these initiatives were steps on the road to war. Vietnam and the Soviet Union formalized their alignment by signing a Treaty of Friendship and Cooperation on 3 November 1978 and later supported the establishment of the exile Kampuchean National United Front for National Salvation that challenged the Pol Pot regime. Vietnam's invasion of Cambodia began on 25 December 1978 and ended the power equilibrium in Indochina. Santoli explains that Hanoi 'conceived of its invasion in terms of the Soviet invasions of Hungary and Czechoslovakia: a blitzkrieg operation with quick destruction of all resistance, rapid establishment of a puppet government, and an occupation force that could survive short-term world condemnation'.[16] The DK government was overthrown in early January 1979 and its Deputy Prime Minister Ieng Sary fled to Beijing to seek assistance. A pro-Vietnamese government, the People's Republic of Kampuchea (PRK), was established on 8 January 1979 under the nominal leadership of Heng Samrin. The latter was a former Khmer Rouge official who had found refuge in Hanoi the previous year. Finally, a Treaty of Peace, Friendship and Cooperation was signed on 18 February 1979, which provided Vietnam with a legal justification for maintaining military forces in Cambodia.

The Third Indochina Conflict

The Cambodian conflict originated from a struggle over the distribution of power in Indochina.[17] In addition to its domestic dimension, consisting of a struggle between Cambodian factions, the war had a regional scope defined by a series of hostile bilateral relations, above all, Sino-Vietnamese antagonism. Moreover, the conflict became an element in East–West rivalry and thus part of the strategic calculations of the great powers. It is often argued that Vietnam invaded its neighbour either to establish an Indochinese federation under its control or to respond to a Chinese threat on its southwestern border.[18] Both explanations need to be included in an analysis of Vietnam's policy in Cambodia. The creation of a loose federation should be examined as the outcome of a military doctrine introduced during the First Indochina Conflict. General Vo Nguyen Giap, leading strategist and founding father of the People's Army of Vietnam, had then declared: 'Indochina is a strategic unit; a single theatre of operations. Therefore, we have the task of helping to liberate all of Indochina – especially for reasons of strategic geography, we cannot conceive of Vietnam completely independent while Cambodia and Laos are ruled by imperialism.'[19] Vietnam imposed militarily a relationship of dependency on Cambodia already established in Laos through a Treaty of Friendship and Cooperation. Vietnam was influenced in its military action by the close ties that had developed between Cambodia and the PRC.

Chinese strategic calculations were dominated by the need to avoid a situation where one single state could control Indochina and threaten its south-eastern border. Vietnam's hegemony over Cambodia and Laos was therefore unacceptable to the PRC. Beijing was highly suspicious of Hanoi's alignment with Moscow and perceived the invasion of Cambodia as part of a Soviet regional expansion. The occupation of Cambodia was conditional on military and financial assistance from the Soviet Union. The Soviet regional presence was also intensified in early 1979 through its military deployment at the air and naval bases at Danang and Cam Ranh Bay. Consequently, the Third Indochina Conflict was part of the so-called Second Cold War and became particularly relevant with regard to the Sino-Soviet Split.[20] The Soviet invasion of Afghanistan in December 1979 consolidated fears in Beijing of a Soviet encirclement of its territory and expansion in Asia. Though sharing these apprehensions, the United States had scaled down its military involvement in Southeast Asia and was unwilling to orchestrate a response to the power shift in Indochina.

Rather than being accepted as a fait accompli, Vietnam's invasion of Cambodia was strongly condemned and provoked an international response, with military, diplomatic and economic dimensions. It united China, the United States, Japan and the ASEAN members in an effort to terminate an illegal occupation of a sovereign state. Leifer argues that the 'object of the collective enterprise was to apply a strategy of attrition at Vietnam's expense which over time would subject its government and society to breaking strain so obliging it to abdicate its geopolitical advantage'.[21] Affecting its credibility as a regional player, the PRC reacted most strongly to Vietnam's policy in Cambodia. Deng Xiaoping authorized a punitive offensive across Vietnam's northern border that lasted from mid-February until mid-March 1979. US President Jimmy Carter had tacitly approved the offensive during Deng Xiaoping's visit to the United States in early 1979.[22] Restrained in its objectives to avoid a Soviet response, the operation indicated the inexperience of the People's Liberation Army (PLA) and failed to influence Vietnamese actions in Cambodia. For instance, it did not deter Hanoi from announcing the signing of the Treaty of Amity and Cooperation with the Heng Samrin government. The PRC never attempted to teach Vietnam a second lesson. Nevertheless, the attack served to remind Hanoi of a constant Chinese threat and questioned the reliability of the Soviet Union as a military ally. Afterwards, the PRC imposed military pressure on Vietnam through a large deployment of forces on their joint frontier. This led to a series of border clashes.

In addition to its direct military activities, the PRC actively supported the Khmer Rouge resistance, which had established sanctuaries along the Thai-Cambodian border. By June 1980, the Khmer Rouge disposed of over 40,000 to 50,000 soldiers.[23] Receiving Chinese assistance through Thailand, the Khmer Rouge fought a guerrilla warfare that prevented the Heng Samrin government from fully controlling its territory. Moreover, it obliged Vietnam to commit numerous troops in Cambodia and to hold yearly offensive operations along the eastern border of Thailand. These attacks against the sanctuaries of the Khmer resistance led to military incursions into Thai territory. While less influential in military terms, other opposition groups also developed. The Khmer People's National Liberation Front (KPNLF) was established in October 1979 under the leadership of former Premier Son Sann. A royalist resistance faction, led by King Norodom Sihanouk, was organized into the National United Front for an Independent, Neutral, Peaceful and Cooperative Cambodia (FUNCINPEC). Some limited military assistance was provided by Thailand and Singapore to the so-called non-communist Khmer resistance. In short, Vietnam was confronted with fierce Cambodian nationalism that challenged the legitimacy of the puppet regime in Phnom Penh.

The diplomatic response to the events in Indochina was primarily coordinated by ASEAN and is examined in the next section. It suffices to say now that the member states maintained a common standpoint in relation to the Cambodian question by taking a legalistic position vis-à-vis a case of aggression. Economic isolation was implemented by the United States and Japan, which imposed economic sanctions on Vietnam. Moreover, Washington ended negotiations with Hanoi regarding the establishment of bilateral relations and increased its economic and military aid to the ASEAN states, particularly Thailand.[24]

The Third Indochina Conflict quickly reached a military deadlock. On the one hand, the Chinese intervention of early 1979 and the military assistance provided to the Khmer Rouge did not affect Hanoi's willingness to preserve its Indochinese federation. On the other, it was obvious by the mid-1980s that Vietnam could not expect a complete victory on the battlefield. For instance, despite a successful dry season offensive in 1984–85 that removed the resistance groups from their border sanctuaries, Huxley writes that 'by the time of the 1985–86 dry season the resistance had established new, smaller bases, had trained several thousand more guerrillas and had begun to take their military and political struggle deeper into Cambodia.'[25] In spite of the international significance of the conflict, its military dimension remained confined to a domestic level. With a low level of military intensity, the war could be expected to last in the long term. The unlikelihood of a military victory transformed diplomacy into an important strategic instrument. The outcome of the conflict was dependent on the political interpretation of its nature. Eager to ensure the legitimacy of the PRK, Hanoi described it as a civil war between Cambodian factions. In contrast, ASEAN argued that the Cambodian question was an international conflict that had resulted from Vietnam's illegal invasion and occupation of the country.[26] It refused, therefore, to recognize the pro-Vietnamese government in Phnom Penh. The search for a diplomatic solution was severely affected by Sino-Vietnamese rivalry as Beijing and Hanoi each wished for a distribution of power in Indochina that would benefit their own strategic interests. Vietnam excluded even a partial return to power of the Khmer Rouge while the PRC rejected any initiative that questioned the legitimacy of the overthrown DK government.

The resolution of the Third Indochina Conflict resulted from transformations at the international level rather than from ASEAN's diplomatic proposals or events on the battlefield.[27] The coming to power of Mikhael Gorbachev, as general secretary of the Communist Party in March 1985, led to Soviet attempts to reach détente with the United States and China. Gorbachev's desire to improve relations with the PRC was indicated in a speech in Vladivostok on 28 July 1986. Negotiations on the normalization of relations were initiated in August 1988. The restoration of diplomatic ties with Beijing was dependent, among other issues, on the cessation of Soviet support for Vietnam's occupation of Cambodia. When that occurred, the Sino-Soviet rapprochement terminated the Cold War dimension of the conflict. Sino-Soviet relations were normalized during Gorbachev's official visit to China in May 1989. No longer able to rely on external assistance and in urgent need for domestic economic reforms, Vietnam withdrew its troops in September 1989. Its decision made a Sino-Vietnamese dialogue possible as well as negotiations for a peaceful solution in Cambodia. The settlement of the conflict was signed on 23 October 1991 at the International Conference on Cambodia held in Paris. The organization of the conference and the accord that was reached derived predominantly from the diplomatic efforts made by the permanent members of the United Nations Security Council.

ASEAN's reaction to the Cambodian conflict

The ASEAN member states were shocked by Vietnam's invasion of Cambodia, which broke the assurances given by Prime Minister Pham Van Dong in the fall of 1978, and by the assistance provided by the Soviet Union. The invasion terminated hopes of establishing stable relations with Hanoi and violated the cardinal rule of the international states system, namely respect for national sovereignty, which had been promulgated as the core principle of ASEAN in 1976. A failure to respond would have discredited ASEAN and created a dangerous precedent. Furthermore, Vietnam's policy in Cambodia brought to an end a distribution of power in

Indochina tolerable to the Association. It altered the strategic environment in mainland Southeast Asia by removing Thailand's traditional buffer state against Vietnam with hostile military forces deployed along its eastern border. Subsequently, collective solidarity had to be demonstrated towards a new front-line state.

ASEAN's response to the Third Indochina Conflict assumed two major forms, which were primarily determined by Bangkok. The members followed a common diplomatic position that transformed the Association into a well-respected regional organization. To review this side of its reaction, this section focuses on some achievements and also on failures that denoted ASEAN's limited influence as a diplomatic actor. Only a few specific events are therefore examined. Furthermore, the Association entered a tacit alliance with China to exert additional pressure on Vietnam. ASEAN's reply to the invasion of Cambodia is thus in part analysed as an example of the traditional practice of countervailing power. The Association also relied on the economic sanctions imposed on Vietnam by the United States, Japan and other dialogue partners. This aspect is not addressed in this section, which concludes by discussing how the associative and balance of power dimensions interacted in ASEAN's response to the Third Indochina Conflict. Both perspectives were indeed closely intermingled. Beyond their common position, the member states perceived the Cambodian question according to their respective threat perception. In that respect, it brought to surface differences in strategic outlooks and became a source of tension in intra-mural relations.

Associative dimension: a collective diplomatic response

Indonesia's Foreign Minister Professor Mochtar Kusumaatmadja, as chairman of ASEAN's Standing Committee, formulated the initial ASEAN reply to Vietnam's invasion of Cambodia on 9 January 1979.[28] Restrained in its wording, the statement did not mention Vietnam in order to preserve a possible form of dialogue with the country. A special meeting of the ASEAN foreign ministers was held in Bangkok on 12–13 January 1979 and led to a stronger position that condemned the invasion. The joint statement of 12 January declared: 'The ASEAN Foreign Ministers strongly deplored the armed intervention against the independence, sovereignty and territorial integrity of Kampuchea.' In addition, it asserted the right of the 'Kampuchean people to determine their future by themselves free from interference or influence from outside powers in the exercise of their rights of self-determination' and 'called for the immediate and total withdrawal of the foreign forces from Kampuchean territory'.[29] These points would represent the essence of ASEAN's common diplomatic position throughout the conflict.

ASEAN's standpoint was later repeated in the joint communiqué of the ASEAN Ministerial Meeting organized in Bali on 28–30 June 1979.[30] The significance of that session was raised by the attendance of US Secretary of State Cyrus Vance and ministers from other dialogue partners. The common stand indicated the cohesion of the Association and the recognition of its core principles. By registering a hardline position towards Vietnam, it also demonstrated collective solidarity vis-à-vis Thailand. The joint communiqué declared that the ASEAN foreign ministers agreed that:

> any further escalation of the fighting in Kampuchea or any incursion of any foreign forces into Thailand would directly affect the security of the ASEAN member states, and would endanger peace and security of the whole region. In this regard the ASEAN countries reiterated their firm support and solidarity with the government and people of Thailand, or any other ASEAN country in the preservation of its independence, national sovereignty and territorial integrity.[31]

ASEAN's diplomatic response to Vietnam's invasion of Cambodia was brought to the United Nations in 1979. Under UN auspices, the Association attained a position of leadership in its diplomatic struggle against a case of aggression. Its primary achievements involved the diplomatic isolation of Vietnam and its puppet regime in Phnom Penh, the tenure of the Cambodian seat in the United Nations General Assembly by the DK government and later by establishing a Coalition Government of Democratic Kampuchea (CGDK). In November 1979, ASEAN sponsored a resolution in the General Assembly that demanded a ceasefire in Cambodia, the withdrawal of all foreign troops and called for the right of self-determination for the Cambodian people. Adopted with a large majority, the resolution was a diplomatic defeat for Vietnam, which had expected its action to be rapidly accepted as a fait accompli. From that year onwards, ASEAN lobbied effectively at the UN to ensure the annual condemnation of Vietnam's occupation of Cambodia.

Beyond the violation of the Cambodian national sovereignty, ASEAN was confronted with another development that had first arisen with the communist victory in Indochina in 1975, namely the influx of refugees into different member states. The arrival of refugees severely increased after the invasion of Cambodia. The ASEAN foreign ministers declared on 13 January 1979 that the influx of refugees 'is encountering severe economic, social, political and security problems particularly in those countries bearing the main brunt of the influx, such as Thailand and Malaysia'.[32] The issue was discussed at the ASEAN Ministerial Meeting of June 1979 and included in the joint communiqué. Singapore's Foreign Minister S. Rajaratnam affirmed in his address that the refugee issue: 'is a military exercise to further the ambitions which the Vietnamese have concealed from us but not from their own people and their allies. Their ambition is hegemony in Southeast Asia.'[33] The flow of predominately ethnic Chinese refugees alarmed the ASEAN states. The Thai government feared that some might engage in subversive activities in Thailand. Singapore and Malaysia were concerned by the prospect of instability in their multiracial societies. A first United Nations Meeting on Refugees and Displaced Persons in Southeast Asia was organized in Geneva in July 1979.[34] The Association later succeeded in maintaining this dramatic problem on the international agenda.

The legitimacy and recognition of the DK government was achieved through an ASEAN-sponsored resolution in September 1979. It consolidated the notion that the Cambodian question was an international conflict that had been provoked by Vietnam's invasion of the country. Backing the overthrown DK government posed two serious complications for the ASEAN states however. It was close to impossible to secure long-term international support for a government that had implemented genocidal policies which had cost the lives of 1.7 million Cambodians. The United Kingdom and Australia were, for instance, no longer willing to support the legitimacy of the DK government. In addition, Vietnam radically opposed a return to power of the Khmer Rouge. As a result, ASEAN sought to integrate the DK government in an alternative grouping that would unite the three Khmer resistance factions in a coalition arrangement. After long and tedious negotiations, the leaders of the three factions, Sihanouk, Son Sann and Khieu Samphan, who had replaced Pol Pot as the formal leader of the Khmer Rouge, agreed to meet in Singapore in September 1981.

The CGDK was eventually established in Kuala Lumpur in June 1982 and represented an important diplomatic achievement for the Association.[35] It ensured the tenure of the Cambodian seat and prevented the PRK from gaining international recognition. Buszynski explains that the CGDK 'made it more difficult for the Phnom Penh government to appear as anything more than a foreign-controlled regime whose legitimacy was questionable'.[36] In addition, the coalition government eased the provision of international assistance to the Khmer resistance and offered the possibility of an alternative to a Vietnamese-installed government and the Chinese-supported Khmer Rouge. Finally, the CGDK was presided over by King Sihanouk who was recognized by both the Cambodian people and the international community. Nevertheless, the coalition government was weakened by persistent mistrust and rivalry among the factions, which maintained separate military forces. The Khmer Rouge conserved its leading role and dominant military position. Moreover, the creation of a coalition arrangement did not change Vietnam's standpoint as it continued to declare the situation in Indochina as irreversible.

Prior to the formation of the CGDK, ASEAN succeeded in organizing an International Conference on Kampuchea (ICK) in New York in July 1981 under the auspices of the Secretary-General of the United Nations. Vietnam and the Soviet Union declined to participate which ended hopes of any progress. Hanoi rejected any diplomatic solution that would question the recognition of the Heng Samrin government and limited the conflict to a border problem between Thailand and Cambodia. The Vietnamese position had formerly been reiterated at a conference held in Vientiane in July 1980, which gathered the foreign ministers of Laos, Vietnam and Cambodia. The communiqué had proposed the signing of non-aggression treaties with the ASEAN states, the creation of a demilitarized zone on the Thai-Cambodian border and mutual cooperation to solve the refugee problem.[37] Hence, it suggested a de facto recognition of the PRK.

Yet, the ICK also indicated the existence of opposing views between the Association and the PRC on an eventual peace settlement in Cambodia. ASEAN set forward a diplomatic initiative during the conference, which proposed the withdrawal of foreign troops from Cambodia under UN supervision, the disarming of the different Cambodian factions and the organization of free elections. The member states were keen to avoid a political outcome that would replace a Vietnamese puppet regime by a Chinese dominance of Cambodia. Their attempt to offer a diplomatic solution to the Cambodian issue was rejected by the PRC and the United States. Stressing the legitimacy of the Khmer Rouge, China argued that only the military troops of the PRK should be forced to disarm. Justus van der Kroef writes: 'The Chinese strongly objected on the grounds that these proposals infringed the DK's exclusive sovereign rights as Cambodia's only legitimate government. The United States accepted these Chinese objections, despite evident ASEAN displeasure.'[38] The American position resulted from a need to consolidate ties with Beijing after the opening of relations in January 1979.[39] The Chinese intransigence concerned the ASEAN states, primarily Indonesia and Malaysia. The final declaration of the ICK accommodated the PRC by making no reference to the disarmament of the Khmer Rouge and it failed to have a diplomatic impact on the conflict.[40]

In sum, an associative position was adopted by the ASEAN states during the Third Indochina Conflict that reflected the norms and principles promoted by the Association since 1967. The member states maintained a common stand based on the principles of national sovereignty and non-intervention in the affairs of other states. They demanded the withdrawal of all foreign troops from Cambodia and called for the right of self-determination for the Cambodian people.[41] It should be noted that a similar position was not adopted in response to Indonesia's invasion of East Timor or to China's punitive offensive of early 1979. The member states made considerable efforts and used any diplomatic means available to challenge the occupation of Cambodia. They were successful in isolating Vietnam diplomatically and preventing the Heng Samrin government from gaining international recognition. Through its collective diplomatic activities in the UN, ASEAN indicated its cohesion and enhanced its international standing and credibility as a diplomatic arrangement. In spite of different threat perceptions, the members also closed ranks with Thailand. The degree of solidarity manifested during the Third Indochina Conflict was surprising in light of the cooperative fragility that had defined ASEAN since its creation.

Nonetheless, the common diplomatic response to the Cambodian issue was undermined by significant limitations. Devoid of military capabilities, ASEAN's actions on their own failed to influence events on the battlefield or to affect Vietnam's commitment in Cambodia. By refusing to negotiate with the Association other than on its own terms, Hanoi thwarted ASEAN's collective diplomatic undertakings. These undertakings only evolved into political tactics set forward by ASEAN with little bearing on the final resolution of the conflict. Moreover, Vietnam demonstrated ASEAN's inability to manage the regional order and to influence extra-mural events. China's intransigence also restricted attempts to find a political solution to the conflict. As a result, collective efforts rapidly reached a deadlock. ASEAN's weakness as a diplomatic actor was displayed in the international settlement of the conflict that followed the normalization of Sino-Soviet relations and in which it played only a secondary role. Though Indonesia's foreign minister co-chaired the Paris conference, the Association was not involved in the final diplomatic stages that led to the resolution of the war. Hence, the Third Indochina Conflict revealed the limits of diplomacy without supporting sanctions, which ASEAN lacked. As will be discussed in Chapter 6, this limitation has also restricted ASEAN's involvement in the South China Sea dispute.

Balance of power dimension: ASEAN's tacit alliance with China

Having so far examined the associative dimension, let us now focus on the politics of the balance of power in ASEAN's response to the occupation of Cambodia. Its reaction is analysed in light of its strategic collaboration with outside powers. Despite its objective of national and regional resilience, the Association cooperated with the PRC to exert countervailing pressure on Vietnam and to supplement a necessary military dimension to its collective diplomatic efforts. In that respect, it followed conventional balance of power tactics to counterbalance a Vietnamese hegemony in Indochina. This policy of tacit alliance was imposed by Thailand on its ASEAN partners. It resulted from Sino-Thai relations and not from a common institutional position. While supported by Singapore, the tacit alliance was generally tolerated by Indonesia and Malaysia in the name of ASEAN solidarity. It would still concern and frustrate Jakarta and Kuala Lumpur and affect the cohesion of the Association. A large part of the following discussion deals with the intra-mural consequences of the conventional power balancing policies.

Faced with a direct threat to its security, Thailand could not ensure its defence by relying on a cooperative security regime that lacked joint military capabilities and on a common threat perception among its participants to evolve into a tacit or formal alliance. The members that primarily associated sources of regional instability with internal threats opposed such a shift, despite the invasion of Cambodia. Moreover, the ASEAN states did not dispose of the necessary means to influence the military dimension of the conflict. Singapore's Prime Minister Lee Kuan Yew declared that 'there is no combination of forces in Southeast Asia that can stop the Vietnamese on the mainland of Asia.'[42] There was also a strong desire not to provoke Vietnam or further deepen its reliance on the Soviet Union. Besides, a move towards alliance formation would have been viewed by Indonesia as violating its active and independent foreign policy. Thailand was thus unable to rely on the weak ASEAN states to oppose militarily the occupation of Cambodia, deter incursions on its border or defend its territory in the rather unlikely event of an open Vietnamese offensive. Instead, it sought assistance from the PRC and to a lesser extent from the United States. In short, though regarded as a significant diplomatic instrument, the Association would only receive a secondary position in Thailand's strategic planning during the Third Indochina Conflict.[43]

In contrast to cooperative security, Thailand had traditionally entered power-balancing arrangements to react to changes in the regional distribution of power. A tacit alliance with China, the historic enemy of Vietnam, was concluded in January 1979 in response to the events in Cambodia.[44] Though no formal treaty was signed, the PRC gave assurances to Thailand that it would intervene in the case of Vietnamese aggression. Copper explains that 'China cemented a kind of informal military alliance with Thailand shortly after Vietnam's invasion of Kampuchea and China's invasion of Vietnam, promising to once again invade Vietnam if Vietnamese troops enter Thailand.'[45] Besides acting as a deterrent, the PRC contributed to Thailand's defence capabilities through the transfer of military equipment. Bangkok was also reliant on increased financial and military aid from the United States. During a visit to Washington in February 1979, Thailand's Prime Minister Kriangsak Chomanan received confirmation from President Carter that the United States would honour its security commitments under the Manila Pact of September 1954. The United States also accelerated the supply of arms to the Thai military.[46] Yet, it was unwilling to play a direct military role in the Cambodian issue mainly due to its bitter experience in the Second Indochina Conflict.

In addition to its defensive character, the special relationship with the PRC aimed to end Vietnam's control over Cambodia. Thailand allowed the passage through its territory of Chinese military supplies for the Khmer Rouge resistance operating in Cambodia and the border area. The use of Thai facilities was thus indispensable to sustain the guerrilla warfare. In return, Thailand was strongly criticized by Hanoi and faced a flow of refugees and repeated incursions into its territory. China's punitive offensive in early 1979 also indicated its disposition to act as a direct source of countervailing power against Vietnam. Yet, the attack failed to reduce the number of Vietnamese soldiers in Cambodia. It therefore demonstrated the limits of China's capacity to intimidate its neighbour and defend the security of Thailand. Nevertheless, the PRC maintained a large military presence on its south-eastern border to exercise pressure on Hanoi. The fear of a second attack forced Vietnam to deploy numerous troops along its frontier, which was expected in Beijing to divert its military commitment in Cambodia. In sum, the conventional operation of the balance of power factor was dependent on China's commitment to a war of attrition against Vietnam.

The tacit alliance was a function of a common opposition to Vietnam's occupation of Cambodia. It served the Chinese and Thai narrowly defined interests. It enabled Beijing to enhance its Southeast Asian influence after the downfall of the Khmer Rouge and to offset the rising Soviet power in the region. In the absence of Thai collaboration, China would have been unable to assist the Khmer resistance. The tacit alliance promoted Thai security interests by challenging the PRK and led China to end its support for the Communist Party of Thailand (CPT). This greatly reduced the activities of the subversive movement. Moreover, Beijing gradually decreased its aid to communist insurgencies operating in other ASEAN states. Yet, the partnership was also affected by several constraints.[47] Thailand and the PRC disagreed on an eventual political settlement of the conflict. Though aiding its military efforts, Thailand opposed a return to power of the Khmer Rouge, which would replace a Vietnamese with a Chinese domination of Cambodia. Additionally, Bangkok was fearful of China's hegemonic ambiions in Southeast Asia and concerned about its remaining subversive influence in Thailand. Finally, China's influence as a deterrent against Vietnam was restricted, particularly with reference to Vietnam's military activities on the Thai-Cambodian frontier.

Thailand succeeded in imposing on its partners its tacit alliance with China and thus to integrate a power balancing dimension into ASEAN's reaction to the Cambodian crisis. Under the Thai guidance, the Association took sides with the PRC in its struggle against Vietnam and was integrated within a larger international effort to oppose Vietnamese and Soviet policies in Indochina. Concerned about China's intentions in mainland Southeast Asia, Bangkok was eager though to preserve the unity of the Association and its operation as a credible diplomatic arrangement. Forming the link between the PRC and ASEAN, Thailand wished to rely both on military and diplomatic pressure to oppose Vietnam's occupation of Cambodia. General Prem Tinsulanond, Thailand's prime minister from 1980 to 1988, and Siddhi Savetsila, who served as foreign minister until 1990, played an important role in challenging Vietnam and preserving the cohesion of the Association. Siddhi, in particular, was gifted at keeping options open and managing bilateral relations with China and Indonesia.[48] Hence, he took a decisive part in successfully combining the two major forms that characterized Thailand's reaction to the Third Indochina Conflict.[49]

Still, ASEAN's diplomatic efforts were reliant on traditional balance of power tactics. Doubtlessly, the tacit alliance was a prerequisite for Bangkok's stand against the occupation of Cambodia. Leifer writes: 'had China not made absolutely clear its unrelenting opposition to Vietnam's policy in

Kampuchea, then Thailand would have almost certainly been obliged to accommodate itself to the political *fait accompli.*'[50] This suggests that the diplomatic response of the Association was conditional on China's willingness to exert countervailing power on Vietnam. The associative dimension was dependent in particular on the Chinese support to the Khmer Rouge resistance. Without ongoing guerrilla warfare against the PRK, Vietnam would have won the conflict despite ASEAN's diplomatic efforts in the UN.[51] This argument is developed in the final part of this section when the interaction between the associative and balance of power dimensions is examined.

Besides ASEAN's balance of power strategy with China, the member countries upgraded and modernized their military capabilities in response to the changing strategic environment in Indochina and as a deterrent to Vietnam. Moreover, a web of bilateral collaborations over defence issues was undertaken to strengthen intra-mural security cooperation. Although not formally part of ASEAN, such defence ties included the exchange of information, cross-border agreements, training exercises and naval operations. The member states viewed this limited form of bilateral military cooperation as contributing to the development of confidence, stability and regional resilience. One can question, however, whether the upgrading of national defence forces and the formation of extra-ASEAN defence cooperation ever deterred Vietnam's military actions. In short, the strategic impact that these unilateral military capabilities and bilateral defence ties had on Vietnam during its occupation of Cambodia should be dismissed when compared to the importance of China's countervailing power and the Khmer Rouge resistance.

ASEAN's tacit alliance with the PRC evolved into a source of division in intra-mural relations. The response of the different member states to a balance of power strategy with China was subject to their respective threat perception. Contradictory positions on the tacit alliance soon appeared within ASEAN owing to contesting views on regional order and the balance of power. Singapore advocated a confrontational stance against Vietnam and accepted Thailand's reliance on China to oppose the PRK. Due to its own strategic situation, the city-state could not tolerate Vietnam's act of hegemony towards its smaller neighbour. In addition, it was fearful of a growing Soviet naval influence in the region enhanced from March 1979 by a deployment of its aircrafts and naval vessels at Cam Ranh Bay. Though fully aware of China's potential menace, Singapore regarded the special relationship with the PRC as necessary to limit Vietnam's control of Indochina backed by Moscow. Moreover, the city-state supported China's punitive offensive across Vietnam's northern border. Lee Kuan Yew would later write in his memoirs that 'Deng Xiaoping deterred any assault against Thailand by attacking Vietnam in February 1979.'[52] In short, Singapore perceived the Soviet Union and its alliance with Vietnam as posing the most immediate threat to regional security. The Philippines, least affected by the Cambodian crisis, supported Thailand's position.

Indonesia and Malaysia favoured a more accommodating line towards Vietnam that would take into account its regional security interests as well as its difficult relations with China. They also opposed the international isolation of Vietnam as it was expected to increase its reliance on the Soviet Union. Taking a more insular approach to security, the military leadership in Jakarta did not feel threatened by the events in Indochina. Indonesia, and to a lesser extent Malaysia, perceived the PRC as their primary source of external threat and judged the Soviet rising presence in the region as less menacing. Both members were troubled by China's military intervention against Vietnam in early 1979.[53] The ASEAN foreign ministers had responded to the Chinese attack by calling 'for the withdrawal of all foreign troops from the areas of conflict in Indochina to avoid the deterioration of peace and stability in Southeast Asia'.[54] Finally, Indonesia and Malaysia comprehended that the long-term weakening of Vietnam would enable the PRC to consolidate its Southeast Asian influence. Indonesia regarded Vietnam as necessary to constrain China. It thus opposed the tacit alliance with Beijing as a result of its own view of the balance of power. Yet, keen to preserve the cohesion of the Association, Indonesia and Malaysia were left with no choice but to accept the tacit alliance with China. Though expressing their concern, they recognized that breaking ranks with Thailand would only increase its dependence on the PRC. Bangkok itself repeated this point frequently.[55]

Indonesia's policy on the Cambodian question was rather ambivalent due to the different positions adopted by the ministry of foreign affairs and the Armed Forces of the Republic of Indonesia (ABRI).[56] Professor Mochtar Kusumaatmadja, Indonesia's foreign minister from 1978 to 1988, was mostly inclined to adjust the official governmental line with ASEAN's stance against the invasion. He viewed Vietnam's undertaking primarily as an act of aggression and focused on the restoration of the Cambodian national sovereignty. The notion of ASEAN solidarity, supported by Suharto himself, was thus respected. In addition, foreign ministry officials realized that the PRC needed to be involved in a settlement of the war. Yet, they were 'also obliged to avoid the impression that by siding with ASEAN's stance, Indonesia indirectly supported China's position in the Cambodian conflict'.[57] This would have been unacceptable to the military. General Benny Murdani, commander of Indonesia's armed forces from 1983 to 1988 and later minister of defence until 1993, favoured a resolution of the conflict that would exclude China and reckon with Vietnam's security interests. The military elite argued that Vietnam was primarily acting in self-defence in response to a border conflict provoked by the Khmer Rouge and supported by Beijing. ABRI admired the Vietnamese armed forces and shared with them the experience of a military struggle for independence. Contrary to Thailand, which was said to follow a 'bamboo policy', Vietnam was perceived as a safeguard against Chinese expansionism in Southeast Asia. Bangkok was aware of Indonesia's ambivalent stand on the Cambodian crisis.

While in contradiction with its security perspective, the imposition of a tacit alliance with China also violated Indonesia's preference for an autonomous management of the regional order. The integration of Vietnam within a regional order was regarded as indispensable to achieve long-term autonomy in Southeast Asia. Through its strategic relations with the PRC and the United States, ASEAN opposed the Soviet Union and its regional ally. Indonesia was distressed by the fact that the situation in Cambodia had led to external interference in Southeast Asia, chiefly from China and the Soviet Union. The reliance on the PRC and a deeper involvement in Cold War antagonism delayed the implementation of the ZOPFAN principle and frustrated Indonesia's managerial disposition. Jakarta hoped that the Third Indochina Conflict would become the last manifestation of external military intervention in Southeast Asia.[58]

Finally, ASEAN's reaction to the Cambodian issue questioned Indonesia's position of natural leadership within the Association. As discussed later on, Indonesia and Malaysia set forward various diplomatic initiatives to find a regional solution to the conflict. Yet, Thailand dictated the ASEAN stand on Cambodia and used its right as a front-line state to reject or modify proposals. Thailand became the Association's political centre of gravity. Polomka points out when discussing Thailand's leading role in the formulation of collective policies that it 'had the consequence of shifting the centre of gravity of decision-making on ASEAN/Indochina relations away from Jakarta and Kuala Lumpur, where it resided in the early post-1975 period, towards Bangkok and Singapore'.[59] The demand for cohesion and uniformity prevented Indonesia from formulating an independent foreign policy towards Vietnam and to influence the regional order. In short, Indonesia was confined by a common diplomatic position that aimed to oppose Vietnam's policy in Cambodia.[60] The Thai guidance and its restraining impact on Jakarta were negatively perceived by Indonesian public opinion.

Differences over the tacit alliance with China were best demonstrated in March 1980 when talks between President Suharto and Malaysian Prime Minister Tun Hussein Onn led to the formulation of the Kuantan principle. Despite the common position adopted by the Association, two member states bilaterally expressed contrasting views on Cambodia. The preference for regional autonomy and the integration of Vietnam into a Southeast Asian pattern of power were at the core of the statement. Weatherbee argues that 'the Kuantan principle was a reiteration of the 1971 ZOPFAN declaration but with direct applicability to the Kampuchean crisis.'[61] Both leaders agreed that a political settlement of the conflict required a broader Vietnamese autonomy from the Soviet Union and China and the recognition of its security interests in Indochina. They suggested the legitimacy of some Vietnamese control in Cambodia in exchange for greater independence from the Soviet Union, which would reduce the Sino-Vietnamese struggle in the region.[62] In short, the Kuantan principle rejected ASEAN's tacit alliance with the PRC. It acknowledged Vietnam's hegemonic disposition in Indochina and implied that external intervention was the primary threat to regional stability.

Vigorously opposed by Thailand and Singapore, the Kuantan principle caused tension in intra-mural relations. Indonesia and Malaysia, which were unwilling to break ranks with their partners, quickly dropped a proposal that might have led to the fragmentation of the Association. Solidarity towards Thailand was thus maintained. Both would also restrain in the future their official opposition to the special relationship with the PRC. The Kuantan principle remained relevant, however, as it had shown a division within ASEAN. Two influential members had demonstrated their concern for a collective policy that contradicted associative principles and opposed their desire for regional autonomy. Interestingly, the Kuantan principle was also received negatively in Hanoi, which rejected the implication that Vietnam was dependent on external powers.[63] Instead of taking advantage of intra-mural frictions, Vietnam made a brief military incursion into Thailand on 23 June 1980 as a response to a Thai repatriation programme of Cambodian refugees. Issued on 25 June, an ASEAN statement affirmed that Vietnam's action 'constitutes a grave and direct threat to the security of Thailand and the South East Asian region'.[64] Vietnam's incursion into Thailand served to reinforce the hardline position on Vietnam's occupation of Cambodia during the ASEAN Ministerial Meeting held in Kuala Lumpur on 25–26 June 1980.

Despite the rapid withdrawal of the Kuantan principle, Indonesian and Malaysian concerns regarding the tacit alliance with China were strengthened. Jakarta criticized Thailand's flexible foreign policy and argued that the resolution of the conflict could only result from a negotiated settlement with Vietnam. Indonesia took a more active part in the Cambodian question partly due to its frustration over the ASEAN position. It was eager to reach a settlement that would serve its own regional design and indicate its position of regional leadership. A core motivation of the initiatives proposed by Indonesia but also Malaysia was to reduce Thailand's dependence on China and to keep out external players from a regional solution to the conflict. Hence, these undertakings were a response to the Chinese strategy of attrition against Vietnam. They provoked additional discord within the Association.

At the Seventh Non-Aligned Conference in New Delhi in March 1983, Malaysia's Foreign Minister Tan Sri Mohamad Ghazali Shafie suggested a 'five-plus-two formula' that would bring together Laos, Vietnam and the ASEAN states in a series of talks without the Khmer factions. While accepted by Hanoi, the proposal was denied, primarily due to Chinese pressure, during a special meeting of the ASEAN foreign ministers in Bangkok. Weatherbee points out that it was 'the failure to follow up on this possible breakthrough that is at least part of the inspiration for what became Indonesia's dual track diplomacy towards Vietnam in 1984'.[65] Indonesia's dual policy aimed at maintaining ASEAN's cohesion while establishing closer relations with Vietnam. In response, the other members provided Indonesia with the role of 'interlocutor' with Vietnam, though on an ad hoc basis, so encouraging its ambition to reach a regional solution within an ASEAN framework.[66] Vietnam's Foreign Minister Nguyen Co Thach visited Jakarta in March 1984 and held talks with Suharto. No progress was made towards a diplomatic settlement. General Murdani had previously declared during an official trip to Hanoi in February 1984 that Indonesia did not perceive Vietnam as a threat to Southeast Asia. This comment had strained intra-mural relations. As a consequence of Indonesia's dual track diplomacy, the Association needed to indicate its unity on the Cambodian question and its solidarity vis-à-vis Thailand. A special meeting of the ASEAN foreign ministers was organized in Jakarta in May 1984.[67] In July, the foreign ministers also 'reiterated ASEAN's firm support and solidarity with the government and people of Thailand in the preservation of Thai independence, sovereignty and territorial integrity'.[68]

Indonesia and Malaysia did not lessen their efforts to find a regional resolution of the conflict that would exclude a direct Chinese involvement in the settlement. While chairman of ASEAN's Standing Committee, Tengku Ahmad Rithauden, Malaysia's new foreign minister since the retirement of Ghazali Shafie in July 1984, suggested in 1985 the notion of 'proximity talks' between the CGDK and the Heng Samrin government. Under Thai and Chinese pressure, the initiative was later modified to consist of negotiations between the coalition arrangement and Vietnam, which then refused to participate. The outcome of the Malaysian proposal once more manifested the influence of Bangkok and Beijing on ASEAN's negotiating position. Furthermore, during an official visit to Hanoi in July 1987, Professor Mochtar and Nguyen Co Thach agreed on the organization of informal discussions, the so-called 'cocktail party', which would first include the different Khmer factions before introducing other regional actors. Reviewed during a special meeting in August, the proposal was renounced by Singapore and Thailand, which feared a de facto recognition of the PRK.

The two-stage proposal was eventually applied in both the first and second Jakarta Informal Meetings (JIMs) held in July 1988 and February 1989.[69] Organized by Ali Alatas, who had been appointed Indonesia's foreign minister in March 1988, the meetings failed to reach a regional solution to the conflict. Yet, they enabled Indonesia to open negotiations with Phnom Penh and Hanoi and to co-chair the International Conference on Cambodia of October 1991. The JIMs also confirmed that the military leadership in Jakarta rejected the Chinese policy of attrition against Vietnam imposed on the Association.[70] By acting as a mediator, Indonesia gained credibility as a responsible and peaceful regional player and indicated its position of leadership within ASEAN.[71] These diplomatic efforts should therefore be regarded as an Indonesian attempt to enhance its managerial position in Southeast Asia. Similar calculations partly motivated Indonesia to launch in 1990 the extra-ASEAN Workshops on the South China Sea. Significantly, Thailand's stand on the Cambodian issue was by the late 1980s dramatically modified by the new prime ministership of General Chatichai Choonhavan (1988–91). Without informing his regional partners, Chatichai called for the need 'to turn Indochina from a battlefield into a market place'. He invited Hun Sen, the prime minister of the PRK, to visit Bangkok in January 1989. This political shift, that again revealed the flexibility of the Thai foreign policy, developed from rapid transformations at the international level and the beginning of Vietnam's withdrawal from Cambodia. Having displayed their solidarity towards Thailand and its hardline position for a decade, most ASEAN states reacted negatively to the sudden change in policy.

Balance of power meets associative perspective

The invasion of Cambodia violated ASEAN's central principle and affected the Southeast Asian distribution of power. Both aspects were included in the ASEAN response, which consisted of collective diplomatic efforts to condemn an act of aggression and a tacit alliance with an external source of countervailing power to challenge a Vietnamese hegemony in Indochina. Bridging ASEAN to the PRC, Thailand relied on both dimensions to oppose the occupation of Cambodia. Let us now discuss how balance of power tactics interacted with the associative perspective.

In order to do so, one needs to define our interpretation of the balance of power in the case of ASEAN's response to the Third Indochina Conflict. In accordance with the prior observations of the balance of power factor – namely the formation and early years of the Association and its expansion of membership in the case of Brunei – the member states indicated a disposition to promote countervailing arrangements, in this case beyond cooperative security. In contrast to the previous illustrations where the power balancing occurred generally through political means, the ASEAN states relied on conventional measures to affect the distribution of power and deny hegemony in Indochina. By entering a tacit alliance with the PRC, even if through diplomatic alignment, the members engaged in traditional balance of power practice. This distinction derives from the fact that the Association was faced with an external military threat rather than an intra-mural hegemonic disposition. Except for some military supplies provided by Thailand and Singapore to the non-communist Cambodian factions, ASEAN's participation in the tacit alliance remained devoid of a direct military content. In fact, the need for an external source of countervailing power partly resulted from ASEAN's inability to evolve into a tacit or formal alliance. The conventional operation of the balance of power was a function of China's commitment to a strategy of attrition against Vietnam. This policy of attrition consisted of a guerrilla warfare in Cambodia and military pressure on Vietnam's northern border. In short, the distribution of power in mainland Southeast Asia would have drastically changed if the PRC had decided during the course of the conflict to end its military support to the Khmer Rouge resistance.[72]

When reviewing the part played by a conventional practice of the balance of power, it is important to analyse its influence not only on ASEAN's diplomatic response to the Cambodian crisis but also its repercussions on intra-mural relations. Let us begin with the former. The Association gained from a favourable strategic context, as it became part of an international response that aimed to undermine Vietnam's policy in Indochina. The associative dimension was conditional, in its early formulation and later development, on the operation of conventional power balancing policies. In the absence of an external source of countervailing power, Thailand would have been obliged to accept the new distribution of power in Indochina and may have been subject to more Vietnamese military pressure and intimidation.[73] ASEAN's initial reaction was therefore made possible by China's strong resistance to a Vietnamese occupied Cambodia. Its diplomatic success in isolating Vietnam internationally was also reliant on its tacit alliance with the PRC. Its limited diplomatic voice was strengthened by China's military role in the conflict. ASEAN's diplomatic significance therefore resulted from specific circumstances, namely the availability of external support and in particular its tacit alliance with China. In sum, the relevance of an associative dimension beyond cooperative security is dependent on access to an external source of countervailing power. This argument is further developed in Chapter 6 when ASEAN's reaction to the Third Indochina Conflict is contrasted with its post-Cold War involvement in the South China Sea dispute.

Nevertheless, the practice of balance of power politics also influenced negatively ASEAN's diplomatic response. While the collective activities were contingent on China's interest in the conflict, the tacit alliance restricted the diplomatic freedom of the member states in their attempt to find a political settlement. Alagappa explains that 'Beijing's own objectives of punishing Vietnam and containing the Soviet threat overrode ASEAN's concerns and its peace proposals on several occasions.'[74] This was illustrated, for instance, by China's rejection of an initiative introduced during the 1981 ICK that questioned the sole legitimacy of the DK government. Although reliant on guerrilla warfare, ASEAN's diplomacy was weakened by the Khmer Rouge as Vietnam rejected any political solution that would include its participation.[75] Thailand gave primary importance to its special relationship with the PRC, which lessened the autonomy of ASEAN's diplomatic efforts. However, Beijing and Bangkok disagreed on the role to be played by the Khmer Rouge in a final resolution of the war.[76] As the weaker part of the tacit alliance, the Association could not influence China's regional policies and was concerned about its aspirations in Southeast Asia.

The engagement in conventional balance of power practice became a factor in intra-mural cooperation. The Cambodian crisis in general and the tacit alliance with China in particular brought to the surface original differences and caused discord among the participants.[77] At issue were contesting views on regional order and the balance of power. Thailand and Singapore viewed China as necessary to balance Vietnam while Indonesia and to a lesser extent Malaysia considered Vietnam as a safeguard to balance China. The tacit alliance with the PRC was a source of great concern for Indonesia and Malaysia as it challenged their security interests and reinforced their perception of a Chinese threat in Southeast Asia. Indonesia, in particular, was frustrated by Thailand's reliance on an external source of countervailing power. The tacit alliance was resented by Indonesia because it questioned its position of natural leadership within the Association and violated its preference for an autonomous distribution of power placed under its guidance. As such, the special relationship with the PRC contradicted the call for regional autonomy registered in the Bangkok Declaration and the ZOPFAN principle.

Walt's research on alliance formation is applicable to an examination of ASEAN's tacit alliance with the PRC and its impact on intra-mural relations.[78] Thailand's partnership with China and the negative response that it provoked among some ASEAN members strengthen the notion that states aim to balance threats rather than aggregate power. In terms only of capabilities, China was a more significant danger to the Southeast Asian security environment than Vietnam but was still perceived in Thailand as less menacing to its national security. This resulted from Vietnam's aggressive policy in Cambodia. These views were not shared by Indonesia and Malaysia. Hence, disagreements over the tacit alliance with the PRC indicated the importance of contradictory threat perceptions within ASEAN.

In light of the level of division, one may wonder how ASEAN preserved its unity and succeeded in operating as an effective associative arrangement until the end of the conflict. Indeed, Indonesia and Malaysia manifested their continuing solidarity towards Thailand and never broke ranks with their partners. The general cohesion of the Association can be explained by several factors. The member states shared an interest in responding to the violation of Cambodia's national sovereignty.[79] Respect for this core principle was a uniting element that defined ASEAN's collective position. In spite of the differences, all the members wanted a political settlement that would ensure Vietnam's withdrawal from Cambodia. This concealed to a certain extent the divergence in strategic outlooks. Moreover, Vietnam's inflexible position on the Cambodian crisis helped to preserve the unity of the Association by frustrating the efforts of those who favoured a regional solution. Hanoi's negative response to the Kuantan principle needs to be noted for instance. Vietnam might have succeeded in exacerbating intra-mural tensions by adopting a more conciliatory attitude towards Indonesia and Malaysia.

Furthermore, Indonesia had since 1967 benefited from the Association, which had become the central pillar of its foreign policy. Its dissatisfaction was also in part accommodated by the integration of its dual-track diplomacy within an ASEAN framework and by its role of co-chair at the 1991 International Conference on Cambodia. In addition, Thailand was aware of the frustration of some of the member states and made efforts to preserve the unity of the Association. ASEAN had by the 1980s gained a life of its own and its dissolution over Cambodia never seemed conceivable. As discussed in Chapter 3, the risks of fragmentation had been much higher during the early years of the Association. In short, associative benefits and a common willingness to ensure the lasting viability of the cooperative security regime received precedence over individual power balancing considerations. Intra-mural disparities were constrained by judgements about long-term interests. Indonesia and Malaysia were also influenced by the geo-strategic consequences of breaking ranks with Thailand. Such an action would have increased its dependence on Beijing and therefore enhanced China's influence in Southeast Asia.

5 The post-Cold War regional security context

The role of the balance of power factor within the ARF

Introduction

The role of the balance of power factor within regimes for cooperative security is analysed in this chapter by examining the formation and workings of the ARF. Its establishment and institutional evolution were discussed in Chapter 1 through an associative perspective. The object of this chapter is not to provide an adverse interpretation but rather to complement our previous analysis by illustrating one specific aspect of the creation and operation of the Forum, namely the possible influence of the balance of power factor on the calculations of some participants. This factor can influence the modalities of a cooperative security regime by aiming to contain a disposition to hegemony on the part of a rising power.

This chapter consists of three sections. The first describes the strategic environment that emerged in the Asia-Pacific at the end of the Cold War. The second section discusses the role of the balance of power factor in the formation of the ARF noting, in particular, the chairman's statement of the ASEAN-PMC Senior Officials Meeting (SOM) in May 1993. Beyond the founding moments of the ARF, it is considered how the influence of this factor has carried over in the workings of the institution. It is argued that the ARF has failed as an instrument for constraining China in a way that corresponds to ASEAN's degree of success with Indonesia. Finally, attention is given to the existence of different perceptions within the framework of the ARF and specifically to China's preference for multipolarity in the Asia-Pacific that can be defined with particular reference to the United States.

Post-Cold War strategic architecture in the Asia-Pacific

The cessation of Soviet–US and Sino-Soviet rivalries contributed to a sense of relief and optimism and also to a feeling of strategic uncertainty in East Asia.[1] ASEAN's transformed security environment at the end of the Cold War derived from the resolution of the Third Indochina Conflict and in the broader regional context from a shifting distribution of power in East Asia.

The settlement of the Cambodian conflict followed the normalization of Sino-Soviet relations and resulted directly from the nature of the end of the Cold War.[2] ASEAN played only a secondary role in the final settlement of the conflict despite its high profile diplomatic activities during the war to oppose Vietnam's occupation of Cambodia.

The resolution of the Cambodian conflict was indicative of the rapid transformations occurring at the international level and of a shifting distribution of power in East Asia. The disintegration of the Soviet Union in December 1991 dramatically limited Russia's regional role and influence as Moscow was now primarily concerned with domestic changes.[3] The Soviet Union had already announced in October 1990 its decision to withdraw its troops from Cam Ranh Bay. The reduction in regional influence was less significant in the case of the United States, the sole global superpower, which had demonstrated its military capability in Operation Desert Storm in January 1991. The collapse of the Soviet Union and budgetary constraints obliged Washington to reconsider its military deployment in East Asia.[4] This led to a measured reduction of US forces in the region. In addition, the Philippine Senate denied a new base treaty with the United States in September 1991 leading to a complete withdrawal from Subic Bay Naval Base and Clark Air Base by November 1992. At issue were the terms of extending leases. By then, Clark Air Base needed to be closed down as its operational use had been undermined by the volcanic eruption of Mount Pinatubo in June 1991. In sum, the long-term US commitment to regional security seemed uncertain in the early 1990s.

Even so, the US strategic retrenchment from East Asia at the end of the Cold War should not be exaggerated. Washington reached an agreement with Singapore in November 1990 allowing the US Air Force and Navy to use the city-state's military facilities more extensively. The agreement that offered the United States compensating facilities in Singapore mitigated the strategic consequences of its departure from Subic Bay Naval Base and Clark Air Base. Initially critical of the memorandum, Malaysia and Indonesia were prepared after the US withdrawal from the Philippines to provide access to the US Navy so enhancing their military ties with Washington. A US Navy logistics facility was also transferred in 1992 from Subic Bay to Singapore. Later on, the United States redefined its alliance with Japan through the Joint Declaration of April 1996 and subsequent provision for new guidelines. Moreover, it demonstrated its security commitment to the region. For example, the 1996 Taiwan Straits crisis led the United States to deploy two carrier squadrons near Taiwan to deter further Chinese actions of intimidation.

At the end of the Cold War, the influence of Japan and China became more significant due to the collapse of the Soviet Union and the uncertain nature of US involvement in the region. As a result of the legacy of its experience in the Pacific War, Japan was reluctant to extend its security role in East Asia. Its military power, including its naval force, continued to be limited to self-defence purposes. In these circumstances, China became the prime beneficiary of the changing strategic context. Having reached a rapprochement with Moscow in the late 1980s, China no longer faced a threat on its Northern border and could now focus on other security interests, including its territorial claims in the South China Sea. Furthermore, since the 1980s, China had experienced a sustained economic development that had accelerated up to a point the modernization of its military capabilities.[5] Consequently, China's regional influence was viewed with apprehension at the end of the Cold War. Some Southeast Asian states, Singapore being the prime example, feared that a US military disengagement in East Asia might encourage China or even Japan to fill 'the power vacuum' left by retreating external powers.[6] Indonesia recognized China's rising influence and normalized relations with Beijing in August 1990.[7] In sum, the post-Cold War strategic architecture in the Asia-Pacific was primarily dependent on a triangular power relationship between the United States, Japan and China.

The emergence of an uncertain multipolar structure was regarded by the ASEAN states as a source of concern. In response to the changing security environment, most members wanted the United States to remain militarily engaged in the region to promote peace and stability and contain China's rising power. In the new strategic context, the problem of the overlapping claims in the South China Sea had become a major security issue and complicated relations between the PRC and some members of the Association. The US deployment in the region was regarded by most Southeast Asian states as a means to constrain China's hegemonic aspirations and prevent possible violations of the freedom of navigation, especially in the South China Sea. In addition, the US presence in East Asia obviated the need for an active and independent Japanese security role.

Role of the balance of power factor in the formation and workings of the ARF

The ARF is based partly on ASEAN's model of cooperative security, which focuses on confidence building, an informal process of dialogue and a mode of conflict avoidance. While the Forum was an attempt by the Association to expand to the wider region its approach to cooperative security, its establishment also involved power-balancing considerations. The ASEAN states feared that a reduced US regional deployment might give rise to regional instability and were concerned about China's growing influence. China's rising power was the most central issue facing the ASEAN members at the end of the Cold War.[8] Leifer writes:

> For ASEAN, a constructive regional order would ideally be based on the balancing military engagement of the United States. This would allow Japan to continue its limited security policy which in turn would be critical in encouraging China to conduct its regional relations according

to those norms that had served the general interests of the ASEAN states so well.[9]

The institutional steps that led to the formation of the ARF should first be identified. The members of the ASEAN Post-Ministerial Conference (PMC), that included the United States, needed in the post-Cold War to cope with the changing security environment in East Asia and particularly with the potential American strategic retreat from the region. The ASEAN-PMC had initially been developed after the second summit of the ASEAN heads of state and government held in Kuala Lumpur in August 1977, which had been followed by a series of bilateral meetings with the heads of government of Australia, Japan and New Zealand. Subsequently, the ASEAN-PMC took place after the annual ASEAN Ministerial Meeting (AMM). By the early 1990s, the ASEAN-PMC consisted of serial discussions on economic matters with seven dialogue partners, namely Japan, South Korea, Australia, New Zealand, the United States, Canada and the European Union (EU). Although the PMC was primarily limited to economic issues until 1992, ASEAN had used the dialogue structure in the 1980s to address the Cambodian conflict and the Indochinese refugee problem. In short, the Association succeeded through the PMC in establishing formal and regular contacts with a number of key states and thus in enhancing its international diplomatic influence.

The idea of using the ASEAN-PMC as a forum for a regional security dialogue was first proposed in 1990 by the ASEAN Institutes of Strategic and International Studies (ASEAN-ISIS). The proposal was then discussed at the AMM organized in Kuala Lumpur in July 1991 where it was received differently by the various ASEAN foreign ministers. In his opening statement, Singapore's Foreign Minister Wong Kan Seng suggested that the ASEAN-PMC could evolve 'into a structure for political and security cooperation in the Asia-Pacific'.[10] Indonesia and Malaysia, however, were somewhat reluctant to widen the scope of the conference. Consequently, no consensus was reached in Kuala Lumpur on the need for a regional security dialogue.[11] The AMM Joint Communiqué only stated that the foreign ministers 'were of the view that ZOPFAN, the Treaty of Amity and Cooperation in South East Asia and the PMC (Post Ministerial Conferences) process are appropriate bases for addressing the regional peace and security issues in the nineties'.[12] At the ASEAN-PMC that followed, which was attended by China and Russia as observers, Japan's Foreign Minister Taro Nakayama suggested that the conference be used to address security issues. He declared: 'it would be meaningful and timely to use the ASEAN Post Ministerial Conference as a process of political discussions designed to improve the sense of security among us.'[13] In contrast to ASEAN's equivocal response, the United States openly opposed Nakayama's proposal. The United States was suspicious of a multilateral security dialogue that might undermine its bilateral arrangements with regional players.

The fourth summit of the ASEAN heads of state and government was held in Singapore in January 1992. It followed the US announcement in November 1991 of its forthcoming withdrawal from the Philippines and the collapse of the Soviet Union in December. The ASEAN leaders acknowledged the dramatic political and economic changes that had taken place since the end of the Cold War.[14] In contrast to the AMM of 1991, the member states agreed to address security matters through the ASEAN-PMC. The Singapore Declaration stated that 'ASEAN should intensify its external dialogues in political and security matters by using the ASEAN Post-Ministerial Conference (PMC)'.[15] It is interesting to distinguish ASEAN's decision to extend the scope of the PMC from the common position adopted by the members at their third summit in Manila in December 1987.[16] The Manila Declaration had simply affirmed that 'each member state shall be responsible for its own security' and that cooperation on security matters would continue to be conducted by the members on a non-ASEAN basis.[17] By 1992, the Association was forced to adjust to a changing strategic context and to acknowledge the limits of its sub-regional approach to security.

The next annual meeting of the ASEAN foreign ministers was held in Manila in July 1992 and was dominated by the problem of the overlapping claims in the South China Sea. On 25 February 1992, Beijing had passed the Law of the People's Republic of China on the Territorial Waters and Contiguous Areas that had reiterated China's claims in the South China Sea and stipulated the right to use force to protect islands, including the Spratlys, and their surrounding waters. ASEAN responded through formulating a Declaration on the South China Sea. At the ASEAN-PMC that followed the AMM, the first discussions on regional security were held, though on a serial rather than on a multilateral basis. During the ASEAN-US dialogue session, US Secretary of State James Baker referred to the American withdrawal from Clark and Subic Bay and reassured the member states by stating: 'this development has not altered our interest in, nor our commitment to, Asian security. The form of our presence may have changed, but the substance of our commitment is firm.'[18] The South China Sea question and the closure of the US bases in the Philippines by the end of 1992 further influenced the ASEAN states to establish a new multilateral security dialogue that would include non-PMC members.

A first ever ASEAN-PMC SOM was organized in Singapore in May 1993 and joined the permanent secretaries of the ASEAN countries and of the seven dialogue partners. One should note here the significance of Singapore as chair of ASEAN's Standing Committee during 1992–93. The city-state was keen to establish a multilateral structure of security dialogue in the Asia-Pacific and succeeded in collaborating successfully with Japan and Australia. Singapore's Ministry of Foreign Affairs (MFA), led by Foreign Minister Wong Kan Seng, played a key role therefore in the formation of the ARF. It may be argued that no other foreign ministry in Southeast Asia would have been capable of reaching similar results.

The senior officials discussed in May 1993 the political and security context in the Asia-Pacific. They agreed on the need to form a multilateral process of cooperative security to promote cooperation in the region.[19] Significantly, the ASEAN-PMC SOM registered balance of power considerations in signalling the forthcoming establishment of the ARF. The chairman's statement affirmed: 'The continuing presence of the United States, as well as stable relationships among the United States, Japan and China, and other states of the region would contribute to regional stability.'[20] The prime object of a region-wide cooperative security arrangement therefore would be to secure a continuing US involvement in the Asia-Pacific and to address China's rising influence in the region. Excluding a policy of containment, the permanent secretaries expressed a willingness to engage China, and other non-PMC members, within an extended security dialogue. The chairman's statement declared: 'the senior officials felt that it was important to develop an open process to take into account the presence of other regional countries that could contribute to the regional dialogues.'[21] It was decided to invite the foreign ministers of China, Russia, Vietnam, Laos and Papua New Guinea to a special session of foreign ministers in Singapore in July 1993 that would coincide with the AMM. In their conclusion, the senior officials stated that it was 'important for ASEAN and its dialogue partners to work with other regional states to evolve a predictable and constructive pattern of relationships in the Asia-Pacific'.[22] The last part of the sentence would later be repeated in the chairman's statement of the first ARF meeting.[23]

The Association also introduced the TAC at the ASEAN-PMC SOM.[24] By acknowledging the legitimacy of the TAC, the member states aimed to advance the Association's diplomatic centrality within the forthcoming Forum. Most regional players supported the position of leadership adopted by ASEAN. Its diplomatic centrality and managerial role were essential, for instance, to ensure an initial Chinese participation. The ASEAN states were keen to promote their code of conduct for regional inter-state relations, which was based primarily on respect for national sovereignty. The ASEAN Declaration on the South China Sea had made reference to the TAC in July 1992.[25] The ASEAN members appeared to believe that a collective code of conduct based on standard international norms would help to restrain the larger participants in the forthcoming ARF. They hoped that this source of constraint might encourage China not to threaten its smaller partners. Indeed, any aggressive action would undermine such norms and rebound adversely on the political cohesion of the arrangement as well as on the interests of larger participants with a stake in its viability. The TAC would later be endorsed at the first ARF meeting 'as a code of conduct governing relations between states and a unique diplomatic instrument for regional confidence-building, preventive diplomacy, and political and security co-operation'.[26]

The inaugural dinner of the ARF was held in Singapore on 25 July 1993 and was attended by eighteen foreign ministers, including China's Foreign

Minister Qian Qichen. It was agreed that the Forum's first working session would take place in Bangkok one year later. The following day at the start of the ASEAN-PMC, Singapore's Foreign Minister Wong Kan Seng stated that peace and stability 'in the Asia-Pacific depend not only on whether the United States continues to lead as she has in the past. It also depends on how America settles her relationships with other major powers – Russia, China and Japan.'[27] A key purpose of the ARF was therefore to engage the US, Japan and the PRC in a structure of multilateral dialogue in order to promote a stable distribution of power in the Asia-Pacific. This core ASEAN objective has not changed since the formation of the Forum. For example, Singapore's Foreign Minister Professor S. Jayakumar affirmed in 1996 that for ASEAN 'the issue now is not how to avoid entanglement in big power conflict. It is how to maintain a stable balance of the major powers at a time of immense fluidity.'[28]

The establishment of the ARF was dependent on the participation of the three main regional players. At the end of the Cold War, the United States had been unwilling to support multilateralism in the Asia-Pacific, as it feared that a multilateral security structure might undermine its bilateral arrangements with regional actors. This position had changed by the end of the Bush administration. In an article published in *Foreign Affairs* in 1991, US Secretary of State James Baker had referred to three pillars for regional security and prosperity, namely economic integration, democratization and a new defence structure.[29] Elected in November 1992, US President Bill Clinton welcomed the establishment of a multilateral security forum. The ARF was seen in Washington as a diplomatic instrument to complement US bilateral security relations and to convince regional allies to take a more active part in their own security.

Japan played an active role behind the scene in the formation of the ARF. In addition to Nakayama's proposal of July 1991, Japan's Prime Minister Kichii Miyazawa had declared during a tour of Southeast Asia in January 1993 that Japan would actively participate in a multilateral security dialogue. Furthermore, Yukio Satoh, a senior official at the Japanese foreign ministry, explains that 'Tokyo played a significant role in impressing upon Washington the importance of multilateral security dialogue for the Asia-Pacific region, when Washington was sceptical about a multilateral approach.'[30] The ARF was viewed in Japan as supplementary to its alliance with the United States and as a tool to improve relations with South Korea and China. By backing the ASEAN initiative, Japan succeeded in advancing its national interests without hurting the sensitivities of other East Asian countries. However, the ARF also symbolized the persisting constraints on its foreign policy as it indicated Tokyo's capacity to participate but not to take a leading position within a multilateral security arrangement.

From its perspective, Beijing perceived multilateralism as an attempt to encircle China as a threatening rising power and to interfere in its domestic affairs. Nonetheless, it was reassured by the fact that the ASEAN states were leading the new cooperative process. Beijing was willing to support an informal and flexible security dialogue sponsored by middle powers that did not represent a potential threat to its security interests. China also agreed with ASEAN's emphasis that progress should be gradual within the ARF.[31] A US or Japanese led arrangement would have been unacceptable to the PRC. However, China could also not afford to be left out of a multilateral security forum that included the most significant regional states. Despite its initial suspicion, the PRC would quickly learn to use the ARF to its advantage.

The creation of the ARF was regarded by ASEAN as a diplomatic instrument to promote a continuing US involvement in the region, thus avoiding the need for an independent Japanese security role, and to encourage the PRC in habits of good international behaviour.[32] Interestingly, US Secretary of State Warren Christopher confirmed during the 1993 ASEAN-PMC that 'the United States will remain actively engaged in Asia. America is and will remain an Asia Pacific power.'[33] A driving factor behind the organization of the first ever ASEAN-PMC SOM had been the need to cope with the potential US strategic retreat from the region. Yet, regional concerns about the uncertain long-term US involvement in the Asia-Pacific had primarily disappeared by May 1993. President Clinton had indicated by then his views on regional security and his support for the formation of a new multilateral institution. The United States had also actively taken part in the ASEAN-PMC SOM. By July 1993, China's rising power had therefore become the main source of concern. The ARF was perceived by the ASEAN members as a tool to encourage China to act with good international citizenship in mind. As part of its calculations, the Association wanted the PRC to be constrained through its participation in an embryonic security regime and respect for its norms and principles. The establishment of the ARF was thus influenced by balance of power practices. These practices should be understood as constraining power through political means within the cooperative process rather than a reliance on traditional military tactics. Leifer argues: 'the very attempt to lock China into a network of constraining multilateral arrangements underpinned hopefully by a sustained and viable American military presence would seem to serve the purpose of the balance of power by means other than alliance.'[34]

The formation of the ARF indicated, however, that ASEAN's sub-regional approach to security was insufficient in the new regional security context. The extension of the ASEAN model of cooperative security to the Asia-Pacific represented an informal abdication of the commitment to realize ZOPFAN. The latter was made obsolete by the establishment of the Forum. Promulgated in 1971, the principle had registered a call for regional autonomy and repeated a determination, previously announced in the 1967 Bangkok Declaration, to avoid external intervention. The Association had previously ignored ZOPFAN during the Third Indochina Conflict, claiming that its application would only become possible after the end of the war.[35]

As the strongest supporter of ZOPFAN, Indonesia was most concerned about the creation of the ARF due to its own aspiration for a regional order based on the exclusive managerial role of the Southeast Asian states. Keen to avoid external interference, Jakarta had for instance opposed a Thai-Singaporean proposal made prior to the Singapore Summit to invite the permanent members of the UN Security Council to sign the TAC.[36] Still, Indonesia supported the formation of the ARF primarily due to balance of power considerations.[37] Jakarta was apprehensive of China's rising influence and was increasingly fearful of its potential hegemonic disposition in the South China Sea. With China's growing power in mind, in December 1995 Indonesia would also sign a security agreement with Australia and support Singapore's initiative to give India the status of dialogue partner.

By concentrating on security cooperation, the ARF was expected to complement the Asia-Pacific Economic Cooperation (APEC) forum, which had been created in Canberra in November 1989. The rise in regional multilateralism was indeed not limited to the politico-security realm but also included economic cooperation. The sustained economic 'miracle' in the Asia-Pacific had generated a great source of optimism. Driven by market forces, the rise in economic regionalism had been closely linked to the growth of regional economies over the last twenty years. APEC was established as a regional economic dialogue as opposed to a negotiating group.[38] The goal from the outset was to encourage trade and investment liberalization. APEC is based on a concept of 'open regionalism', which means that the outcome of accords on liberalization is applied without discrimination within the regional grouping but also to non-APEC economies. The majority of Asian participants have preferred APEC to remain a dialogue on trade and investment rather than an institutionalized body.

Both APEC and the ARF are region-wide arrangements that include the United States, Japan and China. In contrast to the ARF, APEC also includes Taiwan. Beijing regards Taiwan as a renegade province of China and would not tolerate its participation in the ARF. While the ARF's institutional structure has to this day been limited to ministerial meetings, the first summit of the APEC heads of state and government was organized in Seattle in November 1993 after the scheduled session of finance ministers. The summit derived from a proposal made by President Clinton at the meeting of the Group of Seven (G7) in Tokyo in July 1993. Consequently, APEC has developed into an institutional structure that combines ministerial and heads of state and government meetings. By providing a framework for both multilateral and bilateral discussions, the arrangement has assumed a security significance beyond its focus on economic issues. For instance, in response to the terror attacks in the United States on 11 September 2001, the APEC summit in Shanghai in October that year produced a declaration on terrorism, even before the ARF had a chance to discuss the issue.[39] At their next annual summit in Mexico two weeks after the Bali bombings of 12 October 2002, the APEC leaders adopted a series of anti-terror measures. In a joint statement issued on the sidelines of the summit meeting, the United States, South Korea and Japan also called on North Korea to dismantle its nuclear weapons development programme.

The relevance of the balance of power factor within the ARF was further demonstrated through ASEAN's initiative to admit India during the ARF's third session in Jakarta in July 1996. India had automatically become a participant of the ARF after having received the status of dialogue partner at the summit of the ASEAN heads of state and government in Bangkok in December 1995. Strongly pushed by Singapore and supported by Indonesia, ASEAN's initiative was motivated by power balancing considerations.[40] Da Cunha explains that leaders in Singapore 'are clearly concerned about the staying power of the United States in the region, and are likely to see India as one possible counterweight to China's expanded power in the future'.[41] India is a growing regional actor and perceived in Jakarta as a natural countervailing power to Chinese ambitions in Asia. India's participation in the ARF was thus viewed as beneficial in light of the uncertain long-term US involvement in Southeast Asia. ASEAN's decision to enlarge the geographical scope of the Forum was not welcomed by the United States and Japan but supported by the PRC that favours multipolarity in the Asia-Pacific.

The role of the balance of power factor in the formation of ASEAN and the ARF are comparable. The participants of the Forum, in particular the ASEAN states, needed to deal with China's rising power just as some ASEAN members had been anxious in 1967 to constrain any disposition towards hegemony by Indonesia. The various ASEAN states had been forced to rely on institutional and political channels as they were in no position in a post-Confrontation period to contain Indonesia through conventional methods. Similarly, in the post-Cold War the ASEAN members were not able to depend on a policy of containment against China due to their lack of countervailing power. To complicate matters further, the ASEAN states shared no common security perspective and had differential relationships with Beijing. In addition, the economic opportunities provided by China's growing economy made a policy of confrontation unattractive. As part of their calculations, the ASEAN countries wanted China to be constrained through its participation within a cooperative security arrangement and respect for its standard international norms and principles. Moreover, they may have anticipated that the PRC would find itself isolated within the institution if it failed to follow a policy of self-restraint. Among other objectives, the ARF was therefore expected to become a structure of dialogue helping regional states to deal with the 'China problem'. Yong Deng writes that since the ASEAN members 'do not have the capability or the willingness to rely on traditional balance of power allying with other great powers to "constrain" China, institutional entrapment appears to be the only way to manage China's power ascension'.[42]

Yet, in contrast to the founding moments of the Association, it is far from clear if China was willing in 1993 to follow a policy of political self-abnegation along Indonesian lines in order to reassure its cooperative partners and to be constrained through developing a stake in an emerging regime for cooperative security. The PRC could promote some of its national interests by adopting restrained behaviour within the ARF and vis-à-vis its different participants. The benefits of such a constrained policy could include sustained economic development, which is highly dependent on access to capital, technology and foreign markets, the avoidance of regional and international isolation and stable Sino-ASEAN relations. However, Beijing's assertiveness in foreign policy caused a sense of insecurity and vulnerability among other regional states. For instance, China's seizure of Mischief Reef, discovered in February 1995, and its military exercises in the Taiwan Straits in March 1996, which led the United States to deploy two carrier squadrons to deter further Chinese undertakings, were assertive actions that complicated relations with ARF participants. Beijing seemed ready after joining it to undermine the premises of confidence building and trust on which the Forum was based. The PRC ameliorated its relations with the Association after the Mischief Reef incident but mainly to promote multipolarity in the Asia-Pacific in view of its worsening relations with the United States and Japan. In short, China's participation in the Forum has not led to a policy of self-imposed containment comparable to Indonesia within ASEAN.

This limited experience suggests that the ARF has failed as an instrument for constraining China in a corresponding way to ASEAN's degree of success with Indonesia. This measure of failure can be explained by several factors. The PRC still feels subject to US containment and perceives multilateralism as a Western attempt to restrain its growing regional influence. In contrast, Indonesia was acknowledged within the Association as the primary state. This was, for instance, indicated by the fact that its preference for a regional order based on the exclusive managerial role of the Southeast Asian states was registered in the Bangkok Declaration of August 1967. Indonesia's expectations were later further incorporated in the Association through the principles of national and regional resilience. An ASEAN Secretariat was also established in Jakarta in 1976 after a decade of co-operation and confidence building during which Indonesia had adopted a policy of self-restraint within the Association.

Furthermore, Indonesia's and China's respective diplomatic and economic conditions at the time of the formation of ASEAN and the ARF should be distinguished. In a post-Confrontation period, Indonesia was keen to restore its credibility and was willing to follow a policy of self-constraint in order to promote domestic economic development within a framework of regional stability. It therefore attained international rehabilitation by acting according to standard international norms. In short, ASEAN's success 'derived, in great part, from an initial willingness by a potential but economically prostrate hegemon to give up challenging the regional status quo and to inspire trust among new-found partners through a self-abnegating political role'.[43] In contrast to Indonesia in 1967, the PRC joined the ARF as the prime beneficiary of the changing strategic environment in East Asia. It was not in any need of institutionalizing a process of reconciliation with its neighbouring states. Moreover, China had experienced sustained economic development since the 1980s and was already becoming well integrated in the regional and international economy. Hence, the ARF did not contain sufficient incentive to counter a disposition towards hegemony by the PRC.

Nonetheless, Indonesia's lack of constraint over East Timor should be noted. Indonesia's annexation of the Territory in December 1975 was an act of regional hegemony that demonstrated that its practice of constraint did not apply outside the walls of the Association. Still, the case of East Timor should not be compared to China's irredentist claims in the South China Sea or its policy vis-à-vis Taiwan. Indonesia's invasion of the Territory was a special case of strategic denial within its own archipelago that did not transform the regional pattern of power. This may be contrasted with a future PRC dominant in the South China Sea. Moreover in 1975 East Timor was not an issue in Indonesian domestic politics. The annexation of the Territory was influenced by a defensive consideration rather than linked to a question of domestic legitimacy. The military action was perceived in Jakarta as having eliminated a possible threat of communist influence and intervention within the archipelago. This distinguishes the case of East Timor from China's policy towards Taiwan.

Indonesia only renounced its sovereignty over East Timor in 1999. Indonesian President B.J. Habibie announced unexpectedly in January that year the holding of a forthcoming popular vote in East Timor on the future of the Territory. The United Nations organized a referendum in East Timor on 30 August 1999 that led to an overwhelming vote in favour of independence. Following these results, anti-independence militias, orchestrated by the Indonesian military, perpetrated killings and massive destructions throughout East Timor. These dramatic events led to the formation of a humanitarian intervention, the International Force in East Timor (INTERFET), authorized by a UN Security Council (UNSC) resolution. Australia provided the backbone of the intervention. While Thailand, Malaysia, Singapore and the Philippines contributed among others to the operation on an individual basis, ASEAN and the ARF did not become involved in the East Timor crisis.[44] The UN Transitional Administration in East Timor (UNTAET) managed the Territory until it gained its independence on 20 May 2002.

East Timorese leaders rejected until recently the prospect of joining the Association. ASEAN members had demonstrated for many years their solidarity towards Indonesia and had played an active diplomatic role in the

UN to oppose resolutions that demanded an Indonesian withdrawal. The same political leaders are now more realistic about the geo-strategic condition of East Timor. Moreover, the ASEAN states have been careful since the events of 1999 to indicate their support. East Timor's Foreign Minister Jose Ramos-Horta was invited to the thirty-fifth AMM in Brunei in July 2002. He announced his country's intention to attend future ASEAN meetings as an observer and to adhere to the TAC.[45] East Timor may wish to take part in ASEAN as a means of managing its relations with Indonesia. It could therefore follow the example of Brunei which became a member of the Association in January 1984 partly to protect and confirm its newly obtained sovereignty. ASEAN's expansion to include the Sultanate involved power balancing considerations. At issue was the constraint imposed on Indonesia and Malaysia through their stake in the Association from which Brunei could benefit to promote its own security and consolidate its position vis-à-vis its neighbours.

In sum, the ARF has so far failed to operate as a structure of constraint on China's regional foreign policy; at least, as indicated by its sustained irredentist claims in the South China Sea. Partly due to the limits of multilateralism as a constraining factor on the PRC, various ASEAN states have continued to depend on bilateral relations with external players to ensure their security. Individual members have adopted traditional balance of power practices, primarily on a bilateral basis with the United States, outside of an ASEAN framework. Singapore relies on the United States to operate as a conventional source of countervailing power in the region. Despite its often anti-Western rhetoric, Malaysia has also perceived the US presence as necessary to preserve regional stability. The Philippines signed a Visiting Forces Agreement with the United States in February 1998.[46] Moreover, Malaysia and Singapore are parties to the Five Power Defence Arrangements (FPDA), a defence grouping that also includes Britain, Australia and New Zealand. Malaysia withdrew from the FPDA exercises in September 1998, officially because of economic difficulties but also as a result of the deterioration of its relations with the city-state.[47] The activities of the arrangement were resumed in 1999. Brunei has relied on a private agreement reached with Britain in 1983 and renewed in December 1994 that ensures an ongoing presence of a battalion of Gurkha Rifles in the Sultanate. Significantly, Indonesia signed a security agreement with Australia in December 1995. The bilateral agreement terminated Indonesia's declaratory reliance on non-alignment and questioned the utility of the ARF as an instrument to restrain China's foreign policy. Indonesia's need to deter China influenced Suharto's decision to sign the security agreement. However, the security agreement was repudiated in September 1999 over East Timor. Finally, the ASEAN states have aimed to modernize their defence forces and acquire naval capabilities to patrol claimed maritime territories in the South China Sea. The modernization programmes were delayed by the East Asian financial crisis of 1997–98.

Influence of the balance of power factor within the ARF: unilateralism versus multipolarity

The role of the balance of power factor in the formation of the ARF has so far been examined. Beyond its establishment, it has been indicated that the influence of this factor has also carried over in the workings of the institution. In addition to relating to a denial of a potential Chinese hegemony, the balance of power factor has an additional significance within the Forum, when the calculations made by some of its participants are examined. Central to a second relevance of the balance of power factor is the existence among some ARF participants of alternative views on the role of the regime for cooperative security. Indeed, this section argues that China has perceived the Forum as a vehicle for promoting multipolarity in the Asia-Pacific to counter America's unipolar status in the post-Cold War. This suggests that the ARF is essentially dominated by major power relationships; above all, that between China and the United States.

The three key regional players – namely the United States and Japan on the one hand and China on the other – hold opposing expectations on the cooperative security arrangement. The United States views the multilateral security dialogue as a means of complementing its bilateral arrangements with regional states. For example, US Secretary of State Warren Christopher affirmed at the ASEAN-PMC held in Singapore in July 1993 that while 'alliances and bilateral defense relationships will remain the cornerstone of American strategy in Southeast Asia, the Clinton Administration welcomes multilateral security consultations – especially within the framework of the PMC'.[48] America's reliance on bilateral security structures has been further demonstrated since the creation of the ARF. The joint US–Japanese Declaration of April 1996 on regional security and subsequent provision for new guidelines confirmed the post-Cold War significance of the Mutual Security Treaty. Similar to Washington, Tokyo examines the Forum as a means to complement rather than replace existing bilateral alliances. Japan regards the ARF as supplementary to its alliance with the United States and as an instrument to preserve an ongoing US engagement in East Asia.[49]

This latter security perspective is shared by most ASEAN states. By establishing the ARF, they recognized the need for a new security structure in the post-Cold War that could supplement existing bilateral alliances. A consensus had already emerged during the separate session of the ASEAN-PMC SOM in May 1993 that the Forum would only complement a bilateral approach to security. It is interesting to note, however, that all the participants at the meeting, except for Indonesia and Malaysia, had formal bilateral agreements with the United States. This security perspective has not changed since May 1993. For instance, Singapore's Foreign Minister Professor S. Jayakumar declared in 1999 that the ARF 'is an important vehicle to supplement our bilateral relations with the major powers'.[50]

In contrast to the United States and Japan, China has come to perceive the ARF as a vehicle for promoting multipolarity defined with reference to countering US unilateralism. The PRC supports a multipolar rather than a multilateral perspective in the Asia-Pacific that would include the traditional Chinese–Japanese–US triangle but also recognize India, Russia and the ASEAN states as relevant regional actors. Beijing favours a multipolar system based on equality and partnership between the main regional states. It has embraced ASEAN's diplomatic centrality and managerial role within the ARF as a way to enhance multipolarity in the Asia-Pacific and to avoid US domination of the institution. This position has also been adopted by Russia and by India since it joined in 1996. In addition, the PRC supported India's participation during the ARF's third annual meeting as a means for promoting a multipolar regional order. In essence, China has regarded the ARF as an instrument for opposing a new US policy of containment. For instance, Segal already explained in 1997 that 'Chinese officials now privately admit that they see virtue in regional multilateralism as a way to exert counter-pressure against a United States that now seems more prepared to threaten the use of force in order to balance China.'[51] The Forum provides the PRC with a diplomatic tool to preserve its political ties with the ASEAN states and to avoid potential isolation in the Asia-Pacific. China has also used the ARF as a means to question US bilateral alliances by arguing that these agreements may no longer be required in a less menacing regional environment.[52] On this question, it has the support of India and Russia. Beijing has openly addressed Southeast Asian leaders on the superiority of cooperative security over the use of 'outdated' Cold War alliances.

In the post-Cold War, the PRC has become deeply concerned about the US unipolar status, which Beijing viewed as having been demonstrated by the Gulf War of 1991. Tense after the events in Tiananmen Square in June 1989, Sino-US relations have also been complicated since the creation of the ARF. For example, Beijing resented the US decision to offer Taiwanese President Lee Teng Hui a visa for a private visit to the United States in June 1995. Bilateral relations worsened due to the events in the Taiwan Straits in March 1996 that demonstrated a US willingness to act as a source of countervailing power against the PRC. Beijing was also critical of the joint US–Japanese Declaration of April 1996, which 'unambiguously reinforced Chinese anxiety about these two powers' joint efforts to counterweight Chinese power'.[53] Sino-US relations improved following the official trip of the Chinese President Jiang Zemin to the United States in November 1997 and the return visit of President Clinton to China in June 1998. Bilateral relations again deteriorated as a result of the US bombing of the Chinese Embassy in Belgrade in early 1999, which was regarded in Beijing as part of a new US policy of containment. The coming to power of US President George W. Bush in January 2001 led to a resurgence of unilateralism in US foreign policy. Sino-US relations were repeatedly tested during the first few months of the Bush administration. The terror attacks on 11 September and

Beijing's anti-terrorism efforts have to some extent contributed to a more cooperative and constructive relationship. Yet, 11 September has also reinforced a unilateralist US foreign policy. The PRC is still therefore deeply concerned about the US unipolar status that derives from its growing preponderance in military power, as indicated once again by the war in Afghanistan.

Beyond its participation in the ARF, China has aimed to oppose US unilateralism in the Asia-Pacific through other diplomatic means. It has tried to improve relations with Southeast Asian states. It normalized relations with Indonesia in 1990 and with Vietnam in 1991. China also opened diplomatic ties with Singapore and Brunei respectively in 1990 and 1991. Moreover, the PRC supported Malaysia's initiative for an East Asian Economic Group (EAEG) that would have excluded non-Asian states. First initiated by Malaysia in 1990, the EAEG lapsed after strong US objection because Washington refused to be excluded from East Asian economic cooperation and also as a result of coolness within ASEAN. In response, Malaysia's Prime Minister Dr Mahathir Mohamad modified it to an East Asian Economic Caucus (EAEC) in October 1991. The project has revived through the ASEAN + Three (China, Japan and South Korea) summit of heads of state and government that first met in Kuala Lumpur in December 1997. It was decided a year later in Hanoi that the summit would be held annually. Yet, Malaysia's proposal for setting up an ASEAN + Three Secretariat in Kuala Lumpur was rejected during the 2002 AMM, as the other ASEAN members feared that it would undermine the significance of the ASEAN Secretariat in Jakarta. The PRC also takes part in the Asia–Europe Meeting (ASEM) that was inaugurated in Bangkok in March 1996 and which brings together the heads of state and government from the EU and ASEAN states as well as from Japan, China and South Korea. The ASEAN + Three and ASEM are structures of dialogue that exclude the United States and provide China with alternative economic and strategic partners.

Malaysia has stood behind China's preference for a multipolar security structure in the Asia-Pacific. Sino-Malaysian relations improved in the 1990s as a result of economic cooperation but also due to a shared desire for a multipolar regional order and a common apprehension of US interference in their internal affairs.[54] Malaysia has opposed a US domination of the ARF and APEC. Acharya explains that 'Malaysia, more than any other ASEAN state, wants neither Beijing nor Washington to dominate the region.'[55] The PRC has supported Malaysia's often anti-Western stand as indicated by the Chinese willingness to go along with its initiative to establish the EAEC. Interestingly, Malaysia's original proposal to form an economic grouping was initially announced during the visit of Chinese Premier Li Peng to Malaysia in December 1990 and without prior consultation with ASEAN partners.[56] Most ASEAN members have feared some of the potential consequences of the US unipolar status in the post-Cold War. In particular, they have shared China's concerns about US pressure on human rights, trade issues and the need for democratic reforms. Malaysia, Singapore, Indonesia and Vietnam have also been 'uneasy about the possibility of the United States attempting to link its security presence to such domestic issues'.[57] In the post-11 September context, China, Vietnam, Indonesia and Malaysia have opposed a greater US military presence in the region. Significantly, the ASEAN–US declaration on counter-terrorism signed in July 2002 did not mention the deployment of US troops in Southeast Asia.[58] Prior to its adoption, Vietnam and Indonesia rejected any clause that might be regarded as allowing the involvement of US forces in the region and thus undermining the principles of national sovereignty and non-intervention in the affairs of other states. The declaration explicitly recognized these principles as well as the importance of the UN in the combat against terrorism.

Beyond its support for a multipolar security perspective in the Asia-Pacific, China has at least paid lip service to the standard international norms promoted by the ASEAN states through the ARF. The PRC has introduced since the mid-1990s an element of relative moderation in its foreign policy and has not attempted to pose challenges to the regional order. Huxley explains that:

> There is considerable evidence that, in general, China recognises that its emerging superpower status entails huge responsibilities, particularly in terms of requiring international behaviour which gives priority to regional and global stability and adherence to international norms over a sense of historical entitlement.[59]

The PRC has not been acting as a revisionist power. Self-restraint characterized China's reaction to the construction in 1996 of a lighthouse on Diaoyu (Senkaku) Islands by Japanese right-wingers. These islands, located in the East China Sea, are claimed by the PRC and Japan. It is also important to note China's muted response to the victory of Chen Shui-bian, the pro-independence leader of the Democratic Progressive Party, in the Taiwanese presidential election of March 2000.[60] This should be distinguished from China's military exercises in the Taiwan Straits in March 1996 to intimidate Taiwan and influence its coming presidential election. The relative moderation in China's foreign policy can also be observed in the context of the South China Sea dispute. Although the PRC expanded its structures on Mischief Reef in late 1998, it has not seized additional disputed features in the Spratlys since 1995. This may be contrasted with Malaysia's seizure of Investigator Shoal in March 1999. The PRC has stood firm on the question of sovereign jurisdiction. The other claimants, however, have also refused to make any concession on this matter. Significantly, Beijing has been careful not to allow the South China Sea question to become an issue in Chinese domestic politics. Miles writes that even 'during the 1995 Mischief Reef dispute with the Philippines, China avoided turning the issue into a major subject of domestic propaganda'.[61] In short, Beijing's policy towards the South China Sea question has included some moderation since 1995. The element of control in China's foreign policy can be explained by a desire not to antagonize the ASEAN states and its fear of the entire region becoming infected with the virus of irredentism.

China's response to the question of preventive diplomacy within the ARF should also be mentioned. Beijing has strongly opposed any attempt to move towards the second stage of development, primarily due to the fear of external interference in its domestic affairs. The United States has also rejected the implementation of formal measures that would constrain its regional policy and bilateral ties. Still, the PRC has been supportive of the process of preventive diplomacy. It has taken part in the ARF track-two seminars on the subject held respectively in Seoul in May 1995, in Paris in November 1996 and in Singapore in September 1997. Moreover, it was a participant at a workshop on preventive diplomacy organized by the CSCAP Working Group on Confidence- and Security-Building Measures (CSBMs) in Bangkok on 28 February–2 March 1999.

Conclusion

The establishment of the ARF involved balance of power considerations. The balance of power perspective and the associative dimension, discussed in Chapter 1, were closely intermingled in the formation of the Forum. Indeed, the anticipated political constraint likely to be imposed on the major participants was primarily dependent on their stake in the emerging cooperative security regime. Yet, it is questionable whether the ARF has so far succeeded in constraining China's foreign policy through non-military means. The Mischief Reef incident indicated a Chinese readiness to undermine the premises of confidence building and trust on which the Forum was initially based. The ARF does not entail sufficient incentive to counter a disposition towards hegemony by China. However, since the mid-1990s the PRC has generally respected the standard international norms promoted by the ARF and has aimed not to upset the regional order. It has also viewed its participation in the Forum in balance of power terms. In contrast to the United States, Japan and most ASEAN states, China has regarded the ARF as a vehicle for promoting multipolarity in the Asia-Pacific to counter America's unipolar status in the post-Cold War.

6 ASEAN's post-Cold War involvement in the South China Sea dispute

The relevance of associative and balance of power dimensions

Introduction

This chapter focuses on the South China Sea dispute in relation to ASEAN's ability to conduct itself as an associative body and considers its initiatives to bring the balance of power to bear. The associative dimension is examined as involving the promotion of a code of conduct for the South China Sea respected at least by the member states. The balance of power perspective is analysed in a conventional sense. It is argued that ASEAN's involvement in the territorial dispute has been defined by the absence of both dimensions. The lack of associative conduct results from the absence of intra-mural cohesion over the territorial dispute and ASEAN's failure so far to establish a code of conduct for the South China Sea. Its inability to practise conventional balance of power politics arises from the limitations associated with cooperative security and the lack of access to an external source of counter-vailing power. Finally, it is asserted that China's participation in the ARF has not led to any concessions or compromises regarding its territorial claims in the South China Sea.

The chapter consists of three sections. The first reviews the nature of the South China Sea dispute by discussing the relevance of international law, the conflicting territorial claims and the economic and strategic interests involved. The second section deals with the emergence of the territorial dispute as a regional security issue at the end of the Cold War. Additionally, it points out that the ASEAN members have contradictory views on China's potential threat as a rising power. Finally, ASEAN's post-Cold War involvement in the South China Sea dispute is addressed by studying its conduct through both associative and balance of power perspectives.

The nature of the South China Sea dispute

The overlapping territorial claims over the Spratly Islands represent a difficult area of dispute between China, Taiwan, Vietnam, the Philippines, Malaysia and Brunei. Also, the Paracel archipelago, controlled by the PRC since 1974, is claimed by Vietnam and Taiwan. This chapter focuses only on the Spratly issue. The South China Sea dispute may be examined in the context of international law. The Third United Nations Convention of the Law of the Sea (UNCLOS III) was adopted on 30 April 1982 and came into force on 16 November 1994. It was ratified, among others, by Indonesia, the Philippines, Vietnam, Thailand, Singapore, and eventually by China, Malaysia and Brunei in 1996. The Convention aims to establish a new maritime regime by calling for closer cooperation on maritime issues, offering procedures for the resolution of territorial disputes and introducing new concepts, rights and responsibilities.[1]

The 1982 Convention imposes conditions to regulate internal waters, archipelagic waters, territorial seas, contiguous zones, exclusive economic zones (EEZs), continental shelves and high seas. Maritime zones are measured from base points on land. The Convention provides coastal states with the authority to extend their sovereign jurisdiction under a specific set of rules. It authorizes expansion of the territorial sea to 12 nautical miles and limits the contiguous zone to 24 nautical miles. The EEZ 'shall not extend beyond the 200 nautical miles from the baselines from which the breadth of the territorial sea is measured'.[2] The sovereign rights of a coastal state over the EEZ are limited to the exploration and exploitation of its living and non-living resources. Continental shelves may not be extended beyond a limit of 350 nautical miles from territorial baselines. The sovereign rights of a coastal state over the continental shelf are reduced to the exploration and exploitation of its non-living resources. The Convention defines the rights and privileges of archipelagic states and recognizes that archipelagic waters fall within their sovereign jurisdiction. It also ensures the freedom of navigation, the right of innocent passage and the passage through straits.

A peaceful maritime regime in Southeast Asia depends on the interpretation and application of the Law of the Sea by the various regional states. Moreover, the 1982 Convention is based on assumptions of agreement on sovereignty and does not provide for resolution of disputes, except through a diplomatic compromise. International or regional arbitration is therefore not compulsory under the terms of the Law of the Sea. The claimants have not agreed on the problem of sovereign jurisdiction over the islands of the South China Sea and the overlapping claims have not been presented to the International Court of Justice (ICJ) or the International Tribunal for the Law of the Sea. On the contrary, some of the parties have misused the Convention to extend their sovereign jurisdiction unilaterally and justify their claims in the South China Sea. Yet, the question of whether the Spratly Islands may generate maritime zones needs to be mentioned. UNCLOS III defines an island as 'a naturally-formed area of land, surrounded by water, which is above water at high tide'.[3] An island is also capable of naturally supporting life. In contrast, UNCLOS declares that 'rocks which cannot sustain human habitation or economic life of their own shall have no exclusive economic zone or continental shelf.'[4] Features that cannot sustain human life and artificial islands are only entitled respectively to a 12 nautical mile territorial sea and a 500 metre safety zone. These terms of the 1982 Convention seem to apply to most features in the Spratly archipelago. In short, due to their status the disputed features in the South China Sea may not be a legitimate basis for claiming maritime jurisdiction.

The claims made by the parties involved in the South China Sea dispute can be separated into historical claims of discovery and occupation and claims that rest on the extension of sovereign jurisdiction under interpretations of the provisions of UNCLOS. The PRC views the South China Sea as an exclusive Chinese sea and claims nearly its entire territory. Its historical claims are based on the discovery and occupation of the territory.[5] In 1947, the Nationalist government of Chiang Kai-shek defined China's traditional claims by an area limited by nine interrupted marks that cover most of the South China Sea. Zhou En-lai formalized the claims for the PRC in 1951 as a response to the San Francisco Peace Treaty in which Japan renounced all claims over the Spratly and Paracel islands without stating their new ownership. China's territorial claims in the South China Sea have not changed since 1951. Relying on its claim to historical administration of the area, Beijing has not provided a legal explanation for or given specific delimitations to its territorial claims. In fact, historically based claims over nearly an entire maritime territory, rather than specific islands, seem legally indefensible.[6] Claiming a comparable area in the South China Sea, Taiwan relies on similar historical arguments. Taipei has occupied since 1956 the island of Itu Aba, the largest feature in the Spratly group. Despite the Taiwan question, the PRC has tolerated Taipei's territorial claims in the South China Sea and its control of Itu Aba. Until the reunification of Vietnam, Hanoi had recognized Chinese sovereignty over the Paracel and Spratly islands. Since 1975, it has claimed both groups based on historical claims of discovery and occupation. Its claims rely on the Vietnamese administration of these islands in the nineteenth century and on French involvement in the area as a colonial power. Vietnam also established in May 1977 a 200 nautical mile EEZ.

The original ASEAN members involved in the dispute present conflicting claims that differ from those discussed above. They are limited to specific parts of the Spratly archipelago and tend to rely on international law, including the extension of the continental shelf, rather than on historical arguments.[7] Among the member states, the Philippines claims the largest area of the Spratlys, a zone referred to as *Kalayaan*. These claims are largely based on the so-called discovery of the area by an explorer, Tomas Cloma, in 1956. First officially proclaimed in 1971, a 1978 presidential decree declared the *Kalayaan* part of the national territory. The Philippine claims also rest on a 200 nautical mile EEZ, which is said to cover the *Kalayaan*. Malaysia extended its continental shelf in 1979 and included features of the Spratlys in its territory.[8] Brunei established in 1988 an exclusive economic zone of 200 nautical miles that extends to the south of the Spratly Islands and comprises Louisa Reef. Yet, the Sultanate does not claim the reef as such. Finally, Indonesia is not a party to the Spratly dispute. It was neutral in the South China Sea issue until 1993 and the suspected extension of the Chinese claims to the waters above the Natuna gas fields, currently exploited by Indonesia.

Important economic, strategic and domestic interests are involved in the South China Sea dispute. The area is rich in fishery resources and expected to hold substantial oil and gas reserves.[9] Brunei, Malaysia and Vietnam are already important oil producers but China became a net energy importer from 1994 to sustain its economic growth and development. However, the oil reserves of the South China Sea are uncertain and initial estimations have been reduced. Also, none of the claimants have so far gained from their oil or gas exploration. The exploitation has until now been limited to continental shelves. The situation in the South China Sea could quickly change for the worst if proof was found of sufficient oil reserves for commercial usage. The free navigation of commercial vessels in the South China Sea is essential for regional and international trade. Major shipping lanes used by the United States, Japan and other maritime powers cross these waters. Valencia explains that 'Japanese tankers carry 70 per cent of Japan's oil through the South China Sea and the US Seventh Fleet requires free, flexible and, for its nuclear submarines, undetected passage in the area.'[10]

The South China Sea dispute has a strategic dimension. If it succeeds in realizing its territorial claims, the PRC would 'be able to extend its jurisdiction some one thousand nautical miles from its mainland so as to command the virtual Mediterranean or maritime heart of Southeast Asia with far-reaching consequences for the strategic environment'.[11] A Chinese naval presence at the heart of the sub-region would be threatening for Vietnam and the Philippines but also for Malaysia, Brunei and Indonesia. The control of the maritime communication routes would also have a strategic value, as it would endanger the economic and security interests of the United States, Japan and others.[12] Finally, the territorial claims have assumed a nationalist importance in the states concerned, above all in the PRC. The claimants have been inflexible on the sovereignty issue. Retracting territorial claims or a willingness to make concessions on the question of sovereign jurisdiction would be costly domestically and perceived regionally as a sign of weakness.

Following a strategy of southward expansion, the PRC has used force to consolidate its position in the South China Sea. In January 1974, China completed its control over the Paracel archipelago by acting militarily against South Vietnam before the expected fall of Saigon and the reunification of the country.[13] This military action should be examined as part of the Sino-Soviet struggle and fear of a Soviet encirclement of the PRC.[14] Beyond the Cold War calculations, the events of 1974 reinforced China's influence in the South China Sea. In part due to its limited capacity to project power, the PRC remained absent from the Spratly Islands until the second half of the 1980s. Except for Brunei, all the other parties involved already controlled features in the Spratlys. Claiming the entire archipelago, China needed urgently to secure a military presence in the Spratlys and occupied some features in 1987. Most claimants have viewed the construction of permanent foundations on uninhabitable and occasionally submerged features as a way to manifest their sovereign jurisdiction. A naval confrontation with Vietnam on 14 March 1988 led to a new Chinese seizure of territory.[15] Despite the ongoing Third Indochina Conflict, the regional strategic context had dramatically changed by 1988. Eager to achieve a rapprochement with the PRC, the Soviet Union failed to assist or support Vietnam. The lack of a reaction further undermined the reliability of the Soviet Union as a military ally, which had been previously questioned by the absence of a Soviet response to China's punitive attack against Vietnam in early 1979. On 8 February 1995, the Philippines discovered the Chinese occupation of Mischief Reef located in the *Kalayaan*. It was the first time the PRC had taken territory claimed by an ASEAN member. China has not seized disputed features in the Spratlys since the Mischief Reef incident, but Malaysia did in 1999.

ASEAN's post-Cold War relations with China and the South China Sea question

During the Third Indochina Conflict, the problem of the overlapping claims in the South China Sea was set aside in Sino-ASEAN relations. Thailand needed access to an external source of countervailing power to oppose Vietnam's occupation of Cambodia while the PRC was reliant on Thai collaboration to assist the Khmer Rouge militarily. Some regional states, primarily Singapore, were also concerned about the growing Soviet naval influence in Southeast Asia. Though the naval clash of 1988 revived the issue in some ASEAN capitals, the tacit alliance with China and the regional isolation of Vietnam meant that the territorial question was overlooked during most of the decade. The PRC did not act aggressively against any of the ASEAN claimants during that period. The Paris Accords of October 1991 and Vietnam's military withdrawal from Cambodia put an end to the complementary security interests that had united China and the Association. Rather than a threat to Southeast Asian stability, Vietnam was now keen to reach a détente with the United States and the ASEAN members.[16]

In the regional strategic context of the post-Cold War, the territorial dispute over the Spratly Islands has become a major regional security concern. However, the dispute is still primarily a political rather than a military issue thanks to the limited naval capabilities available to the different claimants. For instance, the modernization of China's naval force since the late 1980s, which has included the slow acquisition of limited blue water capabilities, has been modest and should not be exaggerated. Its naval position in the South China Sea has continued to be weak, particularly in the Spratly Islands, due to its limited power projection. Moreover, the ASEAN states have been eager not to antagonize the PRC or to overemphasize the South China Sea question in their bilateral as well as multilateral talks with Beijing. Before analysing ASEAN's response to the Spratly dispute, attention should be given to the intra-mural disparities. Though all the members are confronted with China's rising power, they have differential relationships with the PRC that derive from various aspects that include: contrasting historical experiences, ethnicity and economic relations as well as domestic and international conditions. Contradictory views on China have complicated the establishment of a common position on the South China Sea.

The Philippines maintained good ties with China after the opening of bilateral relations in July 1975. Isolated from mainland Southeast Asia, the Philippines supported ASEAN's tacit alliance with the PRC during the Cambodian conflict. Yet, post-Cold War bilateral relations have been complicated by the South China Sea question and affected by the Mischief Reef incident. Moreover, since the 1992 US withdrawal the Philippines has become the most vulnerable actor in the Spratly dispute. Manila has aimed to internationalize the issue and proposed in 1992 to organize an international conference on the problem under the auspices of the United Nations.[17] In contrast, the PRC has constantly refused any form of international mediation.

Indonesia has perceived the PRC as its primary external security concern. Bilateral relations were only normalized in August 1990, after having been suspended by Jakarta in 1965, and feelings of mistrust and suspicion towards China have remained strong in Indonesia, especially among the armed forces. Indonesia fears external interference from China and is concerned about its remaining subversive influence. It is also apprehensive that China's rising military and economic power may increase its role in Southeast Asia. Bilateral relations have been complicated by the suspected inclusion of the waters above the Natuna gas fields into the Chinese claims in the South China Sea. As Indonesia favours a Southeast Asian order based on its own managerial role, Beijing and Jakarta should also be viewed as geopolitical competitors for regional influence in the post-Cold War.[18] During the 1980s, Malaysia generally shared Indonesia's threat perception. This has changed in the post-Cold War as a result of a more cooperative relationship with China. Political and economic ties have been enhanced since the early 1990s, as first manifested by the visit of Chinese Premier Li Peng to Malaysia in December 1990. Rather than perceiving the PRC as a threat, Malaysia has concentrated on the opportunities provided by its economic growth and expects China to be constrained by regional economic interdependence.

Singapore and Thailand have no territorial claims in the South China Sea and have maintained strong links with the PRC. While Bangkok is more concerned about China's rising influence in Myanmar, the city-state is eager not to alienate Beijing and to see the non-violation of the freedom of navigation in the South China Sea. Singapore's interest in the territorial dispute therefore results from its concern for regional stability and economic prosperity. Singapore's long-term economic links with the PRC include large-scale investments in the Suzhou and Shenzhen special economic zones. Khong points out that Singapore aims to respond to China's growing power by engaging the PRC economically and politically but also by modernizing and consolidating its own military forces.[19] As an ethnic Chinese state in Southeast Asia, Singapore has traditionally been concerned with its Malay neighbours, primarily Malaysia and Indonesia. To demonstrate its Southeast Asian identity, the city-state decided to be the last ASEAN member to open relations with the PRC. Despite the prior existence of excellent economic ties, Singapore and China only formalized their relations in November 1990.

ASEAN's involvement in the South China Sea dispute

Absence of an associative dimension

The Association has so far never attempted to address the problem of sovereign jurisdiction over the Spratly Islands. The ASEAN claimants have been unable to agree on the territorial question and attention should therefore be given to a form of intra-mural cooperation that focuses on confidence building and conflict avoidance rather than conflict resolution. Accordingly, ASEAN's response to the South China Sea question should be analysed in relation to its ability to conduct itself as an associative body. An associative dimension could involve the promotion of a code of conduct respected at least by the member states. This sub-section argues that the absence of such an associative dimension has resulted from the lack of intra-mural cohesion over the territorial dispute and ASEAN's failure, so far, to establish a code of conduct for the South China Sea.

ASEAN's involvement in the territorial dispute started in the late 1980s after the Sino-Vietnamese naval confrontation of March 1988. The member states wished to take a conciliatory approach towards China in light of the economic and security interests at stake and to engage it in a peaceful and stable regional order. It was believed that the search for a collective diplomatic stand on the South China Sea could alienate the PRC.[20] Moreover, China was leading a peaceful campaign towards the Association and seemed willing to show restraint vis-à-vis the ASEAN claimants. The Philippine President Corazon Aquino travelled to China in April 1988 and was supposedly told that Chinese naval forces would not attack Philippine troops located in the Spratlys.[21] Visiting Singapore in August 1990, Prime Minister Li Peng declared that the PRC was prepared to set aside the territorial dispute and proposed joint exploration and development of the Spratlys with the Southeast Asian states. China's accommodating position with regard to the ASEAN claimants was in sharp contrast to its policy towards Vietnam, which was devoid of any concession. Sino-Vietnamese relations were normalized in November 1991 during the official visit of Vietnam's Prime Minister Vo Van Kiet to Beijing but bilateral tensions remained despite Li Peng's return trip to Vietnam in November 1992.

The first attempt to establish a multilateral dialogue on the South China Sea was independent from the Association. Launched in 1990, the Workshops on Managing Potential Conflicts in the South China Sea is an Indonesian-sponsored project financed by Canada that has focused on confidence building over maritime issues. By avoiding the question of sovereign jurisdiction, the Workshops have attempted to encourage a multilateral dialogue and enhance a peaceful management of the conflict.[22] In January 1990, an initial Workshop was organized in Bali that gathered the six ASEAN states to a preliminary meeting. Held in Bandung in July 1991, the second event brought together the members of the Association, China, 'Chinese Taipei', Vietnam and Laos. In his opening statement, Indonesia's Foreign Minister Ali Alatas declared that 'our attention and efforts have been and should continue to be directed towards finding ways to transform potential sources of conflict into constructive forms of cooperation for mutual benefit.'[23] Indonesia was then neutral in the South China Sea issue. This changed at the 1993 Workshop where Chinese officials released a map of the Chinese claims that included the waters above the Natuna gas fields. By hosting the Workshops, Indonesia as a non-claimant introduced a new dimension to its foreign policy and consolidated its position as a peaceful and leading regional player. The initiative should also be viewed as an Indonesian attempt to enhance its managerial role in Southeast Asia. Despite their partial success, the Workshops have never been incorporated within the institutional framework of the Association.

China's willingness to show restraint vis-à-vis ASEAN claimants was questioned when on 25 February 1992 Beijing passed the Law of the People's Republic of China on the Territorial Waters and Contiguous Areas. It reiterated China's claims in the South China Sea and stipulated the right to use force to protect islands, including the Spratlys, and their surrounding waters. Though only repeating the traditional Chinese claims in the South China Sea, the law questioned the peaceful management of the territorial dispute and was regarded by the Association as a political provocation that contradicted prior diplomatic gestures towards the member states. In May 1992, the PRC also granted an oil exploration concession to the US-based Crestone Energy Corporation in the Vanguard Bank, a zone claimed by Vietnam as part of its continental shelf. The PRC guaranteed to protect these installations by force if necessary. China's first oil concession contradicted Li Peng's proposal for joint exploration and development of the Spratlys and challenged the Vietnamese leadership. In 1994, Hanoi granted an oil exploration concession to Mobil Corporation within an area of the Vanguard Bank claimed by the PRC.

The ASEAN members responded to the Chinese law during their annual meeting of the foreign ministers held in Manila in July 1992. The ministerial session led to the formulation of the ASEAN Declaration on the South China Sea, which was an outcome of the joint statement of the Bandung Workshop of July 1991.[24] As ASEAN's first common position on the South China Sea, the Declaration was an attempt to promulgate an informal code of conduct based on self-restraint, the non-use of force and the peaceful resolution of disputes. It relied on the norms and principles initially introduced in the Treaty of Amity and Cooperation (TAC). Hence, it was a non-specific document that failed to move beyond the simple assertion of standard international principles to the context of the dispute. The Philippines had argued for a more precise document.[25] The Declaration stated that the foreign ministers: 'emphasize the necessity to resolve all sovereignty and jurisdictional issues pertaining to the South China Sea by peaceful means, without resort to force'; and 'urge all parties concerned to exercise restraint with the view to creating a positive climate for the eventual resolution of all disputes'.[26] They also 'command all parties concerned to apply the principles contained in the Treaty of Amity and Co-operation in Southeast Asia as the basis for establishing a code of international conduct over the South China Sea'.[27]

The Manila Declaration did not deal with the problem of sovereign jurisdiction over the Spratly Islands. It was not an expression of consensus on the territorial question but rather an attempt to ensure a peaceful management of the dispute. This informal code of conduct for the South China Sea should thus be associated with the notion of conflict avoidance rather than conflict resolution. Through its formulation, ASEAN conducted itself as an associative body by reaching a compromise on the South China Sea. The adoption of a broad diplomatic stand was an achievement as it reflected the cohesion of the Association despite intra-mural differences.[28] The Philippines, Malaysia and Brunei have conflicting claims in the Spratlys. The sovereignty question has also further complicated Philippine–Malaysian relations that have been strained since the 1960s by the territorial dispute over Sabah. For instance, Malaysian military forces intercepted in April 1988 three Philippine vessels, which were fishing in areas claimed by Malaysia and the Philippines as part of their EEZs. Thailand and Singapore have no territorial claims in the South China Sea and had therefore no benefit in taking a stand that implicitly criticized the Chinese law on Territorial Waters and Contiguous Areas. Despite these disparities, the member states shared an interest in promoting Southeast Asian stability and avoiding any confrontation with China. It was believed that a potential source of threat could be reduced by the emergence of an embryonic regime in the South China Sea based on ASEAN's norms and principles. Mak argues that the Manila Declaration was 'an attempt by the ASEAN members to handle China using non-military means as a specific response to a situation which could potentially disadvantage all the ASEAN countries'.[29]

Nevertheless, the relevance of the 1992 Declaration was reduced by the lack of external support. In contrast to its involvement in the Third Indochina Conflict, the ASEAN members were unable to rely on external players to advance their associative position. Leifer writes: 'The Declaration on the South China Sea was ASEAN's attempt to maintain its role in shaping regional order, but its diplomatic impact was far less than that registered during the Cambodian conflict. The changed pattern of international and regional alignments had reduced ASEAN's political significance.'[30]

While strongly supported by Vietnam that had adhered to the TAC during the 1992 ASEAN Ministerial Meeting (AMM), China was not receptive to the Declaration and did not formally adhere to its principles. Having a limited stake in ASEAN, Beijing could easily ignore the document and repeat its preference for bilateral rather than multilateral discussions on the South China Sea. The United States was unsupportive and maintained its position of neutrality in the territorial dispute despite the attendance of US Secretary of State James Baker at the 1992 Post-Ministerial Conference (PMC). Hence, ASEAN's associative position was not assisted by a favourable strategic context that would strengthen internationally the relevance of its norms and principles.

Some members of the Association aimed to internationalize the South China Sea dispute by putting it forward in multilateral meetings and international forums. Indonesia and other ASEAN states introduced the issue on the agenda of the Non-Aligned Conference held in Jakarta in September 1992. The South China Sea question was also addressed one month later in the ASEAN–European Union Dialogue. China's inclination to show restraint vis-à-vis the ASEAN claimants was repeated in 1993. While visiting Kuala Lumpur in May, China's Defence Minister Chi Haotian declared that the PRC would not resort to force to promote its claims in the Spratlys. Significantly, China agreed to participate in the ARF, which was inaugurated in July 1993. ASEAN's ambition to apply its norms and principles to the South China Sea was an underlying factor in the creation of the Forum. The Chinese participation in a multilateral dialogue was regarded as an approach to contribute to the peaceful management of the territorial dispute. Yet, the formation of the ARF undermined the traditional call for regional autonomy. However, regional autonomy had been affected since the end of the Cold War by increased security interdependence between North and Southeast Asia and the revival of some security concerns, above all the Spratly issue.

The first ARF meeting was held in Bangkok on 25 July 1994. The Spratly issue was mentioned briefly but not included in the 1994 chairman's statement. Though refusing to discuss the question of sovereign jurisdiction in a multilateral forum, China's Foreign Minister Qian Qichen repeated Beijing's peaceful intentions and rejected the resort to force as a means to solve the dispute. By limiting itself to bilateral negotiations with the other claimants, China aimed to dominate the discussions and avoid being outnumbered during multilateral sessions. This complicated ASEAN's attempt to develop a code of conduct for the South China Sea.

ASEAN's efforts were shattered by the 1995 Mischief Reef incident. China's assertive action in the Spratlys violated the norms and principles included in the 1992 Declaration and repeated in the context of the ARF. In spite of the first ministerial meeting held in July 1994, the construction of structures on the disputed reef had taken place during the second half of that year.[31] The PRC being dependent on investments and technology from ASEAN states, Segal writes that the 'conventional wisdom in East Asia was that China would no doubt continue to take territory claimed by Vietnam, but it would not encroach on territory claimed by ASEAN states'.[32] Instead, Beijing used force and broke the informal code of conduct that the Association had aimed to establish for the South China Sea. The Philippine President Fidel Ramos strongly criticized China's policy in the Spratlys and attempted to build up international support to condemn its latest action. The PRC and the Philippines agreed to hold talks and on 10 August 1995 signed a bilateral statement that rejected the use of force and called for the peaceful resolution of their bilateral disputes in accordance with the principles of the 1982 Convention on the Law of the Sea.[33]

The ASEAN states formulated no common complaint. Singapore, Thailand and Malaysia were eager not to antagonize China in light of the economic and security interests at stake. This provoked disunity among the member states. Leifer explains that 'ASEAN's initial corporate response to the revelation of China's act of assertiveness was a deafening silence, indicative of internal dissent on how to cope with China as a rising power.'[34] ASEAN did not have the political will or necessary means to confront the PRC. Under pressure from the Philippines, the Association eventually repeated its commitment to the ASEAN Declaration on the South China Sea during a meeting held in Singapore on 18 March 1995. Though China was not mentioned, the ASEAN foreign ministers expressed their 'serious concern over recent developments which affect peace and stability in the South China Sea'.[35] They also called 'for the early resolution of the problems caused by the recent developments in Mischief Reef'.[36] The statement was supported by Vietnam. On the eve of the first ASEAN–China Senior Officials Meeting (SOM) in Hangzhou in April 1995, Chinese and ASEAN officials met for an informal meeting during which the latter expressed their concern about China's aggressive action. This diplomatic initiative surprised the Chinese representatives who were made to understand the political consequences of the Mischief Reef incident. Still, ASEAN's constructive and informal approach indicated the need to avoid any diplomatic confrontation with the PRC.

The second annual ARF meeting was held in Brunei on 1 August 1995. The ministerial meeting was influenced by the Mischief Reef incident and a deterioration of Chinese relations with Washington and Tokyo. Sino-US ties had worsened due to a private visit by Taiwanese President Lee Teng Hui to the United States in June 1995. Relations with Japan had been affected by China's testing of an underground nuclear device in May 1995 despite the coming extension of the Nuclear Non-Proliferation Treaty (NPT). The South China Sea issue was alluded to in the 1995 chairman's statement of the ARF. It stated that the participants 'encouraged all claimants to reaffirm their commitment to the principles contained in relevant international laws and convention, and the 1992 Declaration on the South China Sea'.[37] It also referred to the Workshops on the South China Sea. At China's insistence, the Mischief Reef incident was not openly discussed at the ARF meeting. Prior to the annual ministerial session, China's Foreign Minister Qian Qichen made concessions to the members of the Association at the ASEAN-PMC. He declared that the PRC was prepared to hold multilateral discussions on the Spratlys, rather than limit its diplomacy to bilateral talks, and to accept the 1982 Convention on the Law of the Sea as a basis for negotiation.[38] The Chinese concessions were made in an ASEAN context and were not directly raised at the ARF. They resulted primarily from a need to accommodate the Association and ease its worries in light of a deterioration of Chinese relations with the United States and Japan.[39] In addition, these concessions did not alter China's territorial objectives in the South China Sea. The PRC was still unwilling to address the question of sovereign jurisdiction and persistently repeated its territorial claims over nearly the entire area. Consequently, the 1995 concessions should not be associated with a new Chinese desire to respect an informal ASEAN code of conduct for the South China Sea.

After the events of 1995, China's conciliatory attitude towards the ASEAN states continued to emanate from short-term interests. Sino-US relations worsened in 1996 due to the Joint US–Japanese Declaration and the Taiwan Straits crisis. As a result, the PRC needed to preserve its political ties with the members of the Association to avoid potential diplomatic isolation in East Asia. Moreover, an aggressive policy in the South China Sea could entail an important economic cost. China's economic development had greatly benefited from and would continue to be in part dependent on prosperous economic relations with regional states. Finally, China's policy was influenced by its weak naval position in the Spratlys and the absence of concrete evidence on the oil reserves of the South China Sea. These factors led to a Chinese policy of self-restraint regarding the affirmation of its territorial ambitions in the South China Sea.[40] In addition, the PRC ratified the Law of the Sea Convention in May 1996.

Nonetheless, the new peaceful campaign towards the Association should not be overestimated. China did not alter its sovereignty claims over the South China Sea and it misused the 1982 Convention to strengthen its position in the territorial dispute. Though the Philippines and Indonesia are the only archipelagic states in the region, the PRC applied the archipelagic principle when drawing maritime baselines around the Paracel Islands. The illegal use of the principle was a source of concern to some ASEAN states, including the Philippines, Vietnam and Indonesia, which protested because it could be applied to the Spratly Islands in the future. The PRC also extended on 7 March 1997 its oil exploration in Vietnam's continental shelf, an action that Vietnam strongly criticized. ASEAN failed to formulate a statement to support Vietnam diplomatically. The installations were removed before the ASEAN–China SOM of 17–19 April 1997.[41] China again repeated its conciliatory rhetoric towards the Association during a meeting of the heads of state and government held in Kuala Lumpur in December 1997. The ASEAN states and the PRC jointly stated:

> they undertook to resolve their differences or disputes through peaceful means, without resorting to the threat or use of force. The parties concerned agreed to resolve their disputes in the South China Sea through friendly consultations and negotiations in accordance with universally recognized international law, including the 1992 UN Convention on the Law of the Sea.[42]

ASEAN's cohesion on the South China Sea issue was further reduced by the East Asian financial crisis of 1997–98. The need to focus on domestic economic problems diminished intra-mural solidarity and ASEAN's significance as a diplomatic player.[43] However, China did not take advantage of the vulnerability of the ASEAN claimants during the financial crisis to expand its occupation of the Spratly Islands.[44] On the contrary, it contributed to regional stability and enhanced its position in East Asia by not devaluing its currency and providing some financial assistance. The expansion of ASEAN membership in 1997 also complicated the process of consultation and the attainment of a consensus on the South China Sea. The newest members had no interest in the dispute and were eager not to antagonize Beijing. During the sixth formal summit held in Hanoi in December 1998, the ASEAN states only managed to call for the peaceful resolution of the disputes in the South China Sea in accordance with UNCLOS and the 1992 Manila Declaration. They also called on 'all parties concerned to exercise restraint and to refrain from taking actions that are inimical to the peace, security and stability of Southeast Asia and the Asia-Pacific region'.[45] The question of sovereignty was once again avoided. ASEAN seemed incapable of promoting a code of conduct for the South China Sea within as well as beyond the walls of its arrangement.

At the informal Manila Summit of November 1999, Malaysia dissented from a latest version of a code of conduct promoted by the Philippines and supported by Vietnam. The proposed code of conduct was an attempt to peacefully manage the South China Sea question by preventing a deterioration of the situation. In particular, it aimed to avert the additional occupation by the claimant states of disputed and still uninhabited features.[46] Though not a binding document, the initiative was more specific than the 1992 Manila Declaration. It tried to move beyond the simple assertion of standard principles and proposed joint development of the Spratly Islands. Besides Malaysia, the Philippine proposal was also rejected by the PRC. Malaysia's contrary position manifested a lack of intra-mural cohesion and embarrassed the Association. Until the early 1990s, Malaysia was critical of China's actions in the Spratly Islands. Yet, its diplomatic stand on the South China Sea changed over the following years and came closer to the Chinese position. Malaysia refused to address the question of sovereignty. It favoured bilateral negotiations with China and preferred to avoid a constraining regional code of conduct or external mediation.[47] The chairman's press statement at the informal summit only declared that the heads of state and government 'noted the report of the Ministers that ASEAN now has a draft regional code of conduct, and further consultations will be made on the draft with a view of advancing the process on the adoption of the code'.[48]

Preliminary meetings have since then been held with the PRC to identify the elements that ought to be included in the formulation of a joint code of conduct for the South China Sea. At a session in Thailand in March 2000, the member states and China agreed that a regional code of conduct should rely on the principles set forward in the UN Charter, the TAC and UNCLOS and on the Five Principles of Peaceful Coexistence. Moreover, it was decided that 'the code of conduct should include confidence-building measures and areas of cooperation, starting with those that are least controversial and easiest to implement.'[49] By the time of the thirty-fourth AMM in July 2001, the ASEAN–China consultations were still taking place to formulate a code of conduct for the South China Sea.[50]

Malaysia proposed a declaration for the Spratly Islands at the thirty-fifth AMM in Brunei in July 2002. Previously endorsed by the ASEAN senior officials, the non-binding document to regulate conduct in the disputed territory was a prudent and watered down compromise, even failing to mention the Spratlys by name. It was also unclear whether the agreement would be referred to as a code of conduct or as a declaration. The ASEAN foreign ministers hoped to approve the document during their ministerial meeting in order to submit it to China's Foreign Minister Tang Jiaxuan at the ASEAN–China session. The common position would therefore have served as a basis for negotiations with the PRC. Yet, most member states refused to support the Malaysian proposal, Vietnam insisting for instance on the adoption of a binding document on the South China Sea. Unable to reach a consensus, the foreign ministers only announced in their joint communiqué their decision to work closely with China towards a Declaration on the Conduct of Parties in the South China Sea.[51]

The ASEAN foreign ministers and China's Vice Foreign Minister Wang Yi finally signed a Declaration on the Conduct of Parties in the South China Sea on the sidelines of the eighth ASEAN summit in Phnom Penh in early November 2002. The agreement was intended to prevent further tensions over the disputed territories and to reduce the risks of military conflict in the South

China Sea. The parties stipulated their adherence to the principles of the UN Charter, UNCLOS, the TAC and the Five Principles of Peaceful Coexistence and reaffirmed their respect and commitment to 'the freedom of navigation in and overflight above the South China Sea'.[52] They agreed to resolve their territorial disputes by peaceful means, 'without resorting to the threat or use of force, through friendly consultations and negotiations by sovereign states directly concerned, in accordance with universally recognized principles of international law'.[53] The parties also pledged to practise self-restraint in activities that could spark disputes, such as inhabiting still uninhabited features, and to enhance their efforts to 'build trust and confidence between and among them'.[54] They agreed to exchange views among defence officials, to provide humane treatment to any person in danger or distress, and to give advance notice of military exercises on a voluntary basis. Finally, the declaration announced that the parties might cooperate in marine environmental protection and scientific research, safety of navigation, search and rescue operations and in combating transnational crime.

After years of negotiations, the declaration represented a significant move away from the original goal of reaching a detailed and binding code of conduct for the South China Sea. Malaysia had first proposed at the 2002 AMM that ASEAN and China consider issuing a political declaration instead of a long hoped for code of conduct and Kuala Lumpur especially was keen for the document to be approved at the summit in November that year. The political declaration was essentially an interim accord. It stated: 'The Parties concerned reaffirm that the adoption of a code of conduct in the South China Sea would further promote peace and stability in the region and agree to work, on the basis of consensus, towards the eventual attainment of this objective.'[55]

Still, it is legitimate to question whether the ASEAN members and China will ever agree on a code of conduct for the South China Sea. All the claimants have stood firm on the question of sovereign jurisdiction and they failed to make any concession on this matter in the political declaration. Moreover, approval of this watered-down document demanded concessions that demonstrated once again the difficulty of ever concluding a code of conduct. As a result of China's requests, the ASEAN members agreed to include 'on the basis of consensus' when referring to the eventual attainment of a code of conduct and to drop the phrase 'erection of structures' from the paragraph invoking the exercise of self-restraint. Vietnam had demanded that the declaration include a commitment not to build new structures on the islands and China's refusal might have indicated its intentions to erect additional foundations to strengthen its military presence in the Spratlys. Finally, the political declaration made no reference to its specific geographical scope, primarily because China opposed any mention of the Paracel Islands. In short, the document could not be expected to prevent the occurrence of incidents over territorial claims in the South China Sea.

Besides the ASEAN–China consultations, no advance on a code of conduct for the South China Sea has been made by the ARF. Due to China's pressure, the dispute has been addressed in general terms but never directly in the annual ministerial sessions or in the context of the Inter-Sessional Support Group on Confidence-Building Measures (CBMs). The South China Sea was mentioned in the chairman's statement that concluded the third ARF meeting in Jakarta in July 1996. It welcomed the efforts of the parties involved to seek solutions in accordance with UNCLOS and referred to the contributions of the Workshops on the South China Sea.[56] Similar points were repeated in the statements that concluded the following annual ministerial meetings. The 1999 chairman's statement emphasized the freedom of navigation and noted the commitment made by the claimants to exercise self-restraint and to resolve peacefully the disputes in the South China Sea.[57] The issue was not addressed in any meaningful way at the seventh and eighth ARF meetings organized respectively in Bangkok in July 2000 and in Hanoi in July 2001. The chairman's statement of the 2002 meeting simply 'noted that the adoption of a code of conduct in the South China Sea would further promote peace and stability in the region'.[58] China argues that the problem of sovereign jurisdiction concerns only a few states and that it should therefore not be raised within an ARF framework. The PRC does not want the Forum to become an institutional vehicle available to the ASEAN claimants to internationalize the territorial dispute. Moreover, it is keen to avoid US involvement in the issue. The United States has so far only indicated its concern regarding the absence of diplomatic progress.

ASEAN's failure to develop a code of conduct among the claimant states results from several factors. The PRC has constantly repeated that its sovereignty over the South China Sea is indisputable. Partly due to a need to preserve their domestic political legitimacy, Chinese leaders refuse to make any concession on the issue. China has held bilateral talks with ASEAN claimants and has succeeded in dividing them by offering bilateral codes of conduct that would benefit their separate interests. This has further weakened ASEAN's ability to conduct itself as an associative body. Beijing seems only prepared to support a non-binding multilateral code of conduct that would be limited to the Spratly Islands and focus on dialogue and the preservation of regional stability rather than the problem of sovereign jurisdiction. In short, the formulation of an ASEAN diplomatic stand has been undermined by China's intransigence and its ability to control negotiation on the territorial question. Unable to impose its initiatives, ASEAN's influence on the South China Sea dispute is clearly limited.

Nevertheless, the absence of a consensus among the ASEAN states over the South China Sea needs to be kept in mind. The members have differential relationships with the PRC and contrasting views on its potential threat. In addition, some members have conflicting claims in the Spratlys while others are not concerned about the problem of sovereignty. These sources of disunity have complicated the attainment of a collective stance.

The ASEAN claimants involved in the dispute are unwilling to make concessions with regard to their territorial claims and have failed to address the problem of sovereign jurisdiction. This has weakened ASEAN in its talks with the PRC. The question of sovereignty is central to the calculations of the member states and is the cause of most bilateral disputes within the Association.[59] The constant search for solidarity and consensus building has resulted in the failure even to discuss these matters. Finally, cooperation on the South China Sea has been affected by persisting mistrust among the ASEAN claimants. The strained relations between Malaysia and the Philippines are significant for instance when examining the lack of consensus.

The absence of cohesion also results from the fact that the problem of sovereignty over the Spratly Islands does not yet represent a direct danger to the national security of individual members.[60] In contrast, Vietnam's invasion of Cambodia in December 1978 affected Thailand's security environment and located hostile military forces on its eastern border. Additionally, the events in Indochina had a domestic relevance due to the communist insurgencies operating within the ASEAN states. These explicit threats do not exist in the case of the South China Sea. Still, Vietnam and the Philippines feel endangered by China's actions in the Spratlys. Vietnam perceives its relation with the PRC over the South China Sea as a reflection of its traditional antagonism and patterns of power with Beijing. By seizing Mischief Reef, China has demonstrated the Philippine weakness that has resulted from the 1992 US withdrawal.

In sum, the enlarged and weakened Association, which lacks the political will and cohesion to address the South China Sea problem, cannot be compared to the entity that collectively opposed the Vietnamese occupation of Cambodia. Despite conflicting interests and the lack of a shared threat perception, the ASEAN states showed unity in their diplomatic stand against the puppet regime in Phnom Penh. A similar associative position has not been achieved in the case of the Spratlys. If an embryonic regime seemed to be emerging in the early 1990s, it was seriously affected by the Mischief Reef incident. Only applied to the Association, the 1992 Manila Declaration has not been respected by all the member states. Frictions over the disputed territories have occurred between the ASEAN claimants and in August 2002 Vietnamese troops based on one islet fired warning shots at Philippine military planes. Moreover, some members have used military means to take control of reefs claimed by other states. For example, Malaysia's seizure in March 1999 of Investigator Shoal, claimed by the Philippines, strained relations with Manila but was also criticized by Vietnam, Brunei and China. Recent attempts to formulate a code of conduct for the South China Sea have failed. As an interim accord, the Declaration on the Conduct of Parties in the South China Sea is a step in the right direction, though certainly not a landmark agreement as stated in the ASEAN rhetoric. Yet, it may also be regarded as an abdication on the part of the Association regarding its original objective of attaining a detailed and binding code of conduct.

Undoubtedly, ASEAN is short of external backing, which significantly reduces its associative influence. Yet, the lack of external assistance seems to result to a certain extent from the absence of cohesion among the ASEAN members over the South China Sea dispute.

Balance of power dimension

ASEAN's inability to conduct itself as an associative body with reference to the South China Sea problem has been discussed. Let us now examine its initiatives to bring the balance of power to bear. The South China Sea dispute is directly related to the issue of the regional distribution of power. If it succeeds in realizing its territorial claims, China will gain an hegemonic position in maritime Southeast Asia. This final sub-section argues that ASEAN is unable on its own to constrain Chinese actions in the Spratly Islands and lacks access to an external source of countervailing power.

It is important though not to exaggerate the current Chinese military threat in the South China Sea. Despite the ongoing modernization of its navy, China's naval position in the Spratly Islands remains weak. Disposing of a small power projection, the PRC has not extensively increased its ability to sustain naval operations away from its mainland bases. Most features in the Spratly archipelago are too small to offer bases for further naval activities. China's lack of air power in the Spratlys also limits its influence. Hence, the PRC does not currently possess the necessary capabilities to control the Spratly group militarily. Furthermore, command over the maritime communication routes that cross the South China Sea may only result from a significant naval dominance and superiority in the region rather than the occupation of tiny features that may not offer a legitimate basis for claiming maritime jurisdiction.[61] The PRC does not yet possess the technology, military capabilities and power projection to impose such a naval hegemony in Southeast Asia. Still, military power should also be examined in relative terms and in light of regional standards.[62] China disposes of a significant military advantage when compared to some vulnerable Southeast Asian states that fear its regional hegemonic ambitions. Moreover, China's conciliatory attitude towards the ASEAN states 'may be interpreted as a pragmatic but impermanent tactic intended to buy time, and to foster complacency in Southeast Asia, until China possesses sufficient military power to back up its South China Sea claims with force'.[63] In sum, the South China Sea dispute is still a political rather than a military issue that challenges the ASEAN claimants. In the longer run, it could become a military threat and the dominant security concern in Southeast Asia. In the meantime, an armed conflict seems unlikely although risks exist of miscalculations or accidents that could lead to limited confrontation.

The Association is unable on its own to act as an effective source of countervailing power in the South China Sea. A conventional practice of balance of power politics is unachievable due to the limitations associated with cooperative security, which excludes military cooperation and relies on an intra-mural basis. Focusing on conflict avoidance and management, ASEAN is devoid of two elements essential for any formal or tacit alliance: joint military capabilities and the existence of a common threat perception. A move towards alliance formation to contain a Chinese threat would be in accordance with a realist interpretation of security cooperation. Yet, ASEAN has not indicated in the post-Cold War any disposition to evolve into a defence arrangement. Even if such a transformation occurred, it would not have the joint military capabilities to deter Chinese actions in the Spratly Islands. Contradictory security perspectives within the Association have also undermined the potential development of an alliance in Southeast Asia. The lack of a common position on the PRC caused intra-mural tensions during the Third Indochina Conflict and has led to divisions with regard to the South China Sea dispute in the post-Cold War. In short, any kind of military cooperation over the Spratly issue seems particularly unlikely.

The absence of a common threat perception among the ASEAN states was, for example, demonstrated in 1995. The PRC took advantage of Philippine vulnerability to expand its presence in the Spratly Islands but perhaps also to test the US reaction and involvement in the South China Sea problem.[64] Manila viewed the Chinese occupation of Mischief Reef as a danger to its national security mostly because it represented 'a breach of the regional *modus vivendi* which regional states had been painstakingly trying to develop'.[65] The Philippines responded firmly to the discovery of the Chinese occupation of Mischief Reef by seeking multilateral support and taking retaliatory measures that included the destruction of Chinese territorial markers on other features and the arrest of Chinese fishermen in March 1995. The Philippines also announced a defence modernization programme. However, its navy has remained so ill-equipped that it cannot even be expected to patrol the *Kalayaan*.

Indonesia's traditional threat perception was confirmed by the Mischief Reef incident and the suspected extension of Chinese claims to include the Natuna region.[66] China's behaviour reinforced the fear among the military elite of a Chinese irredentist policy in the South China Sea. During his visit to the PRC in July 1995, Indonesia's Foreign Minister Ali Alatas was provided with no clarification regarding the Chinese claims to the waters above the Natuna gas fields. Indonesia's involvement in the territorial dispute and the need to develop a deterrence strategy against the PRC played a part in Suharto's decision to sign a security agreement with Australia in December 1995. Initiated by Paul Keating, the Australian prime minister at the time, the agreement was influenced by three considerations.[67] It was an attempt to reduce persisting mistrust between two states that had no territorial designs on each other. In particular, the agreement indicated that Indonesia should not be perceived in Australia as a possible threat to its security. It also tacitly acknowledged that both states shared a common strategic outlook and similar security concerns. Finally, it was influenced by the close personal links that existed between Suharto and Keating. The two leaders discussed the forthcoming agreement during private meetings held in Jakarta in June 1995 and at the APEC summit in Osaka in November.[68] Jakarta failed to inform its ASEAN partners prior to the joint announcement made by Australia and Indonesia at the ASEAN heads of state and government meeting in Bangkok in December 1995.

Both Ali Alatas and Lt General TNI Agus Widjojo explained to the author that the security agreement was not developed with a common external threat in mind.[69] They pointed out that it should therefore not be considered as a defence arrangement against the PRC. The bilateral agreement had mostly a political and psychological significance and did not modify Indonesia's defence capabilities. Yet, it marked a revision of strategic outlook by Indonesia and could still be examined as an example of conventional balance of power politics. Indonesia and Australia shared a security interest in constraining Chinese actions in the South China Sea. The agreement mentioned the possibility of joint military operations and was regarded regionally as formalizing existing defence ties between the two states. It declared that Indonesia and Australia would consult 'in the case of adverse challenges to either party or to their common security interests and, if appropriate, consider measures which might be taken either individually or jointly and in accordance with the processes of each party'.[70] The agreement sent a political signal to Beijing and indirectly consolidated Indonesia's defence ties with the United States. In addition to cooperative security, Indonesia seemed now willing to rely on traditional countervailing tactics to manage its relations with the PRC and restrain China's irredentist ambitions in the South China Sea. In September 1996, Indonesia also held extensive military exercises in the Natuna region. Discussing these exercises, a security analyst at the Indonesian Institute of Science declared that though Indonesia is engaged diplomatically with the PRC, it 'would be foolish for us to be completely naive. China respects strength. If they see you as being weak, they'll eat you alive.'[71]

In the meanwhile, Malaysia and Singapore adopted a more conciliatory attitude towards the PRC. Malaysia was eager to preserve and further develop its economic ties with China, even at the cost of collective solidarity towards another ASEAN member. In January 1995, Malaysia's Prime Minister Dr Mahathir Mohamad declared that 'it is high time for us to stop seeing China through the lenses of threat and to fully view China as the enormous opportunity that it is.'[72] While indicating the shift in Malaysia's threat perception, the statement was also an implicit criticism of the Philippines. As noted above, bilateral relations have long been strained by the territorial dispute over Sabah and complicated by conflicting claims over the Spratlys, as for example manifested by Malaysia's seizure of Investigator Shoal in March 1999. Additionally, the two states have followed contrasting approaches with regard to the PRC and the South China Sea problem. The

Philippines has aimed to internationalize the territorial question while Malaysia has been more inclined to negotiate bilaterally with China. During his visit to the PRC in May 1995, Singapore's Prime Minister Goh Chok Tong mentioned the need to discuss the feeling of insecurity that the Chinese policy in the South China Sea provoked among the ASEAN members.[73] Yet, rather than an actual sign of concern, this declaration was meant to confirm the Southeast Asian identity of the city-state and express ASEAN solidarity.[74] In an interview with the *Straits Times*, Senior Minister Lee Kuan Yew played down the Mischief Reef incident and China's aggressiveness in the South China Sea.[75] In short, Singapore was keen not to alienate the PRC.

Despite its limitations, ASEAN's diplomatic position on the Spratly issue was strengthened by its enlargement to include Vietnam at the AMM in July 1995. The Paris Accords of 1991 and Vietnam's withdrawal from Cambodia had started a process of détente between Vietnam and the ASEAN states. Suharto had already travelled to Vietnam in 1990. In November 1991, Vietnam's Prime Minister Vo Van Kiet had visited Indonesia, Malaysia and Singapore. Prior to the trip, Vietnam had indicated its desire to become a member of the Association. Regional relations had thus been radically transformed by the time of the fourth ASEAN summit held in Singapore in January 1992. Vietnam adhered to the TAC in July 1992 during the annual meeting of the ASEAN foreign ministers and was invited to participate as an observer to future occasions. Its forthcoming membership was announced in December 1994. The enlargement presented some difficulties. ASEAN became more deeply embroiled in the Spratly issue and lost its neutral position in the territorial dispute over the Paracel Islands. Different security outlooks also coexisted among the original members. Indonesia regarded Vietnam as an ally against China's regional ambitions and actively supported its participation. In contrast, Thailand was in competition with Vietnam over influence in Cambodia and Laos. In addition, Thailand and Singapore were still concerned about a potential Vietnamese threat and wished to maintain their strong ties with the PRC.

The first post-Cold War enlargement should be analysed through both associative and balance of power perspectives. It was related to the original hope of uniting the entire sub-region under ASEAN auspices and symbolized the institutionalization of a process of diplomatic reconciliation between Vietnam and the member states. An analogy can be made with the associative origins of ASEAN, which primarily resulted from an act of reconciliation between Indonesia and Malaysia. Though Vietnam had been invited to join the TAC in 1976, its membership was unthinkable until the end of the Cold War due to the ideological polarization of the region and the Cambodian conflict. The enlargement enabled the original members to cope peacefully with Vietnam and strengthen the political unity and cohesion of Southeast Asia.[76] Balance of power politics played a part in the expansion process. Kissinger writes: 'Though they will disavow it, the nations of Southeast Asia are including the heretofore feared Vietnam in their grouping (ASEAN) largely in order to balance China and Japan.'[77] At issue was the need to constrain China's actions in the South China Sea. The rapid inclusion of Vietnam was perceived by the PRC as a means for the Southeast Asian states to restrain its manoeuvres in the Spratlys and combine against its territorial claims. Although ASEAN did not provide Vietnam with a source of countervailing power, Hanoi joined the cooperative security regime with the regional distribution of power in mind. The new membership provided Vietnam with a countervailing factor in its relations with the PRC. It expected more Chinese restraint towards the Vietnamese claims in the South China Sea due to its participation in the political association.

Nevertheless, the institutionalization of the process of reconciliation between Vietnam and the original ASEAN states, which influenced the normalization of US–Vietnamese relations on 11 July 1995, has not modified the regional distribution of power to their advantage. On the contrary, the PRC has been the prime beneficiary of the changing strategic circumstances in East Asia in the post-Cold War. Moreover, Vietnam's membership has not improved ASEAN's ability to practise conventional balance of power politics to constrain Chinese actions in the Spratlys. ASEAN's relevance as an effective countervailing force has also been undermined by the loss of Indonesian leadership. As the largest member of the Association, Indonesia may have been expected with the assistance of Vietnam and Australia to lead a common stand in opposition to China's potential hegemonic ambitions in Southeast Asia. This is now unlikely in view of its deep internal problems. Its relations with Australia were also complicated during 1999 by the issue of East Timor, which led Jakarta to repudiate its security agreement with Canberra in September that year. Except for some support from Vietnam, the Philippines is therefore isolated in its attempt to resist the Chinese claims in the Spratlys.[78] The Association failed, for example, to support Manila in its protest against the Chinese expansion of its structures on Mischief Reef discovered in November 1998. The Philippine Foreign Affairs Under-Secretary Lauro Baja expressed a sense of isolation on 15 April 1999. Pointing out the lack of support, he declared in a speech to the Rotary Club that 'some of our ASEAN friends are either mute, timid or cannot go beyond espousal of general principle of peaceful settlement of disputes and polite words of understanding given in the corridors or meeting rooms.'[79]

In short, the Association cannot operate on its own as an effective source of countervailing power and needs to rely on external military support to constrain China's actions in the Spratlys. Yet, ASEAN does not enjoy access to an external source of countervailing power. The member states involved in the territorial question, above all the Philippines, do not benefit from external military assistance to contain the PRC in the South China Sea. Discussing the dispute, Leifer explains that the Association 'has no power to deploy because it is neither a defence community nor a party to a countervailing structure of alignments'.[80] In that respect, the Third Indochina Conflict and the South China Sea dispute indicate very different patterns of power. The favourable strategic circumstances that prevailed during the Cambodian conflict, which resulted from a convergence of interests between China, the US and the ASEAN members, have disappeared in the post-Cold War. The new distribution of power and the transformed security relations in East Asia account for ASEAN's limited influence on the South China Sea dispute.

The US departure from its military bases in the Philippines removed a source of deterrence against Chinese actions in the *Kalayaan*, as an ongoing US presence might for instance have dissuaded the PRC from taking control of Mischief Reef. China has become a dominant strategic player in the South China Sea due to the 1992 US withdrawal, Japan's limited involvement in the area and the scaling down of Russian naval activities in Vietnam.[81] However, Singapore reached an agreement with Washington in November 1990. Despite its good relations with the PRC, the city-state was eager to secure a US engagement to uphold a stable distribution of power in Southeast Asia. Singapore's decision to accommodate US facilities was first not well received in Malaysia and Indonesia. These views later changed with the planning of the US withdrawal from the Philippines. After 1992, Malaysia and Indonesia were prepared to provide access to the US Navy. The Royal Malaysian Navy had already been conducting annual joint exercises with the US Navy since 1984.[82] Singapore extended its links with the United States in 1992 when a US Navy logistics unit was relocated from the Philippines to the city-state. In January 1998, Singapore announced that US aircraft carriers would have access to the Changi Naval Base after its completion in the year 2000.[83] Even the Philippines has attempted to lessen the effect of the 1992 US withdrawal. Initially signed on 10 February 1998, the Philippine Senate ratified in May 1999 a Visiting Forces Agreement with the United States that enabled the resumption of joint military exercises. The Philippine desire to reach a bilateral agreement with Washington only seven years after the American departure can be associated with its inability to patrol and protect the *Kalayaan*. Hence, the US deployment in Southeast Asia has not been overly affected by its withdrawal from Subic Bay Naval Base and Clark Air Base. Furthermore, the US strategic involvement in Southeast Asia has increased after the terrorist attacks on 11 September 2001. The Bush administration deployed around 1,000 soldiers to the southern Philippines in late January 2002 for a period of six months to train, advise and provide logistical assistance to the Philippine army combating Abu Sayyaf. Washington has linked the rebel group to the al-Qaeda network. The Philippines is the only ASEAN member that has so far welcomed US military troops on its territory since the terror attacks in the United States.

The absence of an external source of countervailing power to constrain Chinese actions in the Spratlys does not result from a US strategic retreat. Instead, it arises from a US unwillingness to get involved with the question of sovereign jurisdiction. In contrast to Taiwan and the Korean peninsula, the US Congress does not consider the South China Sea dispute as a vital security concern.[84] Though following closely the developments in the South China Sea, the United States has consistently limited its interest to the preservation of the freedom of navigation and the mobility of its Seventh Fleet. Joseph Nye, former US assistant secretary of defence for international security, said on 16 June 1995 that the United States would ensure the free passage of ships in the case of a conflict in the Spratlys that would affect the freedom of navigation.[85] Due to its own economic interests, the PRC is not expected to interrupt the shipping lanes that cross the South China Sea. Washington has also stated that the Philippine-claimed territories were not covered by the Mutual Defence Treaty of 30 August 1951 that ties the Philippines to the United States. For instance, the Mischief Reef incident did not lead to a strong US diplomatic reaction, except for a statement on freedom of sea lanes. The US Department of State declared on 10 May 1995:

> The United States takes no position on the legal merits of the competing claims to sovereignty over the various islands, reefs, atolls and cays in the South China Sea. The United States would, however, view with serious concern any maritime claim, or restriction on maritime activity, in the South China Sea that was not consistent with international law, including the 1982 United Nations Convention on the Law of the Sea.[86]

The US unwillingness to get involved in the territorial dispute may result from a desire not to complicate further its relations with the PRC but also from the lack of cohesion among the ASEAN members over the South China Sea dispute. In fact, the benefits provided by a US involvement would most likely be limited due to the absence of an intra-mural consensus.[87] Moreover, some member states, primarily Malaysia and Indonesia, do not support the need for a more direct US participation in the Spratly issue.[88] No other external source of countervailing power exists. The Russian influence in Southeast Asia has dramatically declined since the end of the Cold War. Despite the economic and strategic interests at stake, Japan has not developed a coherent and active policy on the South China Sea problem. As a legacy of the Pacific War, most ASEAN states fear the prospect of Japan extending its security role in East Asia. In short, though China does not dispose of the necessary capabilities to impose a naval hegemony in Southeast Asia, the military imbalance in the South China Sea should be expected to increase and may influence the PRC to use force to solve the territorial dispute.[89]

Conclusion

ASEAN's involvement in the South China Sea has been defined by the absence of associative and balance of power dimensions. No code of conduct is currently applied to the dispute nor does an associative position unite the member states. All the ASEAN countries have not respected the 1992 Declaration on the South China Sea and recent attempts by the Association to formulate a code of conduct have failed. Instead, China and ASEAN signed a Declaration on the Conduct of Parties in the South China Sea, a non-binding and watered-down document that might lead, though this is rather unlikely, to the adoption of a detailed and binding code of conduct. Moreover, the Association has failed to bring the balance of power to bear in the South China Sea. Its involvement in the dispute has been defined by the absence of conventional balance of power politics due to the limitations associated with cooperative security and the lack of access to an external source of countervailing power. Similar factors help explain the absence of associative and balance of power perspectives. The lack of shared principles and a common threat perception complicate the attainment of a common stand on an extra-mural security issue. The unavailability of external diplomatic and military support, which results to a certain extent from the absence of intra-mural cohesion over the territorial dispute, weakens ASEAN's collective efforts and makes the practice of conventional balance of power politics unachievable.

Conclusion

This book has offered a persistent analysis of the influence of the balance of power factor on the formation and later developments of ASEAN and the ARF. It has done so in the light of claims made in the literature that they are best understood as exemplars of cooperative security, which poses as an alternative to traditional balance of power approaches. The balance of power, defined both in a conventional and unconventional manner, should be focused on when analysing both arrangements. Studying the balance of power factor is required to achieve a good understanding of their history. Its central role has been to deny hegemony within and beyond cooperative security. Its purpose is to keep a cooperative security regime and its participants secure from threatening hegemonic states both at an intra- and extra-mural level. The constraining of power is dependent on political means within cooperative security and on a conventional source of countervailing power when the regime is faced with an external military threat.

In addition to indicating the applicability of balance of power considerations, this book has focused on the coexistence between associative and balance of power dimensions in the case of ASEAN and the ARF. It has thus rejected a dichotomy of interpretations. It has demonstrated instead the presence of coexisting perspectives influencing the operation of associative arrangements and the calculations of their participants. The intention has not been, however, to determine which aspect has been more influential. Indeed, it is impossible to measure the relative importance of the associative and balance of power dimensions, as they have been mutually re-enforcing.

Finally, beyond noting the coexistence of associative and balance of power perspectives, this book has determined the kind of relationship that has existed between them. The associative experience and the constraining of power have been closely intermingled in the modalities of ASEAN and the ARF. Both regimes for cooperative security were partly constructed and later developed with the denial of hegemony in mind. Balance of power considerations are part of the process of cooperative security. On the one hand, the constraining of power needs to be identified in the context of the associative dimension, and especially with reference to norms and principles advanced by a cooperative security regime. The operation of the balance of power factor is reliant on the associative evolution of the regime. On the other hand, norms and principles promoted by an associative arrangement formalize regional power relationships and play a key role in the management of an intra-mural distribution of power by political means. In short, rather than displacing the cooperative security model, the book has shown that it depends upon and cannot preclude the balance of power factor, especially as policy-makers in Southeast Asia frequently draw on a strong sense of realism.

The balance of power factor within and beyond cooperative security

The object of this book has been to indicate a dimension of the balance of power concept that has not often been discussed in theoretical and empirical studies. Beyond its conventional understanding, the balance of power can also be interpreted in political terms. This is based on the premise that potential hegemonic dispositions can be restrained through political and institutional means and without the use of war, the traditional instrument of the balance. Rather than offering a reformulation of the balance of power theory, the study has thus focused on one specific dimension of the traditional concept, which has frequently been ignored in the International Relations literature.

The interpretation of the balance of power factor within cooperative security is based on the general principles and assumptions found in the conventional understanding of the concept. The analysis of this factor needs to be positioned in the traditional problem of security, namely how do states secure themselves from possible external aggressions? To preserve their survival, states focus on the prevention of global or regional dominance by a potential menacing hegemon. The balance of power ensures that no single actor becomes so powerful so as to challenge the sovereignty and independence of other states. By preserving its central logic, the notion of a balance of power factor within cooperative security holds the core simplicity and explanatory qualities of the traditional concept. However, attention needs to be given to the differences between balance of power in its conventional interpretation and practice and the balance of power factor within cooperative security regimes. The constraining of power within cooperative security is dependent on political rather than military means. As a result, the method by which power is constrained distinguishes the balance of power factor from a more conventional application of the concept. This represents an important adjustment to the traditional interpretation of the balance of power.

The balance of power factor within cooperative security needs to be identified in the context of norms and principles promoted by an associative arrangement. At issue is the constraint imposed on larger participants through their stake in a cooperative security regime and from which smaller and medium states can benefit to enhance their own security. Hence, power sensitivities remain prevalent despite the apparent dominance of the coperative process. A common code of conduct based on standard international norms and respected by all the member states constrains the larger participants and ensures that they do not threaten their smaller cooperative partners. Any aggressive action or act of hegemony would undermine these norms and rebound adversely on the political cohesion of a security regime as well as on the interest of larger participants with a stake in its viability. Serving as a means to contain hegemonic dispositions, norms and principles advanced by a regime for cooperative security play a central part in the denial of hegemony. In short, the restraint resulting from political association has a power balancing relevance. In contrast to this interpretation, the application of standard international norms has often been viewed as in conflict with the operation of the balance of power.

The balance of power factor is both a source of strength and weakness within a cooperative security regime. It promotes the cooperative process and the application of associative principles by constraining intra-mural hegemonic dispositions. It provides an additional incentive to cooperate by preventing unrestrained struggles through the institutionalization of the constraining of power. In that regard, the balance of power factor positively influences the creation and institutional evolution of a cooperative security regime. Nevertheless, it provides expression of the limits of the cooperative process. The persistence of contradictory strategic perspectives and competing security interests restrict the institutional development of the regime. The ongoing relevance of the balance of power factor within cooperative security therefore casts doubt upon a neo-liberal analysis that infers a gradual and progressive approach to security cooperation.

This book has focused on the workings of cooperative security regimes but also in the case of ASEAN on its interaction with the outside world. The constraining of power through political and institutional channels has no relevance outside of cooperative security. External players have only a limited stake in the norms promoted by a cooperative security regime, which functions exclusively on an intra-mural basis. Moreover, a conventional practice of balance of power politics is unachievable due to the limitations associated with cooperative security, which excludes alliance formation. A cooperative security arrangement is thus dependent on an external source of countervailing power when faced with an external military threat. Hence, its activities become reliant in these circumstances on a favourable strategic context. In the absence of external military support, an associative arrangement is unable to exert diplomatic influence beyond the walls of its political association.

The balance of power factor within and beyond cooperative security is characterized by a commitment to the preservation of regional order and the national sovereignty of individual states. This factor should be associated with a vision of regional order that emphasizes the sanctity of state sovereignty and non-intervention in the internal affairs of states. The fundamental purpose of the balance of power factor is to keep a cooperative security regime and its participants secure from threatening hegemonic powers both at an intra- and extra-mural level rather than to create and uphold a power equilibrium in the international system. This distinguishes the study of the concept from a systemic interpretation of the balance of power theory. Finally, the operation of the balance of power factor is dependent on the actions of states. The concept is discussed as an expression of policy rather than as a deterministic description of the international system. The notion of choice in the formulation and implementation of foreign policy is clearly present in this study. Great attention has been given to the consequences of individual power calculations, foreign policy choices and inter-state interactions on the regional cooperative process.

The influence of the balance of power on ASEAN and the ARF

This book has aimed to address one core question: to what extent may the balance of power, defined in policy terms, play a part in ASEAN and the ARF and in the calculations of their participants? Both these regimes for cooperative security can be regarded as attempts to move beyond conventional balance of power tactics but not as steps to move beyond the core objective of the balance of power, namely the denial of hegemony through constraining hegemonic dispositions. Yet, the identities and priorities of institutions change over time. Hence, one should not expect a single outcome to arise from the examination of the balance of power factor but rather separate conclusions depending on the particular historical period considered. Three periods come to mind in the case of ASEAN. The formation and early institutional evolution of the Association (1967–75) were dominated by the need to cope with Indonesian power and influence, and constrain its hegemonic dispositions through its integration in an embryonic regime for cooperative security. This first period was defined by a denial of intra-mural hegemony through political measures. A second period (1975–91) was first characterized by the ASEAN states aiming to manage their relations with a reunited Vietnam and then by their diplomatic struggle against its invasion and occupation of Cambodia. An external dimension therefore came into play during these years. The reaction to Vietnam's policy in Indochina was reliant on conventional balance of power tactics that influenced intra-mural relations. In the post-Cold War, the ASEAN members have been confronted with China's rising power in East Asia, as for instance indicated by its irredentist agenda in the South China Sea. In response, the Association partly conceived the ARF with balance of power considerations in mind.

ASEAN and the constraining of Indonesia

The attitude of Indonesia needs to be discussed to understand the role of the balance of power factor within ASEAN. Indonesia was nearly a failed state in 1965. The economy had been terribly neglected by President Sukarno and the Indonesian state was starting to break down. General Suharto was aware that Indonesia would only succeed to play a central role in regional affairs after having first reached a level of domestic socio-economic viability. In fact, Jakarta would later expect ASEAN to represent a synergy between national and regional resilience. In a post-Confrontation period, Indonesia was keen to restore its credibility and was willing to follow a policy of self-constraint in order to promote domestic economic development within a framework of regional stability. The domestic economic imperatives of Indonesia had thus a direct impact on its patterns of behaviour within the emerging regime for cooperative security. Interestingly, ASEAN was originally not much more than a revival of ASA. Suharto sought to transform Indonesia into a good international citizen. The country needed to feel secure regionally and to be accepted and welcomed by former enemies, predominantly Malaysia. Furthermore, Suharto wanted ASEAN to provide Indonesia with a diplomatic barrier that would offer protection against Chinese infiltration and influence. By embracing a policy of self-restraint, Jakarta decisively influenced the formation and later success of the Association.

The original success of a cooperative security regime is dependent on willingness by the dominant power to follow a policy of self-restraint within the cooperative framework. Forced by domestic economic needs, Indonesia respected the intra-mural denial of hegemony and adopted a policy of political self-abnegation. This policy did not include a strategic dimension. Indonesia did not change its regional vision in principle and felt that it was entitled to a position of natural leadership within ASEAN as a result of its size, population, strategic location and military struggle for independence. In addition to its vast land area, the largest in Southeast Asia, Indonesia consists of an extensive maritime territory that derives from its status as an archipelagic state. Moreover, it is the largest Muslim nation in the world though its state identity has never been defined through Islam. Indonesia was recognized by the other members as first among equals and thus as the natural leader of the Association. It expected to become the prime manager of the regional order although its sense of entitlement was not articulated in an hegemonic fashion within ASEAN. It hoped for an autonomous regional order free from external intervention or interference. Its preference was indicated in the Bangkok Declaration, ZOPFAN and later in SEANWFZ and put forward through the principles of national and regional resilience, which were informally adopted as a shared security doctrine among the member states. In short, ASEAN was created partly to cope with Indonesia but also to institutionalize its managerial position in Southeast Asia.

The constraining of Indonesian power and influence within ASEAN should be identified in the context of norms and principles promoted by the regime for cooperative security. The restraint imposed on Indonesia resulted from its growing stake in ASEAN. As originally expressed in the Bangkok

Declaration of 1967, the Association has been committed to the principles of national sovereignty and non-interference in the domestic affairs of other states and has tried to reinforce their application in Southeast Asia. Significantly, Indonesia endorsed the Treaty of Amity and Cooperation (TAC) in February 1976 as a code of conduct to regulate regional inter-state relations. Though giving great importance to the power of norms to enhance order and stability, ASEAN's normative approach to international politics has been unexceptional. It has aimed to advance standard international norms that directly emanate from the principles of the Westphalian states system, constructed on the sovereignty of nation-states. Its approach to cooperative security has continued up to this day to rely on the conventional principles enunciated in the TAC.

Beyond an examination of the role of the balance of power in the formation of ASEAN, this book has shown the relevance of this factor on its initial period and on its expansion of membership in the case of Brunei. The operation of the balance of power factor was reliant on the political evolution of the regime for cooperative security. As a result of its interest in its viability, Indonesia was encouraged to adhere to the standard international norms promoted by ASEAN and particularly to respect the national sovereignty of the member states. The constraint imposed on the larger members directly benefited Brunei's security interests. The Sultanate was keen to secure its newly obtained sovereignty and perceived the arrangement as a form of defence for containing its neighbours, especially Malaysia. The practice of the balance of power by other than conventional means played an implicit role in the rationale for the enlargement and overlapped with the institutionalization of the act of reconciliation.

The member countries attempted during ASEAN's early years to manage an intra-mural distribution of power through political means. ASEAN operated as a grouping through which smaller and medium states could seek to defend their security interests through balance of power choices. The constraining of power within the Association was mostly relevant for the security and stability of maritime Southeast Asia. No equal distribution of power existed in the region as Indonesia continued to be viewed as a natural hegemon. Still, the ASEAN members did not 'bandwagon' with Indonesia as they hoped to restrain its behaviour rather than benefit from its potential aggressive actions. Indonesia displayed its willingness to follow a policy of self-restraint. It should be questioned how its pattern of behaviour evolved over time. Jakarta became restless during the Third Indochina Conflict. Thailand's imposition of a tacit alliance with China violated its preference for an autonomous management of the regional order. Indonesia resented the external interference in Southeast Asia and rejected China's policy of attrition against Vietnam; it regarded Vietnam as necessary to balance the PRC. Nevertheless, Jakarta accepted ASEAN's tacit alliance with Beijing in order to preserve the cohesion and unity of the regime for cooperative security.

Indonesia's status as a regional power has diminished since 1997 and the country has been embarrassed by a series of events. Over the past few years, it has faced deep internal difficulties, which have dramatically reduced its regional influence. It was most affected by the East Asian financial crisis of 1997–98 that drastically worsened its socio-economic problems and provoked the unexpected downfall of President Suharto in May 1998. Indonesia was embarrassed by the imposition of strict IMF conditions on loans required to stabilize its domestic economy. It has yet to recover from the consequences of the financial crisis and has been desperate for foreign investment. Indonesia was also forced to renounce its sovereignty over East Timor. The loss of territory was a deep humiliation for Jakarta and in particular for the armed forces. Separatist movements in Aceh and West Irian and sectarian violence in the Moluccas have brought instability to domestic politics. The issues of Aceh and West Irian need to be distinguished from the case of East Timor. The former were part of the Netherlands East Indies until the independence of the Republic of Indonesia in December 1949 while East Timor was under Portuguese control from 1520 up until 1975. In 1999 the ASEAN members officially declared their support for the territorial integrity of Indonesia in light of the events in Aceh and West Irian.[1] The need for such a collective position humiliated a state that used to represent the core political centre of the Association. Finally, the seriousness of the terrorist threat in Indonesia was demonstrated by the devastating bomb attacks on the island of Bali on 12 October 2002 that killed almost 200 people. The bombings have had severe security, political and economic repercussions on Indonesia and the rest of Southeast Asia. In short, rather than playing a crucial role in Southeast Asia, Indonesia has over the past few years been included in regional calculations as a great source of instability and as a case of a giant neighbouring state on the brink of collapse.

Indonesia's domestic instability has had important consequences on the Association. The current lack of leadership and the absence of a political centre have weakened ASEAN. Its success up until 1997 was dependent on Indonesia's stability and active participation. Suharto's commitment to regional cooperation was viewed regionally as a pillar for Southeast Asian security. The pivotal influence of individual leaders, primarily Suharto and Lee Kuan Yew, on the workings of the Association should therefore be noted. Although Indonesia is still committed to its policy of self-restraint, it is absorbed by domestic difficulties and has lost its managerial position within the cooperative security arrangement. Hence, it can no longer be perceived as the backbone of regional security nor as first among equals in ASEAN.

The importance of the balance of power factor within ASEAN needs to be reassessed due to the new context of Indonesia. The Association's relevance as a source of constraint is questionable because its dominant power is undermined by economic and political difficulties. Should

Indonesia still be regarded as a potential threat to regional stability and to the national sovereignty of some ASEAN members? It can be argued that Indonesia has not represented a conventional threat to the region and its cooperative partners for a long period of time. The primary danger for its neighbouring states presently arises from non-traditional security problems and from the potential consequences of its domestic instability. These issues include the threat of radical Islam, especially since the terror attacks in the United States on 11 September 2001 and the Bali bombings, as well as the illegal migration of Indonesian workers, the fear of Indonesia's fragmentation and the recurrence of ecological disasters with regional repercussions.

ASEAN and the power struggles in Indochina and the South China Sea

In the case of the Third Indochina Conflict, changes in the regional distribution of power were imposed on the ASEAN members. The latter demonstrated during the Cambodian conflict their ability to exercise international political influence, chiefly in the United Nations General Assembly. Still, ASEAN's reaction to the invasion and occupation of Cambodia was limited to collective diplomacy due to its lack of military capabilities and the existence of opposing strategic outlooks within the security regime. The conflict thus revealed the limits associated with cooperative security. Even so, the Association played an important diplomatic role in the Cambodian conflict thanks to favourable strategic circumstances that resulted from a convergence of interests between the PRC, the United States and the ASEAN members. In particular, its diplomatic response was conditional on China's willingness to act as a source of countervailing power against Vietnam. The engagement in conventional balance of power practice also became a factor in intra-mural cooperation. In sum, ASEAN operated successfully as a regime for co-operative security during the Cambodian conflict thanks to the application of balance of power tactics by external actors.

The settlement of the Cambodian conflict, which ensued directly from the nature of the end of the Cold War, changed ASEAN's security environment. It terminated the complementary interests that had united China and the Association during the 1980s and transformed Vietnam into a potential cooperative partner. Significantly, ASEAN's involvement in the South China Sea dispute has been limited, in contrast to its reaction to the Third Indochina Conflict, by the unfavourable strategic circumstances of the post-Cold War. ASEAN has failed to operate as a cooperative security arrangement with regard to the dispute in part due to the absence of an external source of countervailing power to contain China's hegemonic dispositions in the South China Sea. The Vietnamese membership has not improved ASEAN's ability to practise conventional balance of power politics and has more deeply embroiled the institution in the question of sovereign jurisdiction. The lack of external support can partly be explained by ASEAN's inability to develop a common position among its members and to promulgate a code of conduct for the South China Sea.

The ARF and the constraining of China in the post-Cold War

The Asia-Pacific security context at the end of the Cold War was defined by an uncertain multipolar structure. The regional strategic architecture was primarily dependent on a triangular relationship between the United States, Japan and the PRC. The formation of the ARF was an attempt to cope with a potential menacing hegemon through unconventional methods. Its creation, however, illustrated ASEAN's diminished significance in the new regional security context of the post-Cold War and represented an informal abdication of the commitment to realize ZOPFAN. The ASEAN members conceived the Forum partly as a diplomatic instrument for ensuring an ongoing US involvement in East Asia and for including the PRC in a rule-based arrangement to encourage it in habits of good international behaviour. ASEAN wanted China to be constrained in its actions by conforming to standard norms of international conduct. Significantly, the PRC has also come to perceive its participation in the ARF with reference to the balance of power. It has regarded the institution as a vehicle for promoting multipolarity in the Asia-Pacific to counter US unilateralism.

China may have recognized since the mid-1990s the advantages of adopting a restrained regional policy based on established norms. It has introduced an element of relative moderation in its foreign policy and has respected the standard international norms promoted by the ASEAN states through the ARF. For instance, China has played a constructive role with regards to the Korean peninsula and has been an active participant of the ASEAN + Three summit of heads of state and government. Moreover, Beijing's approach towards the South China Sea dispute has been temperate since the Mischief Reef incident.

Yet, it is questionable whether these developments have derived from ARF activities. The element of control in its foreign policy since the mid-1990s can be explained by its desire to improve relations with Southeast Asian nations in light of its complicated ties with the United States and Japan. The PRC has aimed to build up its relations with the ASEAN states, India and Russia as a means to promote a multipolar structure in the Asia-Pacific. It has also sought to maintain stable relations with the United States and Japan. The Chinese leadership has focused on domestic political stability and economic development in order to avoid the experiences of Russia and Indonesia. Moreover, it has been preoccupied with the domestic situation and with the force of nationalism in the PRC. Anti-Western sentiments were indicated, for instance, after the bombing of the Chinese Embassy in Belgrade in early 1999, which was viewed domestically as a direct US attack against Chinese people. Finally, the PRC may have realized that changing its perception abroad by downplaying the image of China as a threat would facilitate its acquisition of a great power status. Yet, it is unclear if its restrained behaviour has resulted from a substantial transformation among its leaders or simply from an exercise in international public relations.

Concluding remarks

Our interpretation of the balance of power factor within and beyond cooperative security has provided a conceptual framework for the study of ASEAN and the ARF. The balance of power factor has played an important part in both regimes for cooperative security and in the calculations of the participants. ASEAN and the ARF were established with the denial of hegemony in mind, but not in a conventional sense. The balance of power also became a factor in their later developments. Hence, an historical examination of both associative arrangements has enabled us to reject the notion that they should be defined as alternatives to the core objective of the balance of power. ASEAN and ARF practices have supported the operation of the balance of power although their rhetoric have implicitly rejected conventional balance of power politics.

The balance of power factor has influenced the creation and institutional evolution of ASEAN by constraining intra-mural hegemonic dispositions and providing some member states with an additional incentive to cooperate. By joining a tacit alliance with the PRC in the 1980s, the members also demonstrated a disposition to promote countervailing arrangements through diplomatic alignment beyond cooperative security. ASEAN has over the years contributed to conflict avoidance and management and has decreased the likelihood of regional states using force to resolve disputes. These achievements, however, have not reduced the role of the balance of power factor within ASEAN due to the persistence of feelings of suspicion, contradictory strategic perspectives and a post-Cold War revival of bilateral disputes. The expansion process has led to the incorporation of additional bilateral contentions. Local struggles for influence have led to a series of competitive distributions of power within the Association. The practice of conventional as well as unconventional balance of power politics by individual members has set a limit to the cooperative process and partly explains why ASEAN has remained a rather weak security regime despite its long existence.

The formation of the ARF involved power balancing considerations. However, its limited experience indicates that it has failed as an instrument to constrain the PRC in a way that corresponds to ASEAN's degree of success with Indonesia. Various ASEAN states have continued to depend on bilateral links with the United States to ensure their security. This measure of failure can be explained by the fact that the PRC joined the Forum as the main beneficiary of the changing strategic environment in East Asia and that it has continued to feel subject to US containment. In short, the ARF does not provide sufficient incentive to encourage China in adopting a policy of political self-abnegation. Nevertheless, it has provided Beijing with a diplomatic forum to promote a multipolar security structure in the Asia-Pacific and thus with a means for countering US unilateralism through other than conventional methods.

Regardless of their limitations and current difficulties, ASEAN and the ARF still serve some of their purposes. Both these regimes for cooperative security operate as diplomatic instruments to avoid the recurrence of conflict by seeking to address the climate of regional relations rather than tackling specific security problems. Instead of concluding on a pessimistic note, it seems therefore more appropriate to refer to a series of challenges they face and to reiterate their ongoing relevance and usefulness.

The fragility of some ASEAN members, primarily Indonesia, has been exposed by the financial crisis. The applicability of ASEAN's basic norms and decision-making process is now also in question. The Association as well as its primary member are currently weak and have lost a great share of international credibility. ASEAN appears in these circumstances to be unable to function as an effective diplomatic instrument. Ironically, this loss of influence and cohesion occurs when for the first time all the ten Southeast Asian states are members of the cooperative security regime. Furthermore, the strategic significance of Southeast Asia has declined in the post-Cold War and China's relative power has increased. The sub-region has lost some of its importance for the great powers, particularly since the end of the Third Indochina Conflict. Yet, the US interest in Southeast Asia has substantially increased since the attacks of 11 September and the Bali bombings. The sub-region has been portrayed as a second front in the war on terror. In spite of the challenges and difficult new prospects, none of the member states have expressed a desire to withdraw from ASEAN. The members still seem convinced by the benefits it provides. Though perceived as a humiliation in Jakarta, the common position on the territorial integrity of Indonesia indicated, for example, ASEAN's continuing purpose and its commitment to the national sovereignty of individual states. In addition, domestic concerns and instability have not affected the rather benign regional security environment. The ASEAN states continue to recognize that it is not in their interest to go to war with each other despite the persistence of numerous bilateral disputes.

ASEAN's declining unity has had a negative impact on the relevance of the ARF. The Association seems currently unable to contribute to the peaceful management of the key triangular relationship in the Asia-Pacific. Moreover, regardless of its original suspicion, China has attained a position in which it can use the Forum. It has increased its influence on the cooperative security arrangement and has gained some control over its decision-making process. The ARF has not become, however, a vehicle for Chinese interests. Instead, it has provided a basis for some restraint by the

PRC. Beijing has several motives to generally respect the standard international norms promoted by the Forum and to introduce an element of relative moderation in its foreign policy. Hence, the importance of the ARF as the first region-wide arrangement for cooperative security should be kept in mind despite the fact that its constraining influence on China may not be as strong as originally hoped for by the ASEAN members.

Notes

Introduction

1 ASEAN was established in Bangkok in August 1967. The original members were: Indonesia, Malaysia, the Philippines, Singapore and Thailand. Brunei joined in 1984, Vietnam in 1995, Laos and Myanmar (Burma) in 1997, and Cambodia in 1999.

2 The founding dinner of the ARF was held in Singapore in July 1993. Its initial participants were: Australia, Brunei, Canada, China, the European Union, Indonesia, Japan, Laos, Malaysia, New Zealand, Papua New Guinea, the Philippines, Russia, Singapore, South Korea, Thailand, the United States and Vietnam. Cambodia was admitted in 1995, India and Myanmar in 1996, Mongolia in 1998 and North Korea in 2000.

3 See for instance William T. Tow, *Subregional Security Cooperation in the Third World*, Boulder, CO: Lynne Rienner, 1990, pp. 13–14, 23–45; Michael Leifer, 'Debating Asian Security: Michael Leifer responds to Geoffrey Wiseman', *Pacific Review*, vol. 5, no. 2, 1992, p. 192; Amitav Acharya, 'A Regional Security Community in Southeast Asia?', *Journal of Strategic Studies*, vol. 18, no. 3, Sept. 1995, p. 191; Tim Huxley, *Insecurity in the ASEAN Region*, London: Royal United Services Institute for Defence Studies, 1993, p. 4. For a comprehensive literature review on this question, see Tim Huxley, 'Southeast Asia in the Study of International Relations: The Rise and Decline of a Region', *Pacific Review*, vol. 9, no. 2, 1996, pp. 215–216.

4 Stephen D. Krasner, 'Structural Causes and Regime Consequences: Regimes as intervening Variables', *International Organization*, vol. 36, no. 2, 1982, p. 186.

5 See Karl Deutsch, S.A. Burrell, R.A. Kann, M. Lee, Jr, M. Lichterman, R.E. Lindgren, *Political Community and the North Atlantic Area: International Organization in the Light of Historical Experience*, Princeton: Princeton University Press, 1957.

6 See Robert O. Keohane, *After Hegemony: Cooperation and Discord in the World Political Economy*, Princeton: Princeton University Press, 1984; Robert O. Keohane, *International Institutions and State Power: Essays in International Relations Theory*, Boulder, CO: Westview Press, 1989; Robert O. Keohane, 'Institutional Theory and the Realist Challenge after the Cold War', in David Baldwin (ed.) *Neorealism and Neoliberalism: The Contemporary Debate*, New York: Columbia University Press, 1993; Kenneth A. Oye, 'Explaining Co-operation Under Anarchy: Hypotheses and Strategies', *World Politics*, vol. 38,

no. 1, October 1985, pp. 1–24; Oran R. Young, *International Cooperation: Building Regimes for Natural Resources and the Environment*, Ithaca, NY: Cornell University Press, 1989.

7 Robert O. Keohane and Lisa L. Martin, 'The Promise of Institutionalist Theory', *International Security*, vol. 20, no. 1, Summer 1995, p. 46.

8 Andrew Hurrell, 'Explaining the Resurgence of Regionalism in World Politics', *Review of International Studies*, vol. 21, 1995, p. 352.

9 Tony Evans and Peter Wilson, 'Regime Theory and the English School of International Relations: A Comparison', *Millennium: Journal of International Studies*, vol. 21, no. 3, 1992, p. 330.

10 See Michael Antolik, *ASEAN and the Diplomacy of Accommodation*, Armonk, NY: M.E. Sharpe, 1990; Pushpa Thambipillai and J. Saravanamuttu, *ASEAN Negotiations: Two Insights*, Singapore: Institute of Southeast Asian Studies, 1985, pp. 10–15. For a critique of the 'ASEAN Way', see Tobias Ingo Nischalke, 'Insights from ASEAN's Foreign Policy Co-operation: The "ASEAN Way", a Real Spirit or a Phantom?', *Contemporary Southeast Asia*, vol. 22, no. 1, April 2000, pp. 89–112.

11 For an understanding of constructivism, see Alexander Wendt, 'Anarchy is what States make of it: The Social Construction of Power Politics', *International Organization*, vol. 46, no. 2, Spring 1992, pp. 391–425 and Alexander Wendt, 'Collective Identity Formation and the International State', *American Political Science Review*, vol. 88, no. 2, June 1994, pp. 384–396.

12 See Richard Higgott, 'Ideas, Identity and Policy Coordination in the Asia-Pacific', *Pacific Review*, vol. 7, no. 4, 1994, pp. 367–379; Amitav Acharya, 'Collective Identity and Conflict Management in Southeast Asia', in Emmanuel Adler and Michael Barnett (eds) *Security Communities*, Cambridge: Cambridge University Press, 1998, pp. 198–227; Amitav Acharya, *Constructing a Security Community in Southeast Asia: ASEAN and the Problem of Regional Order*, London: Routledge, 2001; and Mikolas Busse, 'Constructivism and Southeast Asian Security', *Pacific Review*, vol. 12, no. 1, 1999, pp. 39–60.

13 See Amitav Acharya, 'Ideas, Identity, and Institution-Building: From the "ASEAN Way" to the "Asia-Pacific Way"?', *Pacific Review*, vol. 10, no. 3, 1997, pp. 328–342.

14 Michael Leifer, 'The ASEAN Peace Process: A Category Mistake', *Pacific Review*, vol. 12, no. 1, 1999, p. 27. With regards to the ARF as an example of cooperative security, see Michael Leifer, *The ASEAN Regional Forum. A Model for Cooperative Security in the Middle East?*, Canberra: Research School of Pacific and Asian Studies, 1998, p. 4; and Amitav Acharya, *Reordering Asia: 'Cooperative Security' or Concert of Powers?*, IDSS Working Paper no. 3, Singapore: Institute of Defence and Strategic Studies, July 1999, p. 8.

15 Acharya, *Reordering Asia*, p. 8. For a discussion on the concept of cooperative security, see David Dewitt, 'Common, Comprehensive, and Cooperative Security', *Pacific Review*, vol. 7, no. 1, 1994, p. 7–12.

16 Leifer, 'The ASEAN Peace Process', p. 27.

17 Geoffrey Wiseman, 'Common Security in the Asia-Pacific Region', *Pacific Review*, vol. 5, no. 1, 1992, p. 43.

18 Amitav Acharya, 'ASEAN and Asia-Pacific Multilateralism: Managing Regional Security', in Amitav Acharya and Richard Stubbs (eds) *New Challenges for ASEAN: Emerging Policy Issues*, Vancouver: University of British Columbia Press, 1995, p. 7.

19 Pierre Lizée, 'Sécurité et intégration en Asie-Pacifique: Dynamiques et Implications Théoriques', *Études Internationales*, vol. 28, no. 2, Juin 1997, pp. 346–347.
20 Paul W. Schroeder, 'The Nineteenth Century System: Balance of Power or Political Equilibrium?', *Review of International Studies*, vol. 15, no. 2, April 1989, p. 135.
21 See Michael Leifer, 'The Role and Paradox of ASEAN', in M. Leifer (ed.) *The Balance of Power in East Asia*, London: Macmillan, 1986, pp. 119–131; Michael Leifer, *ASEAN and the Security of South-East Asia*, London: Routledge, 1989; Michael Leifer, 'ASEAN as a Model of a Security Community?', in Hadi Soesastro (ed.) *ASEAN in a Changed Regional and International Political Economy*, Jakarta: Centre for Strategic and International Studies, 1995, pp. 138–142.
22 Michael Leifer, *The ASEAN Regional Forum: Extending ASEAN's Model of Regional Security*, Adelphi Paper no. 302, London: International Institute for Strategic Studies, 1996. See also Khong Yuen Foong, 'Review Article: Making Bricks without Straw in the Asia Pacific?', *Pacific Review*, vol. 10, no. 2, 1997, pp. 289–300.
23 Leifer, *The ASEAN Regional Forum*, p. 59.

1 Regimes for cooperative security

1 Ruggie explains that 'multilateralism refers to coordinating relations among three or more states in accordance with certain principles.' John Gerard Ruggie, 'Multilateralism: The Anatomy of an Institution', *International Organization*, vol. 46, no. 3, 1992, p. 568.
2 The notion of 'security with others' was first developed in the Palme Commission Report. See *Common Security: A Programme for Disarmament. The Report of the Independent Commission on Disarmament and Security Issues under the Chairmanship of Olof Palme*, London: Pan Books, 1982.
3 For an account of *Konfrontasi*, see J.A.C. Mackie, *Konfrontasi: The Indonesia–Malaysia Dispute, 1963–1966*, Oxford: Oxford University Press, 1974; J.M. Gullick, *Malaysia and its Neighbours*, London: Routledge & Kegan Paul, 1967; Donald Hindley, 'Indonesia's Confrontation with Malaysia: A Search for Motives', *Asian Survey*, vol. 4, no. 6, June 1964, pp. 904–913.
4 For a discussion on the Philippines' claim to the territory of Sabah, see Lela Garner Noble, *Philippine Policy toward Sabah: A Claim to Independence*, Tucson: University of Arizona Press, 1977.
5 See Dewi Fortuna Anwar, *Indonesia in ASEAN: Foreign Policy and Regionalism*, New York: St Martin's Press, 1994, pp. 27–29.
6 For a discussion on the end of Confrontation, see Franklin B. Weinstein, *Indonesia Abandons Confrontation: An Inquiry into the Functions of Indonesian Foreign Policy*, Ithaca, NY: Cornell University Press, 1969.
7 Sabam Siagian, former Chief Editor of the *Jakarta Post* and former Ambassador of Indonesia to Australia (1991–1995). The interview was held in Jakarta on 20 March 2000.
8 ASA, Report of the First Meeting of Foreign Ministers of ASA on Economic and Cultural Co-operation Among Southeast Asian Countries and Statement of Policy, Bangkok, Thailand, 1 August 1961.

9 Federation of Malaya, *ASA, Report of the Second Meeting of Foreign Ministers*, Kuala Lumpur, 1963.

10 ASA, Report of the First Meeting of Foreign Ministers of ASA.

11 ASA, Report of the Third Meeting of Foreign Ministers of ASA, Bangkok, Thailand, 3–5 August 1966.

12 Ali Alatas, former Foreign Minister of Indonesia (1988–1999). The interview was held in Jakarta on 21 March 2000.

13 Bernard K. Gordon, *Toward Disengagement in Asia: A Strategy for American Foreign Policy*, Englewood Cliffs, NJ: Prentice-Hall, 1969, p. 111.

14 Tun Abdul Razak, Deputy Prime Minister of Malaysia, Address at the Inaugural Meeting of ASEAN held at the Ministry of Foreign Affairs, Bangkok, Thailand, 8 August 1967.

15 Gordon, *Toward Disengagement in Asia*, p. 98.

16 Michael Leifer, *The ASEAN Regional Forum. A Model for Cooperative Security in the Middle East?*, Canberra: Research School of Pacific and Asian Studies, 1998, p. 6.

17 The offer to participate had previously been declined by Burma, Cambodia and Laos.

18 The ASEAN Declaration (Bangkok Declaration), Bangkok, Thailand, 8 August 1967.

19 Adam Malik, 'Regional Cooperation in International Politics', *Regionalism in Southeast Asia*, Jakarta: Centre for Strategic and International Studies, 1975, p. 162.

20 S. Rajaratnam, Minister of Foreign Affairs of Singapore, Address at the Inaugural Meeting of ASEAN held at the Ministry of Foreign Affairs, Bangkok, Thailand, 8 August 1967.

21 Estrella D. Solidum, 'Security Perspectives in ASEAN', in Werner Pfennig and Mark Suh (eds) *Aspects of ASEAN*, Munchen: Weltforum Verlag, 1984, pp. 115–116.

22 Leo Suryadinata, *Indonesia's Foreign Policy under Suharto: Aspiring to International Leadership*, Singapore: Times Academic Press, 1996, p. 68.

23 Wirjono Sastro Handujo, Fellow Researcher at CSIS and former Ambassador of Indonesia to Austria, France and Australia. The interview was held in Jakarta on 23 March 2000.

24 Adam Malik, Minister for Foreign Affairs of Indonesia, Address at the Inaugural Meeting of ASEAN held at the Ministry of Foreign Affairs, Bangkok, Thailand, 8 August 1967.

25 Tun Abdul Razak, Deputy Prime Minister of Malaysia, Address at the Inaugural Meeting of ASEAN held at the Ministry of Foreign Affairs, Bangkok, Thailand, 8 August 1967 .

26 For information on the establishment of the Federation of Malaysia and the later separation of Singapore from the Federation, see J.M. Gulick, *Malaysia*, London: Ernst Benn, 1969; Stanley S. Bedlington, *Malaysia and Singapore: The Building of New States*, Ithaca, NY: Cornell University Press, 1978.

27 For a discussion on Singapore's sense of vulnerability and its influence on the city-state's foreign policy, see Michael Leifer, *Singapore's Foreign Policy: Coping with Vulnerability*, London: Routledge, 2000.

28 Lee Kuan Yew, *From Third World to First: The Singapore Story, 1965–2000*, Singapore: Times Editions, 2000, p. 369.

29 Suryadinata, *Indonesia's Foreign Policy under Suharto*, p. 68.

30 The ASEAN Declaration (Bangkok Declaration).

31 Frank Frost, 'Introduction: ASEAN since 1967 – Origins, Evolution and Recent Developments', in Alison Broinowski (ed.) *ASEAN into the 1990's*, London: Macmillan, 1990, pp. 4–5.

32 The ASEAN Declaration (Bangkok Declaration).

33 For an account of the Corregidor Affair, see Noble, *Philippine Policy toward Sabah*, pp. 165–175.

34 Michael Leifer, 'The ASEAN Peace Process: A Category Mistake', *Pacific Review*, vol. 12, no. 1, 1994, p. 26.

35 Zone of Peace, Freedom and Neutrality Declaration (Kuala Lumpur Declaration), Kuala Lumpur, Malaysia, 27 November 1971.

36 Treaty on the Southeast Asia Nuclear Weapon-Free Zone, Bangkok, Thailand, 15 December 1995.

37 For a discussion on the different bilateral visits made during these early years that helped to consolidate ASEAN, see Estrella D. Solidum, *Bilateral Summitry in ASEAN*, Manila: Foreign Service Institute, 1982, pp. 20–24.

38 Barry Desker, Director of IDSS and former Ambassador of Singapore to Indonesia (1986–93). The interview was held in Singapore on 17 February 2000.

39 Desker, Singapore, 17 February 2000.

40 Singapore's Foreign Minister S. Rajaratnam said to his colleagues during the AMM of May 1974: 'You might recollect at the very first meeting in 1967, when we had to draft our communiqué, it was a very difficult problem of trying to say nothing in about ten pages, which we did. Because at the time, we ourselves, having launched ASEAN were not quite sure where it was going or whether is was going anywhere at all.' S. Rajaratnam, Minister of Foreign Affairs of the Republic of Singapore, Closing Statement at the ASEAN Ministerial Meeting, Jakarta, May 1974.

41 Desker, Singapore, 17 February 2000.

42 Arnfinn Jorgensen-Dahl, *Regional Organization and Order in South-East Asia*, London: Macmillan, 1982, p. 84.

43 Declaration of ASEAN Concord, Bali, Indonesia, 24 February 1976.

44 Declaration of ASEAN Concord.

45 Michael Leifer, *ASEAN and the Security of South-East Asia*, London: Routledge, 1989, p. 67.

46 Suharto, President of the Republic of Indonesia, Address at the opening of the Summit of the ASEAN Heads of State and Government, Bali, Indonesia, 23 February 1976. Quoted in Solidum, *Bilateral Summitry in ASEAN*, p. 31.

47 See Dewi Fortuna Anwar, *Indonesia's Strategic Culture: Ketahanan Nasional, Wawasan Nusantara and Hankamrata*, Australia-Asia Papers no. 75, May 1996.

48 Suharto, 'Address by the President of the Republic of Indonesia', *Regionalism in Southeast Asia*, Jakarta: Centre for Strategic and International Studies, 1975, p. 8.

49 Michael Antolik, *ASEAN and the Diplomacy of Accommodation*, Armonk, NY: M.E. Sharpe, 1990, p. 98.

50 Tim Huxley, *Insecurity in the ASEAN Region*, London: Royal United Services Institute for Defence Studies, 1993, p. 4.

51 Suharto, 'Address by the President of the Republic of Indonesia', p. 8.

52 A third document was introduced during the summit, the Agreement on the

Establishment of the ASEAN Secretariat, Bali, Indonesia, 24 February 1976. It dealt with various administrative matters including the functions of the Secretariat-General and the members of staff.

53 The TAC mentioned the principles of the UN Charter and the principles endorsed at the Asian–African Conference in Bandung, Indonesia, in April 1955. The Treaty also referred to the 1967 Bangkok Declaration and 1971 Kuala Lumpur Declaration.

54 Treaty of Amity and Cooperation in South-East Asia, Bali, Indonesia, 24 February 1976.

55 Treaty of Amity and Cooperation in South-East Asia. The need to have the consent of all the parties to a dispute was repeated by the ASEAN foreign ministers when they adopted during their 2001 AMM the procedures of the High Council. See Rules of Procedure of the High Council of the Treaty of Amity and Cooperation in Southeast Asia, Hanoi, Vietnam, 23 July 2001.

56 Sheldon W. Simon, 'Security Prospects in Southeast Asia: Collaborative Efforts and the ASEAN Regional Forum', *Pacific Review*, vol. 11, no. 2, 1998, p. 196.

57 Joint Press Communiqué of the Meeting of ASEAN Heads of State and Government, Kuala Lumpur, Malaysia, 4–5 August 1977.

58 Joint Statement of the Special Meeting of the ASEAN Foreign Ministers on the Current Political Development in the Southeast Asia Region, Bangkok, Thailand, 12 January 1979. This common ASEAN position was later repeated in the AMM Joint Communiqué of July 1979.

59 These factions were the Khmer Rouge under the leadership of Khieu Samphan, the Khmer People's National Liberation Front led by the former Prime Minister Son Sann and the royal party, the National United Front for an Independent, Neutral, Peaceful, and Cooperative Cambodia, led by King Norodom Sihanouk.

60 See Nayan Chanda, *Brother Enemy: The War after the War*, New York: Macmillan, 1986.

61 Hussin Mutalib, 'At Thirty, ASEAN looks to Challenges in the New Millennium', *Contemporary Southeast Asia*, vol. 19, no. 1, June 1997, pp. 78–79.

62 Sabam Siagian, Jakarta, 20 March 2000.

63 William T. Tow, *Subregional Security Cooperation in the Third World*, Boulder, CO: Lynne Rienner, 1990, pp. 23–25.

64 Pushpa Thambipillai and J. Saravanamuttu, *ASEAN Negotiations: Two Insights*, Singapore: Institute of Southeast Asian Studies, 1985, p. 15.

65 Amitav Acharya, 'Ideas, Identity and Institution-Building: From the "ASEAN Way" to the "Asia-Pacific Way"?', *Pacific Review*, vol. 10, no. 3, 1997, p. 343.

66 A comparison can be made for instance with the Gulf Cooperation Council (GCC) established in 1981 and which includes Saudi Arabia, Kuwait, Bahrain, Qatar, the United Arab Emirates and Oman.

67 Leifer, *The ASEAN Regional Forum*, p. 6.

68 Bangkok Declaration of 1995, ASEAN Heads of State and Government Meeting, Bangkok, Thailand, 14–15 December 1995.

69 For a description of the constructive policy approach, see Leszek Buszynski, 'Thailand and Myanmar: The Perils of "Constructive Engagement"', *Pacific Review*, vol. 11, no. 2, 1998, pp. 290–305.

70 Joint Statement of the Special Meeting of the ASEAN Foreign Ministers, Kuala Lumpur, Malaysia, 10 July 1997.

71 Joint Communiqué of the Thirtieth ASEAN Ministerial Meeting, Subang Jaya, Malaysia, 24–25 July 1997.
72 John Funston, 'ASEAN: Out of its Depth', *Contemporary Southeast Asia*, vol. 20, no. 1, April 1998, pp. 25–27.
73 Anwar Ibrahim, 'Crisis Prevention', *Newsweek*, 21 July 1997.
74 Professor S. Jayakumar, Minister of Foreign Affairs of the Republic of Singapore, Opening Statement at the Thirty-first ASEAN Ministerial Meeting, Manila, the Philippines, 24 July 1998.
75 See James Cotton, 'The "Haze" over Southeast Asia: Challenging the ASEAN Mode of Regional Engagement', *Pacific Affairs*, vol. 72, no. 3, Fall 1999, pp. 331–351.
76 For a discussion on ASEAN's response to international terrorism and other forms of transnational crime, see Ralf Emmers, *ASEAN's Response to Transnational Crime*, Working Paper no. 70, Canberra: Australian Defence Studies Centre, University of New South Wales, 2002.
77 2001 ASEAN Declaration on Joint Action to Counter Terrorism, Bandar Seri Begawan, Brunei, 5 November 2001.
78 See the Joint Communiqué of the Special ASEAN Ministerial Meeting on Terrorism, Kuala Lumpur, Malaysia, 20–21 May 2002.
79 Declaration on Terrorism, Eighth ASEAN Summit, Phnom Penh, Cambodia, 3 November 2002.
80 S. Jayakumar, Minister of Foreign Affairs of the Republic of Singapore, Opening Statement at the Thirty-first ASEAN Ministerial Meeting, Manila, the Philippines, 24 July 1998.
81 Jorgensen-Dahl, *Regional Organization and Order in South-East Asia*, p. 234.
82 See Hans Indorf, *Impediments to Regionalism in Southeast Asia: Bilateral Constraints among ASEAN Member States*, Singapore: Institute of Southeast Asian Studies, 1984, and Harald David, *Tensions within ASEAN: Malaysia and its Neighbours*, Monographs on Southeast Asian Politics and International Relations, no. 1, University of Hull, Department of South-East Asian Studies, 1996.
83 See Narayanan Ganesan, *Bilateral Tensions in Post-Cold War ASEAN*, Pacific Strategic Papers, Singapore: Institute of Southeast Asian Studies, 1999, pp. 1–81.
84 Amitav Acharya, 'A Regional Security Community in Southeast Asia?', *Journal of Strategic Studies*, vol. 18, no. 3, Sept. 1995, p. 185.
85 Singapore Declaration of 1992, ASEAN Heads of State and Government Meeting, Singapore, 27–28 January 1992.
86 Malaysia's former Deputy Prime Minister Dato Musa Hitam explains for example that 'ASEAN has given each of its members the self-confidence to assert that they are not the objects of international politics – not pawns on a chessboard – but the subjects of international relations, fully fit to participate in the affairs of our region and the wider world.' Dato Musa Hitam, 'ASEAN and the Pacific Rim', in Linda G. Martin (ed.) *The ASEAN Success Story: Social, Economic, and Political Dimensions*, Honolulu: University of Hawaii Press, 1987, p. 9.
87 ASEAN–United States of America Joint Declaration for Cooperation To Combat International Terrorism, Bandar Seri Begawan, Brunei, 1 August 2002.
88 Acharya, 'Ideas, Identity and Institution-Building', p. 322.

89 Singapore Declaration of 1992.
90 Kusuma Snitwongse, 'Achievements through Political Cooperation', *Pacific Review*, vol. 11, no. 2, 1998, p. 189.
91 Donald E. Weatherbee, 'ASEAN and the Political Challenges of Expansion', *Growing Pains: ASEAN's Economic and Political Challenges*, New York: Asia Society, December 1997, p. 33.
92 Amitav Acharya, *Reordering Asia: 'Cooperative Security' or Concert of Powers?*, IDSS Working Paper no. 3, Singapore: Institute of Defence and Strategic Studies, July 1999, p. 9.
93 Chairman's Statement, the First Meeting of the ASEAN Regional Forum, Bangkok, Thailand, 25 July 1994.
94 Chairman's Statement, the First Meeting of the ASEAN Regional Forum.
95 Simon, 'Security Prospects in Southeast Asia', p. 204.
96 Chairman's Statement, the Second ASEAN Regional Forum, Bandar Seri Begawan, Brunei Darussalam, 1 August 1995.
97 The ASEAN Regional Forum: A Concept Paper, Bandar Seri Begawan, Brunei Darussalam, 1 August 1995.
98 The ASEAN Regional Forum: A Concept Paper.
99 The ASEAN Regional Forum: A Concept Paper.
100 IISS, *Strategic Survey: 1995/1996*, London: International Institute for Strategic Studies, 1997, p. 191.
101 See the Chairman's Statement, the Third Meeting of the ASEAN Regional Forum, Jakarta, Indonesia, 23 July 1996.
102 IISS, *Strategic Survey: 1996/1997*, London: International Institute for Strategic Studies, April 1997, p. 193. The PRC also supported the participation of Mongolia in 1998.
103 Chairman's Statement, the Fourth Meeting of the ASEAN Regional Forum, Subang Jaya, Malaysia, 27 July 1997.
104 Chairman's Statement, the Sixth Meeting of the ASEAN Regional Forum, Singapore, 26 July 1999.
105 Chairman's Statement, the Eighth Meeting of the ASEAN Regional Forum, Hanoi, Vietnam, 25 July 2001.
106 The ARF document defines PD 'as consensual diplomatic and political action taken by sovereign states with the consent of all directly involved parties:
   • To help prevent disputes and conflicts from arising between States that could potentially pose a threat to regional peace and stability;
   • To help prevent such disputes and conflicts from escalating into armed confrontation; and
   • To help minimise the impact of such disputes and conflicts in the region.'
   ASEAN Regional Forum (ARF), Concept and Principles of Preventive Diplomacy, Hanoi, Vietnam, 25 July 2001.
107 Chairman's Statement, the Ninth Meeting of the ASEAN Regional Forum, Bandar Seri Begawan, Brunei, 31 July 2002.
108 Trevor Findlay, 'Disarmament, Arms Control and the Regional Security Dialogue', in Gary Klintworth (ed.) *Asia-Pacific Security: Less Uncertainty, New Opportunities?*, New York: Longman, 1996, pp. 238–239.
109 Jayakumar, Opening Statement at the Thirty-first ASEAN Ministerial Meeting, 24 July 1998.
110 James Clad, 'Regionalism in Southeast Asia: A Bridge too Far?', *Southeast*

Asian Affairs 1997, Singapore: Institute of Southeast Asian Studies, 1997, p. 6.

111 See for example Jose T. Almonte, 'Ensuring Security the "ASEAN Way"', *Survival*, vol. 39, no. 4, Winter 1997/98, pp. 80–92.

112 The former UN Secretary-General Boutros Boutros-Ghali defines the notion of preventive diplomacy as an 'action to prevent disputes from arising between two parties, to prevent existing disputes from escalating into conflicts, and to limit the spread of the latter when they occur'. Boutros Boutros-Ghali, *An Agenda For Peace: Preventive Diplomacy, Peace-Making and Peace-Keeping*, New York: The United Nations, 1992, p. 5. The notion of preventive diplomacy was initially developed and used by the former UN Secretary-General Dag Hammarskjold.

113 See the statements of three ARF track-two seminars on preventive diplomacy organized respectively in Seoul on 8–10 May 1995, in Paris on 7–8 November 1996 and in Singapore on 9–11 September 1997. See also Desmond Ball, 'Introduction: Towards Better Understanding of Preventive Diplomacy', in D. Ball and A. Acharya (eds) *The Next Stage: Preventive Diplomacy and Security Cooperation in the Asia-Pacific Region*, Canberra: Research School of Pacific and Asian Studies, Australian National University, 1999, pp. 1–14; and CSCAP Singapore, 'Review of Preventive Diplomacy Activities in the Asia-Pacific Region', paper presented at the CSCAP Working Group on CSBMs, Workshop on Preventive Diplomacy, Bangkok, Thailand, 28 February-2 March 1999.

114 Chairman's Summary: CSCAP Workshop on Preventive Diplomacy, Bangkok, Thailand, 28 February–2 March 1999.

115 Michael Leifer, 'Regional Solutions to Regional Problems?', in David S. Goodman and Gerald Segal (eds) *Towards Recovery in Pacific Asia*, London: Routledge, 2000, p. 115.

116 The ASEAN Regional Forum: A Concept Paper.

117 Simon, 'Security Prospects in Southeast Asia', p. 207.

118 Yoichi Funabashi, 'Bridging Asia's Economics-Security Gap', *Survival*, vol. 38, no. 4, Winter 1996/97, p. 106.

119 Dr Soedjati Djiwandono, former member of CSIS and frequent columnist for the *Jakarta Post*. The interview was held in Jakarta on 17 March 2000.

2 The role of the balance of power factor within and beyond regimes for cooperative security

1 The nine different meanings are: '1. An even distribution of power. 2. The principle that power ought to be evenly distributed. 3. The existing distribution of power. Hence, any possible distribution of power. 4. The principle of equal aggrandizement of the Great Powers at the expense of the weak. 5. The principle that our side ought to have a margin of strength in order to avert the danger of power becoming unevenly distributed. 6. (When governed by the verb 'to hold') a special role in maintaining an even distribution of power. 7. A special advantage in the existing distribution of power. 8. Predominance. 9. An inherent tendency of international politics to produce an even distribution of power.' Martin Wight, 'The Balance of Power', in H. Butterfield and M. Wight (eds) *Diplomatic Investigations: Essays in the Theory of International Politics*, Cambridge: Harvard University Press, 1968, p. 151.

2 Inis L. Claude, *Power and International Relations*, New York: Random House, 1965, pp. 13–39.

3 Claude, *Power and International Relations*, p. 20.

4 Michael Sheehan, *The Balance of Power: History and Theory,* London: Routledge, 1996, p. 53.

5 Sheehan, *The Balance of Power*, p. 20.

6 Sheehan, *The Balance of Power*, pp. 42–51.

7 Inis L. Claude, 'The Balance of Power Revisited', *Review of International Studies*, vol. 15, no. 2, April 1989, p. 79.

8 See Hans Morgenthau, *Politics among Nations: The Struggle for Power and Peace*, New York: Alfred A. Knopf, 1948 and further editions. This book is widely considered to be the first cohesive text on modern realism as both an explanatory and prescriptive theory. See also Kenneth N. Waltz, *Theory of International Politics*, Reading, MA: Addison-Wesley, 1979.

9 Hobbes wrote that the 'power *of a Man,* (to take it Universally,) is his present means, to obtain some future apparent Good'. Thomas Hobbes, *Leviathan*, R. Tuck (ed.), Cambridge: Cambridge University Press, 1991, p. 62.

10 Hans J. Morgenthau, *Politics among Nations: The Struggle for Power and Peace*, first edition, revised and enlarged, New York: Alfred A. Knopf, 1949, p. 14.

11 Morgenthau, *Politics among Nations* (1949), p. 13.

12 Kenneth N. Waltz, 'The Origins of War in Neorealist Theory', in R.I. Rotberg and T.K. Rabb (eds) *The Origins and Prevention of Major Wars*, Cambridge: Cambridge University Press, 1989, p. 40.

13 Richard Little, 'Deconstructing the Balance of Power: Two Traditions of Thought', *Review of International Studies*, vol. 15, no. 2, April 1989, p. 95.

14 Martin Wight, *Power Politics*, London: Leicester University Press, 1978; Hedley Bull, *The Anarchical Society: A Study of Order in World Politics*, London: Macmillan, 1977.

15 Morgenthau, *Politics among Nations* (1949), p. 125.

16 Morgenthau, *Politics among Nations* (1949), p. 155.

17 Henry Kissinger, *Diplomacy*, New York: Touchstone, 1994, p. 21.

18 Hedley Bull, *The Anarchical Society: A Study of Order in World Politics*, second edition, London: Macmillan, 1995, p. 13.

19 Bull, *The Anarchical Society* (1995), p. 8.

20 Bull, *The Anarchical Society* (1995), p. 102.

21 A. Organski, *World Politics*, second edition, New York: Alfred A. Knopf, 1968, p. 274.

22 Claude, *Power and International Relations*, pp. 42–51.

23 Henry Kissinger, *World Restored: Metternich, Castlereagh and the Problems of Peace, 1812–22*, Cambridge, MA: The Riverside Press, 1957, p. 1.

24 Kissinger, *Diplomacy*, p. 835.

25 Kissinger, *Diplomacy*, p. 835.

26 Waltz, *Theory of International Politics*, p. 121.

27 Waltz, *Theory of International Politics*, p. 128.

28 Paul W. Schroeder, 'The Nineteenth-Century System: Balance of Power or Political Equilibrium?', *Review of International Studies*, vol. 15, no. 2, April 1989, p. 135.

29 Robert E. Osgood, *Alliances and American Foreign Policy*, Baltimore, MD: The Johns Hopkins University Press, 1971, p. 30.

30 Hans J. Morgenthau, *Politics among Nations: The Struggle for Power and Peace*,

second edition, revised and enlarged, New York: Alfred A. Knopf, 1955, pp. 166–176.

31 Organski, *World Politics*, pp. 276–279.

32 For a discussion on the study of alliances, see Osgood, *Alliances and American Foreign Policy*; and Julian R. Friedman, C. Bladen and S. Rosen (eds) *Alliance in International Politics*, Boston, MA: Allyn & Bacon, 1970.

33 Martin Wight, *Power Politics*, reprint, London: Leicester University Press, 1995, p. 122.

34 For a discussion on the establishment and early development of NATO, see Robert E. Osgood, *NATO: The Entangling Alliance*, Chicago, IL: The University of Chicago Press, 1962.

35 Stephen Walt, *The Origins of Alliances*, Ithaca, NY: Cornell University Press, 1987, p. 21.

36 Walt, *The Origins of Alliances*, pp. 22–26.

37 Khong Yuen Foong, 'Making Bricks without Straw in the Asia Pacific?', *Pacific Review*, vol. 10, no. 2, 1997, p. 297.

38 Ralph Pettman, *International Politics*, Boulder, CO: Lynne Rienner, 1991, p. 69.

39 Morgenthau, *Politics among Nations* (1955), p. 185.

40 Morgenthau, *Politics among Nations* (1955), p. 189.

41 Wight, *Power Politics* (1995), p. 200.

42 Paul W. Schroeder, *The Transformation of European Politics, 1763–1848*, Oxford: Oxford University Press, 1994, p. 10.

43 See chapter 5 in John Vasquez, *The War Puzzle*, Cambridge: Cambridge University Press, 1994.

44 Wight, *Power Politics* (1995), p. 200.

45 Paul W. Schroeder, 'Historical Reality vs. Neo-realist Theory', *International Security*, vol. 19, no. 1, Summer 1994, p. 116.

46 Schroeder, 'Historical Reality vs. Neo-realist Theory', pp. 116–117.

47 Charles Kupchan and Clifford Kupchan, 'The Promise of Collective Security', *International Security*, vol. 20, no. 1, Summer 1995, pp. 52–53.

48 For a critical assessment of the concept of collective security and its application to the League of Nations, see Inis L. Claude, *Swords into Plowshares: The Problems and Progress of International Organization*, fourth edition, New York: Random House, 1984, pp. 245–265.

49 Edward Vose Gulick, *Europe's Classical Balance of Power*, New York: W.W. Norton, 1967, p. 307.

50 Kupchan and Kupchan, 'The Promise of Collective Security', p. 53.

51 Morgenthau, *Politics among Nations* (1955), p. 175.

52 Kupchan and Kupchan, 'The Promise of Collective Security', p. 54.

53 For a discussion on the relevance of the concept of comprehensive security to the security doctrines of these three ASEAN states, see Muthiah Alagappa, 'Comprehensive Security: Interpretations in ASEAN Countries', in Robert A. Scalapino, Seizaburo Sato, Jusuf Wanandi and Han Sung-joo (eds) *Asian Security Issues: Regional and Global*, Berkeley: Institute of East Asian Studies, University of California, 1988, pp. 50–78.

54 Pierre Lizée and Sorpong Peou, *Cooperative Security and the Emerging Security Agenda in Southeast Asia: The Challenges and Opportunities of Peace in Cambodia*, YCISS Occasional Paper no. 21, Toronto: Centre for International and Strategic Studies, York University, November 1993, p. 2.

55 Stanley Hoffmann, 'Thoughts on the Concept of Common Security', *Policies for*

Common Security, ed. by the Stockholm International Peace Research Institute, London: Taylor & Francis, 1985, p. 54.

56 *Common Security: A Programme for Disarmament. The Report of the Independent Commission on Disarmament and Security Issues under the Chairmanship of Olof Palme*, London: Pan Books, 1982. Quoted in Radmila Nakarada and Jan Oberg, 'We Can Survive – But Only Together', in R. Nakarada and J. Oberg (eds) *Surviving Together: The Olof Palme Lectures on Common Security 1988*, Aldershot: Dartmouth, 1989, p. 12.

57 *Common Security: A Programme for Disarmament*, quoted in E. Rothschild, 'Common Security and Deterrence', *Policies for Common Security*, pp. 92–93.

58 David Dewitt, 'Common, Comprehensive, and Cooperative Security', *Pacific Review*, vol. 7, no. 1, 1994, p. 7.

59 Little, 'Deconstructing the Balance of Power', p. 98.

60 Andrew Hurrell, 'Explaining the Resurgence of Regionalism in World Politics', *Review of International Studies*, vol. 21, 1995, p. 342.

61 Dr Narayanan Ganesan, Senior Lecturer, Department of Political Science at NUS. The interview was held in Singapore on 18 February 2000.

62 Michael Leifer, *Indonesia's Foreign Policy*, London: George Allen & Unwin, 1983, p. 173.

63 Dr Leonard Sebastian, Senior Fellow at IDSS. The interview was held in Singapore on 25 February 2000.

64 Dr Soedjati Djiwandono, former member of CSIS and frequent columnist for the *Jakarta Post*. The interview was held in Jakarta on 17 March 2000.

65 Arnfinn Jorgensen-Dahl, *Regional Organization and Order in South-East Asia*, London: Macmillan, 1982, p. 228.

66 Dr Dewi Fortuna Anwar, Research Professor at the Habibie Centre and former spokesperson of President B.J. Habibie. The interview was held in Jakarta on 24 March 2000.

67 Professor Cornelius Luhulima, Research Associate at CSIS and former ASEAN Secretariat official. The interview was held in Jakarta on 21 March 2000.

68 See Lee Kuan Yew, *From Third World to First: The Singapore Story, 1965–2000*, Singapore: Times Editions, 2000, pp. 369–370.

69 Leifer, *Indonesia's Foreign Policy*, pp. 120–121.

70 Soedjati J. Dijwandono, 'South-East Asia and the South Pacific: The Role of ASEAN', *Security in South-East Asia and the South-West Pacific: Challenges of the 1990's*, New York: International Peace Academy, 1989, p. 160.

71 Leifer, *Indonesia's Foreign Policy*, p. 175.

72 The ASEAN Declaration (Bangkok Declaration), 8 August 1967.

73 Jorgensen-Dahl, *Regional Organization and Order in South-East Asia*, p. 40.

74 Dr Bantarto Bandoro, Head of the Department of International Relations at CSIS. The interview was held in Jakarta on 22 March 2000.

75 Quoted in Leifer, *Indonesia's Foreign Policy*, p. 144.

76 Dr John Funston, Senior Fellow at ISEAS. The interview was held in Singapore on 2 March 2000.

77 Kaw Chong Guan, Head of External Programmes at IDSS. The interview was held in Singapore on 3 March 2000.

78 Hurrell, 'Explaining the Resurgence of Regionalism in World Politics', p. 358.

3 The balance of power factor and the denial of intra-mural hegemony

1 Sabam Siagian, former Chief Editor of the *Jakarta Post* and former Ambassador of Indonesia to Australia (1991–95). The interview was held in Jakarta on 20 March 2000.
2 Adam Malik, 'Regional Cooperation in International Politics', *Regionalism in Southeast Asia*, Jakarta: Centre for Strategic and International Studies, 1975, p. 162.
3 Narayanan Ganesan, *Singapore's Foreign Policy in ASEAN: Major Domestic and Bilateral Political Constraints,* Ann Arbor, MI: University Microfilms International, 1989, p. 55.
4 See Michael Leifer, *Singapore's Foreign Policy: Coping with Vulnerability*, London: Routledge, 2000.
5 Seah Chee Meow, *Singapore's Position in ASEAN Co-operation*, Occasional Paper no. 38, Singapore: Department of Political Science, National University of Singapore, 1989, p. 5.
6 Hasnan Habib, former Ambassador of Indonesia to Thailand (1978–82) and the United States (1982–86). The interview was held in Jakarta on 23 March 2000.
7 Michael Leifer, *ASEAN and the Security of South-East Asia*, London: Routledge, 1989, p. 39.
8 For a discussion on some of Indonesia's domestic constraints, see Michael Antolik, *ASEAN and the Diplomacy of Accommodation*, Armonk, NY: M.E. Sharpe, 1990, pp. 24–28.
9 For an account of Lee Kuan Yew's official visit to Indonesia in May 1973, see Lee Kuan Yew, *From Third World to First: The Singapore Story, 1965–2000*, Singapore: Times Editions, 2000, pp. 300–302; and Lee Khoon Choy, *An Ambassador's Journey*, Singapore: Times Book International, 1983, pp. 213–230.
10 See Lee, *From Third World to First*, pp. 301–306.
11 See Tommy Koh, *The Quest for World Order: Perspectives of a Pragmatic Idealist*, ed. by Amitav Acharya, Singapore: Times Academic Press, 1998.
12 Shee Poon-Kim, 'A Decade of ASEAN, 1967–1977', *Asian Survey*, vol. 17, no. 8, August 1977, p. 757.
13 Koh, *The Quest for World Order*, p. 240.
14 For a discussion on the motives behind the Malaysian initiative, see Dick Wilson, *The Neutralization of Southeast Asia*, New York: Praeger, 1975, pp. 61–70.
15 See Henry Kissinger, *White House Years*, Boston, MA: Little, Brown, 1979.
16 Antolik, *ASEAN and the Diplomacy of Accommodation*, p. 113.
17 Heiner Hanggi, *ASEAN and the ZOPFAN Concept*, Pacific Strategic Papers, Singapore: Institute of Southeast Asian Studies, 1991, pp. 15–16.
18 Adam Malik, Minister of Foreign Affairs of Indonesia, at a meeting of the Press Foundation of Asia, Bali, Indonesia, September 1971. Quoted in Wilson, *The Neutralization of Southeast Asia*, p. 53.
19 See Wilson, *The Neutralization of Southeast Asia*, pp. 68–85.
20 Sinnathamby Rajaratnam, *Will the Real ZOPFAN Stand Up*, Singapore: Library of the Institute of Southeast Asian Studies, October 1989, p. 14.
21 For a discussion on the problems associated with the neutralization proposal, see Professor Tommy Koh, Address to the Commonwealth Society, Singapore, 1972.

Sections of the Address are reprinted in Bilveer Singh, *ZOPFAN and the New Security Order in the Asia-Pacific Region*, Petaling Jaya, Malaysia: Pelanduk Publications, 1992, pp. 71–73.

22 Daljit Singh, Senior Research Fellow at ISEAS. The interview was held in Singapore on 23 February 2000.

23 Leifer, *ASEAN and the Security of South-East Asia*, p. 58.

24 Zone of Peace, Freedom, and Neutrality Declaration (Kuala Lumpur Declaration), Kuala Lumpur, Malaysia, 27 November 1971.

25 Hanggi, *ASEAN and the ZOPFAN Concept*, pp. 18–19.

26 Ali Alatas, former Minister of Foreign Affairs of Indonesia (1988–99). The interview was held in Jakarta on 21 March 2000.

27 Zone of Peace, Freedom, and Neutrality Declaration.

28 Singapore perceived the Five Power Defence Arrangements as an additional means to regulate its relations with Malaysia and to constrain Malaysia's potential aggressive disposition towards the city-state.

29 Chin Kin Wah, *The Defence of Malaysia and Singapore: The Transformation of a Security System, 1957–1971*, Cambridge: Cambridge University Press, 1983, p. 174.

30 Concerned about the movement of its nuclear warships and submarines in Southeast Asia, the United States has refused to support the SEANWFZ Treaty. Beijing has also declined to sign the Treaty as it covers maritime areas claimed by the PRC in the South China Sea.

31 For a history of Brunei, see D.S. Ranjit Singh, *Brunei 1839–1983: The Problems of Political Survival*, Oxford: Oxford University Press, 1984; Graham Saunders, *A History of Brunei*, Oxford: Oxford University Press, 1994; A.V.M. Horton, *A New Sketch of the History of Negara Brunei Darussalam*, first edition, second impression, London: A.V.M. Horton, March 1996.

32 Stanley S. Bedlington, *Malaysia and Singapore: The Building of New States*, Ithaca, NY: Cornell University Press, 1978, p. 260.

33 For additional information on the political ambitions of the People's Party, see Haji Zaini Haji Ahmad (ed.) *The People's Party of Brunei: Selected Documents*, Kuala Lumpur: Institute of Social Analysis (INSAN), 1988.

34 Saunders, *A History of Brunei*, p. 151.

35 Greg Poulgrain, *The Genesis of Konfrontasi: Malaysia, Brunei, Indonesia, 1945–1965*, London: C. Hurst, 1998, p. 283–284.

36 Tim Huxley, *Brunei's Defence Policy and Military Expenditure*, Working Paper no. 166, Canberra: Research School of Pacific Studies, Australian National University, 1988, p. 4.

37 V.G. Kulkarni, 'Family Feuds are giving Way to Fraternal Ties', *Far Eastern Economic Review*, 26 January 1984, p. 33.

38 Michael Leifer, 'Decolonisation and International Status: The Experience of Brunei', *International Affairs*, vol. 54, no. 2, April 1978, p. 243.

39 Dr Khoo Kay Kim, Associate Professor, Department of History at the Malaya University. The interview was held in Singapore on 1 March 2000.

40 Saunders, *A History of Brunei*, p. 158.

41 Bedlington, *Malaysia and Singapore*, p. 266.

42 Huxley, *Brunei's Defence Policy and Military Expenditure*, pp. 7–8.

43 Kwa Chong Guan, Head of External Programmes at IDSS. The interview was held in Singapore on 3 March 2000.

44 Lord Chalfont, *By God's Will: A Portrait of the Sultan of Brunei*, London: Weidenfeld & Nicolson, 1989, p. 114.

45 Tan Sri Mohamad Ghazali Shafie, 'ASEAN's Response to Security Issues in Southeast Asia', *Regionalism in Southeast Asia*, Jakarta: Centre for Strategic and International Studies, 1975, p. 23.

46 Ghazali Shafie, 'ASEAN's Response to Security Issues in Southeast Asia', p. 23.

47 See Lee, *From Third World to First*, pp. 343–346.

48 Huxley, *Brunei's Defence Policy and Military Expenditure*, p. 17.

49 For a history of the invasion, see James Dunn, *Timor: A People Betrayed*, Australia: ABC Books, 1996; and Richard W. Franke, *East Timor: The Hidden War*, New York: East Timor Defense Committee, 1976.

50 Michael Leifer, *Indonesia's Foreign Policy*, London: George Allen & Unwin, 1983, pp. 159–160.

51 Dr Leo Suryadinata, Associate Professor, Department of Political Science at NUS. The interview was held in Singapore on 10 March 2000.

52 Huxley, *Brunei's Defence Policy and Military Expenditure*, p. 9.

53 Antolik, *ASEAN and the Diplomacy of Accommodation*, p. 86.

54 Leifer, 'Decolonisation and International Status', p. 250.

55 Horton, *A New Sketch of the History of Negara Brunei Darussalam*, p. 32.

56 For a discussion on the development of military capabilities in Brunei, see Saunders, *A History of Brunei*, p. 167 and Huxley, *Brunei's Defence Policy and Expenditure*, pp. 3–6.

57 Huxley, *Brunei's Defence Policy and Expenditure*, p. 5.

58 Leifer, *ASEAN and the Security of South-East Asia*, p. 46.

59 Antolik, *ASEAN and the Diplomacy of Accommodation*, pp. 86–87.

60 Timothy Ong Teck Mong, 'Modern Brunei: Some Important Issues', *Southeast Asian Affairs 1983*, Singapore: Institute of Southeast Asian Studies, 1983, p. 82.

61 Ong, 'Modern Brunei: Some Important Issues', p. 82.

62 Leifer, *ASEAN and the Security of South-East Asia*, pp. 46–47.

63 See the Declaration of the Admission of Brunei Darussalam into the Association of Southeast Asian Nations, Jakarta, Indonesia, 7 January 1984.

64 HRH Prince Mohamed Bolkiah, Minister for Foreign Affairs of Brunei Darussalam, Address at the Ceremony of Admission of Brunei Darussalam to ASEAN, Jakarta, Indonesia, 7 January 1984.

65 HRH Prince Mohamed Bolkiah, Minister For Foreign Affairs of Brunei Darussalam, Opening Statement at the Seventeeth ASEAN Ministerial Meeting, Jakarta, Indonesia, 9 July 1984.

66 Quoted in 'Newspaper Reports Welcome its Entry into ASEAN', *The Straits Times*, 23 February 1984, p. 4.

67 Dr Dewi Fortuna Anwar, Research Professor at the Habibie Centre and former spokesperson of President B.J. Habibie. The interview was held in Jakarta on 24 March 2000.

68 Michael Leifer, *The ASEAN Regional Forum. A Model for Cooperative Security in the Middle East?*, Canberra: Research School of Pacific and Asian Studies, Australian National University, 1998, p. 6.

69 See A.J. Crosbie, 'Brunei in Transition', *Southeast Asian Affairs 1981*, Singapore: Institute of Southeast Asian Studies, 1981, p. 91.

70 Richard Little, 'Deconstructing the Balance of Power: Two Traditions of Thought', *Review of International Studies*, vol. 15, no. 2, April 1989, p. 95. See

also Michael Sheehan, *The Balance of Power: History and Theory*, London: Routledge, 1996, pp. 167–169.

71 Donald E. Weatherbee, 'Brunei: the ASEAN Connection', *Asian Survey*, vol. 23, no. 6, June 1983, p. 734.

72 Leifer, *ASEAN and the Security of South-East Asia*, pp. 47–48.

73 Pushpa Thambipillai, 'Brunei in ASEAN: The Viable Choice?', *Southeast Asian Affairs 1982*, Singapore: Institute of Southeast Asian Studies, 1982, p. 108.

74 Lee, *From Third World to First*, pp. 344–345.

75 Kwa Chong Guan, Singapore, 3 March 2000.

76 Barry Desker, Director of IDSS and former Ambassador of Singapore to Indonesia (1986–93). The interview was held in Singapore on 17 February 2000.

77 Daljit Singh, Singapore, 23 February 2000.

4   The balance of power and extra-mural hegemony

1 Press Statement, the Eighth ASEAN Ministerial Meeting, Kuala Lumpur, Malaysia, 15 May 1975.

2 Shee Poon-Kim, 'A Decade of ASEAN, 1967–1977', *Asian Survey*, vol. 17, no. 8, August 1977, p. 759.

3 Declaration of ASEAN Concord, Bali, Indonesia, 24 February 1976.

4 Corrine Phuangkasem, *Thailand's Foreign Relations, 1964–80*, Singapore: Institute of Southeast Asian Studies, 1984, pp. 37–38.

5 Khien Theeravit, 'The United States, Thailand, and the Indochinese Conflict', in Hans H. Indorf (ed.) *Thai-American Relations in Contemporary Affairs*, Singapore: Executive Publications, 1982, pp. 149–150.

6 Grant Evans and Kelvin Rowley, *Red Brotherhood at War*, London: Verso, 1984, p. 182.

7 Gordon R. Hein, *Soeharto's Foreign Policy: Second-Generation Nationalism in Indonesia*, Ann Arbor, MI: University Microfilms International, 1988, p. 343.

8 Bilveer Singh, *Singapore–Indonesia Defence Cooperation: A Case Study of Defence Bilateralism within ASEAN*, ISIS ASEAN Series, Kuala Lumpur: Institute of Strategic and International Studies Malaysia, 1990, p. 5.

9 Michael Leifer, 'The Role and Paradox of ASEAN', in M. Leifer (ed.) *The Balance of Power in East Asia*, London: Macmillan, 1986, p. 125.

10 Robert Ross, *The Indochina Tangle: China's Vietnam Policy, 1975–1979*, New York: Columbia University Press, 1988, pp. 123–125.

11 For a discussion on the growing antagonism in Vietnamese-Cambodian relations that led eventually to open conflict, see Nguyen-vo Thu-huong, *Khmer-Viet Relations and the Third Indochina Conflict*, London: McFarland, 1992, pp. 78–85 and 96–124; Chang Pao-Min, *Kampuchea between China and Vietnam*, Singapore: Singapore University Press, 1985, pp. 51–71; Stephen P. Heder, 'The Kampuchean–Vietnamese Conflict', in David W.P. Elliot (ed.) *The Third Indochina Conflict*, Boulder, CO: Westview Press, 1981, pp. 21–67; Research Institute for Peace and Security, *Asian Security 1979*, Tokyo: Nikkei Business, 1979, pp. 103–104.

12 Michael Leifer, *Conflict and Regional Order in South-East Asia*, Adelphi Paper no. 162, London: International Institute For Strategic Studies, 1980, p. 3.

13 For an analysis of the deterioration of Sino-Vietnamese relations between 1975 and 1978, see Nguyen Manh Hung, 'Sino-Vietnamese Conflict: Power Play among Communist Neighbors', *Asian Survey*, vol. 19, no. 11, November 1979, pp. 1037–1045; Robert Sutter, 'China's Strategy Towards Vietnam and its Implications for the United States', in Elliot (ed.) *The Third Indochina Conflict*, pp. 167–185.

14 Leifer, *Conflict and Regional Order in South-East Asia*, p. 3.

15 Carlyle A. Thayer, 'ASEAN and Indochina: The Dialogue', in Alison Broinowski (ed.) *ASEAN in the 1990's*, London: Macmillan, 1990, pp. 146–147.

16 Al Santoli, *Endless Insurgency: Cambodia*, Washington DC: Center for Strategic and International Studies, Georgetown University, 1985, p. 63.

17 For an examination of the origins and evolution of the Third Indochina Conflict, see Elliot (ed.) *The Third Indochina Conflict*; Evans and Rowley, *Red Brotherhood at War*; Donald E. Weatherbee (ed.) *Southeast Asia Divided: The ASEAN–Indochina Crisis*, Boulder, CO: Westview Press, 1985; Chang, *Kampuchea between China and Vietnam*; Nayan Chanda, *Brother Enemy: The War after the War*, New York: Macmillan, 1986; Nicolas Regaud, *Le Cambodge dans la Tourmente: Le troisième Conflit Indochinois, 1978–1991*, Paris: L'Harmattan, 1992; Nguyen-vo Thu-huong, *Khmer–Viet Relations and the Third Indochina Conflict*.

18 Gareth Porter, 'Vietnamese Policy and the Indochina Crisis', in Elliot (ed.) *The Third Indochina Conflict*, 1981, p. 69.

19 Quoted in Porter, 'Vietnamese Policy and the Indochina Crisis', p. 88.

20 The Sino-Soviet Split gradually developed during the 1960s and resulted from ideological, economic and military factors. These included the issue of nuclear cooperation, which was terminated by the Soviet Union in 1960 to preserve its nuclear monopoly amongst the communist states. The impact of the Chinese Cultural Revolution (1966–69) aggravated an ideological struggle between Moscow and Beijing. The Soviet invasion of Czechoslovakia in August 1968 and the Brezhnev Doctrine of September 1968 deepened the antagonism. A final sign of the Split occurred in March 1969 when military clashes took place along the Ussuri River.

21 Michael Leifer, 'The Indochina Problem', in T.B. Millar and James Walter (eds) *Asian-Pacific Security after the Cold War*, London: Sir Robert Menzies Centre for Australian Studies, University of London, 1992, p. 52.

22 Ross, *The Indochina Tangle*, p. 228.

23 Research Institute for Peace and Security, *Asian Security 1980*, Tokyo: Nikkei Business, 1980, p. 148.

24 Regaud, *Le Cambodge dans la Tourmente*, pp. 261–268.

25 Tim Huxley, 'Cambodia in 1986: The PRK's Eighth Year', *Southeast Asian Affairs 1987*, Singapore: Institute of Southeast Asian Studies, 1987, p. 170.

26 Amitav Acharya, Pierre Lizée and Sorpong Peou, 'The Road to the Paris Conference: The Cambodian Peace Process in Historical Perspective', in A. Acharya, P. Lizée and S. Peou (eds) *Cambodia – The 1989 Paris Peace Process: Background Analysis and Documents*, Millwood, NY: Kraus International, 1991, pp. xxiii–xlviii.

27 For a discussion on the final phase of the Third Indochina Conflict, see Acharya *et al.*, 'The Road to the Paris Conference', pp. xxxiv–xlviii.

28 Professor Mochtar stated: 'The ASEAN member countries strongly regret the

escalation and expansion of the armed conflict now taking place between the two Indochinese states. The ASEAN member countries have expressed their great concern over the implications of this development and its impact on peace, security and stability in Southeast Asia.' Professor Mochtar Kusumaatmadja Foreign Minister of the Republic of Indonesia and Chairman of the ASEAN Standing Committee, Statement on the Escalation of the Armed Conflict Between Vietnam and Kampuchea, Jakarta, Indonesia, 9 January 1979.

29 Joint Statement of the Special Meeting of the ASEAN Foreign Ministers on the Current Political Development in the Southeast Asia Region, Bangkok, Thailand, 12 January, 1979.

30 The communiqué declared: 'The Foreign Ministers reiterated their support for the right of the Kampuchean people to determine their future by themselves, free from interference or influence from outside powers in the exercise of their right to self-determination and called for the immediate and total withdrawal of the foreign forces from Kampuchean territory.' Joint Communiqué of the Twelfth ASEAN Ministerial Meeting, Bali, Indonesia, 28–30 June 1979.

31 Joint Communiqué of the Twelfth ASEAN Ministerial Meeting.

32 Joint Press Statement of the Special Meeting of the ASEAN Foreign Ministers on Indochinese Refugees, Bangkok, Thailand, 13 January 1979.

33 S. Rajaratnam, Minister of Foreign Affairs of the Republic of Singapore, Address at the Twelfth ASEAN Ministerial Meeting, Bali, Indonesia, 28 June 1979.

34 For a discussion on the refugee issue, see William Shawcross, *The Quality of Mercy: Cambodia, Holocaust and Modern Conscience*, London: Andre Deutsch, 1984, pp. 302–328.

35 See Lee Kuan Yew, *From Third World to First: The Singapore Story, 1965–2000*, Singapore: Times Editions, 2000, pp. 375–376.

36 Leszek Buszynski, *Gorbachev and Southeast Asia*, London: Routledge, 1992, p. 77.

37 Vientiane Statement, 18 July 1980. Reprinted in *Documents on the Kampuchean Problem, 1979–1985*, Bangkok: Department of Political Affairs, Ministry of Foreign Affairs, 1988, pp. 148–151.

38 Justus M. van der Kroef, *Dynamics of the Cambodian Conflict*, London: Institute for the Study of Conflict, 1986, p. 6.

39 Discussing the ICK, US President Ronald Reagan declared in 1985 that Washington continues: 'to support the basic principles for the settlement of the Cambodian situation agreed upon at that conference – the complete withdrawal of Vietnamese forces under international supervision; the restoration of Cambodian independence, sovereignty, and territorial integrity; a Cambodian government chosen in free elections under international auspices.' Ronald Reagan, President of the United States of America, Address to the Meeting of ASEAN Foreign Ministers, Bali, Indonesia, on 1 May 1985.

40 ICK Declaration on Kampuchea, New York, 17 July 1981.

41 This was repeated, for instance, in the Appeal for Kampuchean Independence by the ASEAN Foreign Ministers, Jakarta, Indonesia, 20 September 1983.

42 Quoted in Rodolfo C. Garcia, 'Military Co-operation in ASEAN', *Pointer*, vol. 12, no. 3, April–June 1986, p. 9.

43 Michael Leifer, *ASEAN and the Security of South-East Asia*, London: Routledge, 1989, p. 91.

44 Chanda, *Brother Enemy*, pp. 348–349.
45 John F. Copper, 'China and Southeast Asia', in Weatherbee (ed.) *Southeast Asia Divided*, p. 55.
46 See Tim Huxley, *The ASEAN States' Defence Policies, 1975–8: Military Responses to Indochina?*, Working Paper no. 88, Canberra: The Strategic and Defence Studies Centre, Australian National University, October 1984, pp. 31–32.
47 Sukhumbhand Paribatra, 'Dictactes of Security: Thailand's Relations with the PRC since the Vietnam War', in Joyce K. Kallgren, Noordin Sopiee and Soedjati Djiwandono (eds) *ASEAN and China: An Evolving Relationship*, Research Papers and Policy Studies, Berkeley: Institute of East Asian Studies, University of California, 1988, pp. 318–323.
48 Hasnan Habib, former Ambassador of Indonesia to Thailand (1978–82) and the United States (1982–86). The interview was held in Jakarta on 23 March 2000.
49 Dr John Funston, Senior Fellow at ISEAS. The interview was held in Singapore on 2 March 2000.
50 Leifer, *ASEAN and the Security of South-East Asia*, p. 105.
51 Dr Leonard Sebastian, Senior Fellow at IDSS. The interview was held in Singapore on 25 February 2000.
52 Lee, *From Third World to First*, p. 377.
53 Narayanan Ganesan, *Singapore's Foreign Policy in ASEAN: Major Domestic and Bilateral Political Constraints*, Ann Arbor, MI: University Microfilms International, 1989, p. 203.
54 ASEAN Statement on the Vietnam–China Border War, Bangkok, Thailand, 20 February 1979.
55 Dr John Funston, Singapore, 2 March 2000.
56 This paragraph is based on a discussion with Hasnan Habib in Jakarta on 23 March 2000. See also Rizal Sukma, *Indonesia and China: The Politics of a Troubled Relationship*, London: Routledge, 1999, pp. 93–99.
57 Sukma, *Indonesia and China*, p. 95.
58 Ali Alatas, former Minister of Foreign Affairs of Indonesia (1988–99). The interview was held in Jakarta on 21 March 2000.
59 Peter Polomka, 'Intra-Regional Dynamics: ASEAN and Indochina', in T.B. Millar (ed.) *International Security in the Southeast Asian and Southwest Pacific Region*, St Lucia: University of Queensland Press, 1983, p. 126.
60 Barry Desker, Director of IDSS and former Ambassador of Singapore to Indonesia (1986–93). The interview was held in Singapore on 17 February 2000.
61 Donald E. Weatherbee, 'The Diplomacy of Stalemate', in Weatherbee (ed.) *Southeast Asia Divided*, p. 12.
62 Justus M. van der Kroef, 'ASEAN, Hanoi, and the Kampuchean Conflict: Between "Kuantan" and a "Third Alternative"', *Asian Survey*, vol. 21, no. 5, May 1981, p. 517.
63 van der Kroef, 'ASEAN, Hanoi, and the Kampuchean Conflict', p. 518.
64 Joint Statement by the ASEAN Foreign Ministers on the Situation on the Thai-Kampuchean Border, Bangkok, Thailand, 25 June 1980.
65 Weatherbee, 'The Diplomacy of Stalemate', p. 15.
66 Kusuma Snitwongse, 'Thirty Years of ASEAN: Achievements through Political Cooperation', *Pacific Review*, vol. 11, no. 2, 1988, p. 188.
67 The Informal Meeting of the ASEAN Foreign Ministers to Discuss the Recent

Political and Military Developments with Regards to the Kampuchean Problem, Jakarta, Indonesia, 8 May 1984.

68 Joint Communiqué of the Seventeenth ASEAN Ministerial Meeting, Jakarta, Indonesia, 9–10 July 1984.

69 For a discussion on the Jakarta Informal Meetings, see Acharya *et al.*, 'The Road to the Paris Conference', pp. xl–xlv.

70 Dr Dewi Fortuna Anwar, Research Professor at the Habibie Centre and former spokesperson of President B.J. Habibie. The interview was held in Jakarta on 24 March 2000.

71 Dr Bantarto Bandoro, Head of the Department of International Relations at CSIS. The interview was held in Jakarta on 22 March 2000.

72 Kwa Chong Guan, Head of External Programmes at IDSS. The interview was held in Singapore on 3 March 2000.

73 Daljit Singh, Research Fellow at ISEAS. The interview was held in Singapore on 23 February 2000.

74 Muthiah Alagappa, 'Regionalism and Conflict Management: A Framework for Analysis', *Review of International Studies*, vol. 21, 1995, p. 377.

75 Jonathan Stromseth, *Time on whose Side in Cambodia?*, ISIS Paper, Bangkok: Institute of Security and International Studies, Chulalongkorn University, 1988, p. 5.

76 Charles McGregor, *The Sino-Vietnamese Relationship and the Soviet Union*, Adelphi Paper no. 232, London: International Institute for Strategic Studies, 1988, p. 34.

77 Dr Soedjati Djiwandono, former member of CSIS and frequent columnist for the *Jakarta Post*. The interview was held in Jakarta on 17 March 2000.

78 See Chapter 2 for a brief discussion on Stephen Walt's study of alliances and balance of threat theory.

79 Regaud, *Le Cambodge dans la Tourmente*, p. 177.

5   The post-Cold War regional security context

1 Amitav Acharya, *A New Regional Order in South-East Asia: ASEAN in the Post-Cold War Era*, Adelphi Paper no. 279, London: International Institute for Strategic Studies, 1993, p. 12.

2 For a discussion on the changes in Soviet foreign policy under Mikhael Gorbachev and their impact on the Cambodian conflict, see Leszek Buszynski, *Gorbachev and Southeast Asia*, London: Routledge, 1992.

3 See Paul Dibb, *Towards a New Balance of Power in Asia*, Adelphi Paper no. 295, London: International Institute for Strategic Studies, 1995, pp. 17–25, 34–36.

4 For a discussion on the US defence policy in Asia in the post-Cold War, see Douglas T. Stuart and William T. Tow, *A US Strategy for the Asia-Pacific*, Adelphi Paper no. 299, London: International Institute for Strategic Studies, 1995, pp. 6–20.

5 See Gerald Segal and Richard H. Yang (eds) *Chinese Economic Reform: The Impact on Security*, London: Routledge, 1996.

6 Leszek Buszynski, 'Post-Cold War Security in the ASEAN Region', in Gary Klintworth (ed.) *Asia-Pacific Security: Less Uncertainty, New Opportunities?*, New York: St Martin's Press, 1996, p. 121.

7 Michael Yahuda, 'How much has China learned about Interdependence?', in

David S.G. Goodman and Gerald Segal (eds) *China Rising: Nationalism and Interdependence*, London: Routledge, 1997, p. 20. For a study of the normalization of Sino-Indonesian relations, see Rizal Sukma, *Indonesia and China: The Politics of a Troubled Relationship*, London: Routledge, 1999.

8 Ali Alatas, former Minister of Foreign Affairs of Indonesia (1988–99). The interview was held in Jakarta on 21 March 2000.

9 Michael Leifer, *The ASEAN Regional Forum: Extending ASEAN's Model of Regional Security*, Adelphi Paper no. 302, London: International Institute for Strategic Studies, 1996, p. 19.

10 HE Mr Wong Kan Seng, Minister of Foreign Affairs of the Republic of Singapore, Opening Statement at the Twenty-fourth ASEAN Ministerial Meeting, Kuala Lumpur, Malaysia, 19–20 July 1991.

11 Tobias Ingo Nischalke, 'Insights from ASEAN's Foreign Policy Co-operation: The "ASEAN Way", a Real Spirit or a Phantom?', *Contemporary Southeast Asia*, vol. 22, no. 1, April 2000, p. 97.

12 Joint Communiqué of the Twenty-fourth ASEAN Ministerial Meeting, Kuala Lumpur, Malaysia, 19–20 July 1991.

13 HE Mr Taro Nakayama, Minister of Foreign Affairs of Japan, Statement at the Meeting between ASEAN and the Dialogue Partners, Kuala Lumpur, Malaysia, 23 July 1991.

14 Singapore Declaration of 1992, ASEAN Heads of State and Government Meeting, Singapore, 27–28 January 1992.

15 Singapore Declaration of 1992.

16 Nischalke, 'Insights from ASEAN's Foreign Policy Co-operation', p. 96.

17 Manila Declaration of 1987, ASEAN Heads of State and Government Meeting, Manila, the Philippines, 14–15 December 1987.

18 HE Mr James A. Baker, III, Secretary of State of the United States of America, Statement at the ASEAN–US Dialogue Session, Manila, the Philippines, 26 July 1992.

19 Chairman's Statement, ASEAN Post-Ministerial Conferences, Senior Officials Meeting, Singapore, 20–21 May 1993.

20 Chairman's Statement, 20–21 May 1993.

21 Chairman's Statement, 20–21 May 1993.

22 Chairman's Statement, 20–21 May 1993.

23 Chairman's Statement, the First Meeting of the ASEAN Regional Forum, Bangkok, Thailand, 25 July 1994.

24 Chairman's Statement, 20–21 May 1993.

25 ASEAN Declaration on the South China Sea, Manila, the Philippines, 22 July 1992.

26 Chairman's Statement, 25 July 1994.

27 HE Mr Wong Kan Seng, Minister of Foreign Affairs of the Republic of Singapore, Welcoming Remarks at the Meeting between ASEAN and the Dialogue Partners, Singapore, 26 July 1993.

28 Professor S. Jayakumar, Minister of Foreign Affairs of the Republic of Singapore, 'The Southeast Asian Drama: Evolution and Future Challenges', *Georgetown University, Inaugural Distinguished Lecture on Southeast Asia*, Washington DC: Georgetown University, 22 April 1996, p. 18.

29 James A. Baker, III, 'America in Asia: Emerging Architecture for a Pacific Community', *Foreign Affairs*, vol. 70, no. 5, Winter 1991/92, pp. 1–18.

30 Yukio Satoh, 'Emerging Trends in Asia-Pacific Security: The Role of Japan', *Pacific Review*, vol. 8, no. 2, 1995, p. 273.

31 Koro Bessho, *Identities and Security in East Asia*, Adelphi Paper no. 325, London: International Institute for Strategic Studies, 1999, p. 71.

32 Leifer, *The ASEAN Regional Forum: Extending ASEAN's Model of Regional Security*, p. 19.

33 HE Mr Warren Christopher, Secretary of State of the United States of America, Statement at the Meeting Between ASEAN and the Dialogue Partners, Singapore, 26 July 1993.

34 Michael Leifer, 'Truth about the Balance of Power', in Derek da Cunha (ed.) *The Evolving Pacific Power Structure*, Singapore: Institute of Southeast Asian Studies, 1996, p. 51.

35 Acharya, *A New Regional Order in South-East Asia*, p. 55.

36 Acharya, *A New Regional Order in South-East Asia*, p. 62.

37 Michael Leifer, 'Indonesia's Encounters with China and the Dilemmas of Engagement', in Alastair Iain Johnston and Robert S. Ross (eds) *Engaging China: The Management of an Emerging Power*, London: Routledge, 1999, p. 105.

38 APEC's current participants are: the ASEAN states (Indonesia, Thailand, the Philippines, Singapore, Malaysia, Brunei, Vietnam, Myanmar, Laos and Cambodia), the United States, China, Japan, South Korea, Canada, Australia, New Zealand, Papua New Guinea, Taiwan, Hong Kong, Chile, Mexico, Russia and Peru.

39 See APEC Leaders Statement on Counter-Terrorism, Shanghai, China, 21 October 2001.

40 Dr Derek da Cunha, Senior Fellow at ISEAS. The interview was held in Singapore on 22 February 2000.

41 Derek da Cunha, *Southeast Asia's Security Dynamics: A Multiplicity of Approaches amidst Changing Geopolitical Circumstances*, ISEAS Working Papers, Singapore: Institute of Southeast Asian Studies, July 1999, p. 16.

42 Yong Deng, 'Managing China's Hegemonic Ascension: Engagement from Southeast Asia', *Journal of Strategic Studies*, vol. 21, no. 1, March 1998, p. 35.

43 Michael Leifer, *The ASEAN Regional Forum. A Model for Cooperative Security in the Middle East?*, Canberra: Research School of Pacific and Asian Studies, Australian National University, 1998, p. 15.

44 For a discussion on the East Timor crisis of 1999 and the ineffectiveness of regional institutions, see Derek McDougall, 'Regional Institutions and Security: Implications of the 1999 East Timor Crisis', in Andrew Tan and Kenneth Boutin (eds) *Non-Traditional Security Issues in Southeast Asia*, Singapore: Institute of Defence and Strategic Studies, 2001, pp. 166–196.

45 Joint Communiqué of the Thirty-fifth ASEAN Ministerial Meeting, Bandar Seri Begawan, Brunei, 29–30 July 2002.

46 The Visiting Forces Agreement was only ratified by the Philippine Senate in May 1999.

47 Derek da Cunha, *Southeast Asia's Security Dynamics*, p. 21. The deterioration of bilateral relations resulted from a series of issues, including remarks made by Senior Minister Lee Kuan Yew on the crime rate in Johor.

48 HE Mr Warren Christopher, Secretary of State of the United States of America, Statement at the ASEAN–United States Dialogue Session, Singapore, 27 July 1993.

49 For a discussion on Japan's motives to actively take part in the formation of the ARF, see Tsuyoshi Kawasaki, 'Between Realism and Idealism in Japanese Security Policy: The Case of the ASEAN Regional Forum', *Pacific Review*, vol. 10, no. 4, 1997, pp. 480–503.

50 Professor S. Jayakumar, Minister of Foreign Affairs of the Republic of Singapore, Addenda to the President's Address: Ministry of Foreign Affairs, Singapore, 8 October 1999.

51 Gerald Segal, 'How Insecure is Pacific Asia?', *International Affairs*, vol. 73, no. 2, 1997, p. 247.

52 Robyn Lim, 'The ASEAN Regional Forum: Building on Sand', *Contemporary Southeast Asia*, vol. 20, no. 2, August 1998, p. 131.

53 Wang Jisi, 'The United States as a Global and Pacific Power: A View from China', *Pacific Review*, vol. 10, no. 1, 1997, p. 12.

54 For a discussion of Sino-Malaysian relations since the end of the Cold War, see Joseph Liow Chin Yong, 'Malaysia–China Relations in the 1990s: The Maturing of a Partnership', *Asian Survey*, vol. 40, no. 4, July/August 2000, pp. 672–691.

55 Amitav Acharya, 'Containment, Engagement, or Counter-Dominance? Malaysia's Response to the Rise of China', in Johnston and Ross (eds) *Engaging China*, p. 143.

56 Liow, 'Malaysia–China Relations in the 1990s', p. 676.

57 Sheldon W. Simon, 'Security Prospects in Southeast Asia: Collaborative Efforts and the ASEAN Regional Forum', *Pacific Review*, vol. 11, no. 2, 1998, p. 203.

58 ASEAN-United States of America Joint Declaration for Cooperation to Combat International Terrorism, Bandar Seri Begawan, Brunei, 1 August 2002.

59 Tim Huxley, 'A Threat in the South China Sea? A Rejoinder', *Security Dialogue*, vol. 29, no. 1, March 1998, p. 117.

60 James Miles, 'Chinese Nationalism, US Policy and Asian Security', *Survival*, vol. 42, no. 4, Winter 2000/01, pp. 56–57.

61 Miles, 'Chinese Nationalism, US Policy and Asian Security', p. 67.

6 ASEAN's post-Cold War involvement in the South China Sea dispute

1 See Rebecca M.M. Wallace, *International Law*, second edition, London: Sweet & Maxwell, 1992, pp. 128–165.

2 Article 57, 1982 Convention. *Official Text of the United Nations Convention on the Law of the Sea with Annexes and Index*, New York: United Nations, 1983.

3 Article 121, 1982 Convention.

4 Article 121(3), 1982 Convention.

5 For a discussion on the Chinese territorial claims, see Lu Ning, *Flashpoint Spratlys!*, New York: Dolphin Books, 1995, pp. 5–35.

6 R.M. Sunardi, Retired Admiral of the Indonesian Navy (1985–95). The interview was held in Jakarta on 22 March 2000.

7 Amitav Archarya, *A New Regional Order in South-East Asia: ASEAN in the Post-Cold War Era*, Adelphi Paper no. 279, London: International Institute for Strategic Studies, 1993, pp. 33–34.

8 See Lo Chi Kin, *China's Policy Towards Territorial Disputes*, London: Routledge, 1989, pp. 153–154.

9 For a discussion on the economic dimension of the South China Sea dispute, see Bob Catley and Makmur Keliat, *Spratlys: The Dispute in the South China Sea*, Aldershot: Ashgate, 1997, pp. 44–65.

10 Mark J. Valencia, *China and the South China Sea Disputes: Conflicting Claims and Potential Solutions in the South China Sea*, Adelphi Paper no. 298, London: International Institute for Strategic Studies, 1995, p. 28.

11 Michael Leifer, 'Chinese Economic Reform: The Impact on Policy in the South China Sea', in Gerald Segal and Richard H. Yang (eds) *Chinese Economic Reform: The Impact on Security*, London: Routledge, 1996, p. 142.

12 R.M. Sunardi, Jakarta, 22 March 2000.

13 For a discussion on China's seizure of the Paracel Islands, see Gerald Segal, *Defending China*, Oxford: Oxford University Press, 1985, pp. 197–210.

14 See Mark J. Valencia, 'The Spratly Imbroglio in the Post-Cold War Era', in David Wurfel (ed.) *Southeast Asia in the New World Order*, London: Macmillan, 1996, p. 255; and Lo, *China's Policy Towards Territorial Disputes*, pp. 63–68.

15 See Shee Poon Kim, 'The March 1988 Skirmish over the Spratly Islands and its Implications for Sino-Vietnamese Relations', in R.D. Hill, N. Owen and E.V. Roberts (eds) *Fishing in Troubled Waters: Proceedings of an Academic Conference on Territorial Claims in the South China Sea*, Hong Kong: Centre of Asian Studies, University of Hong Kong, 1991, pp. 177–191.

16 For a discussion on Vietnam's foreign policy after the end of the Third Indochina Conflict, see Richard K. Betts, 'Strategic Predicament', in James W. Morley and Nasashi Nishihara (eds) *Vietnam joins the World*, London: M.E. Sharpe, 1997, pp. 94–114.

17 Catley and Keliat, *Spratlys: The Dispute in the South China Sea*, p. 102.

18 Michael Leifer, 'Indonesia's Encounters with China and the Dilemmas of Engagement', in Alastair Iain Johnston and Robert S. Ross (eds) *Engaging China: The Management of an Emerging Power*, London: Routledge, 1999, p. 99.

19 Khong Yuen Foong, 'Singapore: A Time for Economic and Political Engagement', in Johnston and Ross (eds) *Engaging China*, pp. 110–111.

20 Dr Lee Lai To, Associate Professor, Department of Political Science at NUS. The interview was held in Singapore on 14 March 2000.

21 Acharya, *A New Regional Order in South-East Asia*, p. 34.

22 See Ian Townsend-Gault, 'Confidence and Cooperation in the South China Sea: The Indonesia–Canada Initiative', in Jusuf Wanandi (ed.) *Regional Security Arrangements: Indonesian and Canadian Views*, Jakarta: Centre for Strategic and International Studies, 1996, pp. 69–80; and Ian Townsend-Gault, 'Preventive Diplomacy and Pro-Activity in the South China Sea', *Contemporary Southeast Asia*, vol. 20, no. 2, August 1998, pp. 171–190.

23 HE Mr Ali Alatas, Minister for Foreign Affairs of Indonesia, Address Opening the Second Workshop on Managing Potential Conflicts in the South China Sea, Bandung, Indonesia, 15 July 1991.

24 Joint Statement, Workshop on Managing Potential Conflicts in the South China Sea, Bandung, Indonesia, 15–18 July 1991.

25 Lee Lai To, 'The South China Sea: China and Multilateral Dialogues', *Security Dialogue*, vol. 30, no. 2, 1999, p. 170.

26 ASEAN Declaration on the South China Sea, Manila, the Philippines, 22 July 1992.

27 ASEAN Declaration on the South China Sea.

28 Dr Bantarto Bandoro, Head of the Department of International Relations at CSIS. The interview was held in Jakarta on 22 March 2000.

29 J.N. Mak, 'The ASEAN Naval Build-up: Implications for the Regional Order', *Pacific Review*, vol. 8, no. 2, 1995, p. 308.

30 Michael Leifer, *The ASEAN Regional Forum: Extending ASEAN's Model of Regional Security*, Adelphi Paper no. 302, London: International Institute for Strategic Studies, 1996, p. 18.

31 Ang Cheng Guan, *The South China Sea Dispute Re-visited*, IDSS Working Paper Series no. 4, Singapore: Institute of Defence and Strategic Studies, August 1999, p. 13.

32 Gerald Segal, 'East Asia and the "Constrainment" of China', *International Security*, vol. 20, no. 4, Spring 1996, p. 120.

33 Joint Statement on RP-PRC Consultations on the South China Sea and on Other Areas of Cooperation, 9–10 August 1995.

34 Leifer, *The ASEAN Regional Forum: Extending ASEAN's Model of Regional Security*, p. 38.

35 Statement by the ASEAN Foreign Ministers on the Recent Development in the South China Sea, Singapore, 18 March 1995.

36 Statement by the ASEAN Foreign Ministers on the Recent Development in the South China Sea.

37 Chairman's Statement, the Second ASEAN Regional Forum, Bandar Seri Begawan, Brunei Darussalam, 1 August 1995.

38 Sheldon W. Simon, 'ASEAN Regional Forum', in William M. Carpenter and David G. Wiencek (eds) *Asian Security Handbook: An Assessment of Political-Security Issues in the Asia-Pacific Region*, New York: M.E. Sharpe, 1996, p. 47.

39 Gerald Segal, 'East Asia and the "Constrainment" of China', pp. 128–129.

40 Michael Leifer, 'China in Southeast Asia: Interdependence and Accommodation', in David S. Goodman and Gerald Segal (eds) *China Rising: Nationalism and Interdependence*, London: Routledge, 1997, p. 168.

41 Sheldon Simon, 'Security Prospects in Southeast Asia: Collaborative Efforts and the ASEAN Regional Forum', *Pacific Review*, vol. 11, no. 2, 1998, p. 202.

42 Joint Statement of the Meeting of Heads of State and Government of the Member States of ASEAN and the President of the People's Republic of China, Kuala Lumpur, Malaysia, 16 December 1997.

43 'China and the Philippines: Reef-Stricken', *The Economist*, 29 May 1999, p. 83.

44 Dr Chin Kin Wah, Associate Professor, Department of Political Science at NUS. The interview was held in London on 19 May 2000.

45 Hanoi Declaration of 1998, Sixth ASEAN Summit, Meeting of the ASEAN Heads of State and Government, Hanoi, Vietnam, 15–16 December 1998.

46 Dr Termsak Chalermpalanupap, Special Assistant to the Secretary-General of the ASEAN Secretariat. The interview was held in Jakarta on 23 March 2000.

47 Dr Lee Lai To, Singapore, 14 March 2000.

48 Chairman's Press Statement, Third Informal Summit of the ASEAN Heads of State and Government, Manila, Philippines, 28 November 1999.

49 Press Release, ASEAN and China Held a Successful Consultation on Regional Code of Conduct in the South China Sea, ASEAN Secretariat, Jakarta, Indonesia, 15 March 2000.

50 Joint Communiqué of the Thirty-fourth ASEAN Ministerial Meeting, Hanoi, Vietnam, 23–24 July 2001.

51 Joint Communiqué of the Thirty-fifth ASEAN Ministerial Meeting, Bandar Seri Begawan, Brunei, 29–30 July 2002.
52 Declaration on the Conduct of Parties in the South China Sea, Phnom Penh, Cambodia, 4 November 2002.
53 Declaration on the Conduct of Parties in the South China Sea.
54 Declaration on the Conduct of Parties in the South China Sea.
55 Declaration on the Conduct of Parties in the South China Sea.
56 Chairman's Statement, the Third Meeting of the ASEAN Regional Forum, Jakarta, Indonesia, 23 July 1996.
57 Chairman's Statement, the Sixth Meeting of the ASEAN Regional Forum, Singapore, 26 July 1999.
58 Chairman's Statement, the Ninth Meeting of the ASEAN Regional Forum, Bandar Seri Begawan, Brunei, 31 July 2002.
59 For a discussion on the intra-mural territorial disputes, see Harald David, *Tensions within ASEAN: Malaysia and its Neighbours*, Monographs on Southeast Asian Politics and International Relations, no. 1, University of Hull: Department of South-East Asian Studies, 1996.
60 Mak, 'The ASEAN Naval Build-up', p. 308.
61 Michael Leifer, 'The Maritime Regime and Regional Security in East Asia', *Pacific Review*, vol. 4, no. 2, 1991, p. 130.
62 Dr Derek da Cunha, Senior Fellow at ISEAS. The interview was held in Singapore on 22 February 2000.
63 Tim Huxley, 'A Threat in the South China Sea? A Rejoinder', *Security Dialogue*, vol. 29, no. 1, March 1998, p. 114.
64 Brigadier Chris Roberts, *Chinese Strategy and the Spratly Islands Dispute*, Working Paper no. 293, Canberra: Strategic and Defence Studies Centre, Australian National University, April 1996, p. 22.
65 Aileen San Pablo-Baviera, 'Philippine Security in the South China Sea', in Carolina G. Hernandez and Ralph Cossa (eds) *Security Implications of Conflict in the South China Sea: Perspectives from Asia-Pacific*, Manila: Institute for Strategic and Development Studies, 1997, p. 72.
66 Catley and Keliat, *Spratlys: The Dispute in the South China Sea*, p. 167.
67 Sabam Siagian, former Chief Editor of the *Jakarta Post* and former Ambassador of Indonesia to Australia (1991–95). The interview was held in Jakarta on 20 March 2000.
68 Bob Lowry, *Australia–Indonesia Security Cooperation: For Better or Worse?*, Working Paper no. 299, Canberra: Strategic and Defence Studies Centre, Australian National University, August 1996, p. 10.
69 Ali Alatas, former Minister of Foreign Affairs of Indonesia (1988–99). The interview was held in Jakarta on 21 March 2000. Lt General TNI Agus Widjojo. The interview was held in Jakarta on 24 March 2000.
70 Quoted in Leifer, *The ASEAN Regional Forum: Extending ASEAN's Model of Regional Security*, p. 50.
71 Quoted in 'Indonesia Plans War Games to Caution China', *International Herald Tribune*, 16 August 1996, p. 4.
72 *New Straits Times,* 21 January 1995.
73 'Give China Time and Space', *Far East Economic Review*, 25 May 1995.
74 Segal, 'East Asia and the "Constrainment" of China', p. 131.
75 *The Straits Times,* 13 May 1995.

76 Sabam Siagian, Jakarta, 20 March 2000.

77 Henry Kissinger, *Diplomacy*, New York: Touchstone, 1994, p. 827.

78 Robyn Lim, 'Failure of Australian–Indonesian Cooperation is a Loss', *International Herald Tribune*, 30 September 1999, p. 8.

79 'Concern over Spratlys Statement', *The Straits Times*, 27 April 1999.

80 Michael Leifer, 'ASEAN as a Model of a Security Community?', in Hadi Soesastro (ed.) *ASEAN in a Changed Regional and International Political Economy*, Jakarta: Centre for Strategic and International Studies, 1995, p. 141.

81 Shee Poon-Kim, 'The South China Sea in China's Strategic Thinking', *Contemporary Southeast Asia*, vol. 19, no. 4, March 1998, p. 377.

82 Derek da Cunha, *Southeast Asia's Security Dynamics: A Multiplicity of Approaches amidst Changing Geopolitical Circumstances*, ISEAS Working Papers, Singapore: Institute of Southeast Asian Studies, July 1999, p. 19.

83 Da Cunha, *Southeast Asia's Security Dynamics*, pp. 18–19.

84 Dr Lee Lai To, Singapore, 14 March 2000.

85 Valencia, *China and the South China Sea Disputes*, pp. 26–27.

86 Christine Shelly, Acting Spokesperson of US Department of State, 'Spratlys and the South China Sea', 10 May 1995.

87 Daljit Singh, Research Fellow at ISEAS. The interview was held in Singapore on 23 February 2000.

88 Dr Dewi Fortuna Anwar, Research Professor at the Habibie Centre and former spokesperson of President B.J. Habibie. The interview was held in Jakarta on 24 March 2000.

89 Bilveer Singh, 'Security Implications of Conflict in the South China Sea: A Singaporean Perspective', in Hernandez and Cossa (eds) *Security Implications of Conflict in the South China Sea*, p. 53.

Conclusion

1 The ARF participants have also expressed their support for Indonesia's territorial integrity. The chairman's statement of July 2000 declared: 'The Ministers agreed that a united democratic and economically prosperous Indonesia was fundamental to the maintenance of regional security. In this context, they emphasized their support for Indonesia's territorial integrity.' Chairman's Statement, the Seventh Meeting of the ASEAN Regional Forum, Bangkok, Thailand, 27 July 2000. These points were later repeated at the two following ARF meetings organized in Hanoi in July 2001 and in Brunei in July 2002.

Index

Abu Sayyaf 150
Acharya, Amitav 4, 23, 31, 125
adversarial balance of power 42
Afghanistan, Soviet invasion (1979) 91
Alatas, Ali 25, 105, 135, 146, 147
Albright, Madeleine 35
alliances as expression of balance of
    power politics 46–7
Anglo-Malaysian Defence Agreement
    (1963) 59, 69, 82
ANZUS Treaty 30
Anwar Ibrahim 25
Aquino, Corazon 134
ARF *see* ASEAN Regional Forum
Armed Forces of the Republic of
    Indonesia (ABRI) 102
ASEAN: approach to regional security
    38; founding moments 54–9; origins
    11–13; in the Cold War period 13–22;
    weakening since 1997 22–7
ASEAN Foreign Ministers' Retreat 26
ASEAN Institutes of Strategic and
    International Studies (ASEAN-ISIS)
    5, 113
ASEAN Ministerial Meeting (AMM)
    14, 25, 113; (1979) (Bali) 94; (1980)
    (Kuala Lumpur) 104; (1991) (Kuala
    Lumpur) 30, 113; (1997) (Subang
    Jaya) 25; (1998) (Manila) 25; (2002)
    (Brunei) 29, 141, 142; on Terrorism
    (May 2002) 27
ASEAN Post-Ministerial Conference
    (ASEAN-PMC) 21, 113, 114, 139;
    (1990) (Jakarta) 30; (1992) (Manila)
    30, 137; (1993) (Singapore) 123
ASEAN Regional Forum (ARF) 24; cf
    ASEAN 36; balance of power factor
    in the formation and workings of
    112–22; Concept Paper 32, 33, 36, 37,

38; constraining of China and 161–2;
creation and development 30–8; as an
inter-governmental discussion group
for cooperative security 34–8;
involvement in South China Sea
dispute 35; meetings: (1994)
(Bangkok) 31, 138; (1995) (Brunei)
32, 33, 138–9; (1996) (Jakarta) 33;
(1997) (Subang Jaya) 33; (1998)
(Manila) 33, 143; (1999) (Singapore)
33, 143; (2000) (Bangkok) 35, 142,
143; (2001) (Hanoi) 34, 37, 143;
(2002) (Brunei) 34, 35; origins and
institutional progress 30–4; Senior
Officials Meeting (SOM) 31;
Statement on Measures Against
Terrorist Financing 34; unilateralism
vs multipolarity 123–7
ASEAN Secretariat 19
ASEAN Senior Officials Meeting
    (SOM) (1993) 30, 110, 117
ASEAN summits: (1976) (Bali) 18, 19,
    20, 21, 39, 65, 86–7; (1977) (Kuala
    Lumpur) 21, 113; (1987) (Manila)
    114; (1992) (Singapore) 29, 30, 114,
    137; (1995) (Bangkok) 24, 119; (1998)
    (Hanoi) 25; (1999) (Manila) 140;
    (2001) (Brunei) 26; (2002) (Phnom
    Penh) 27, 29, 141; ASEAN Way 3, 6,
    10, 22–7, 36, 39; constructivist
    approach 3
Asia–Europe Meeting (ASEM) 24, 125
Asia Security Conference 34
Asia-Pacific Economic Cooperation
    (APEC) forum 118–19
Association of Southeast Asia (ASA)
    12
Association of Southeast Asian Nations
    see entries under ASEAN